A HISTORY OF
THE CHURCH IN VENEZUELA
1810-1930

A HISTORY OF
THE CHURCH IN VENEZUELA
1810-1930

BY

MARY WATTERS

AMS PRESS
NEW YORK

Reprinted from the edition of 1933, Chapel Hill
First AMS EDITION published 1971
Manufactured in the United States of America

International Standard Book Number: 0-404-06877-4

Library of Congress Catalog Number: 70-137303

AMS PRESS INC.
NEW YORK, N.Y. 10003

TO
MY FATHER AND MY MOTHER

PREFACE

AN INTERESTING and significant feature of the history of the states
that resulted from the dissolution of the Spanish Empire in America
is found in the differences they present in the evolution of the church.
The diversity in the history of this institution is one of the striking
evidences of the individuality and differentiation of these Hispanic-
American groups. It is suggestive, too, of the decentralization and
consequent variations in operation now recognized to have been
fundamental characteristics of the Spanish colonial system; for in the
colonial background, racial, social, and political, lie the roots of this
institutional evolution, whatever may have been the contributions of
the national period.

Although the progress of anti-clericalism and the operation of
other forces have weakened in varying degrees the hold of the church
in all Hispanic-American states, in none did the loss of influence fall
so early, in none was it so complete as in Venezuela. Indeed, the
virtual impotence of the church has been recognized as a peculiar
feature of the history of this people which distinguishes it from all
other Hispanic-American groups. In Colombia, for example, a state
with which Venezuela had special connections both in the colonial
period and in the struggle for independence, the church today is a
prominent social and political force. In Venezuela the institution
has no political power, in spite of the fact that it is still established;
and outside a few centers, notably Mérida and Valencia, its social
effectiveness is slight. A satisfactory explanation of this difference
has been offered neither by native nor foreign students of the institution. The author of this study does not attempt to offer a definitive
explanation, but presents certain events, forces, and developments as
having contributed to it.

For an interest in the politico-ecclesiastical history of Hispanic-
America I am indebted to my teacher, Dr. William Whatley Pierson.
From him came the suggestion that I undertake the particular study
of the church in Venezuela—a work begun in his seminar in Ven-

[vii]

ezuelan history in the University of North Carolina. The instruction received through his general courses in Hispanic-American civilization and his special lectures on the church have been fundamental in my approach to the interpretation of this institutional history. His counsel and direction have been means by which I have been able to effect this preliminary study. I wish to acknowledge my indebtedness to him. For the privilege of the use of his library on Venezuelan history, I am very grateful.

In the course of my research on this study in Venezuela I have received kindly advice and assistance from Dr. Vicente Dávila, director of the Archivo Nacional in Caracas, and Mr. J. C. Bolet, his colleague in that institution; from Dr. Luis Correa, Dr. Vicente Lecuna, and Dr. Manuel Segundo Sánchez, members of the Academia de la Historia; from Dr. José Machado and his assistants in the Biblioteca Nacional; and from Monseñor Nicolás E. Navarro, dean of the chapter of the Metropolitan Cathedral of Caracas and historian of the church. Before going to Caracas, I had the privilege of counsel from Dr. Pedro Arcaya, Venezuelan minister to the United States; from Dr. L. S. Rowe, director of the Pan-American Union, and Dr. Esteban Gil Borges, the vice-director; and from Dr. James A. Robertson, editor of the *Hispanic American Historical Review*. For the guidance and assistance of these I should like to make grateful acknowledgment. I wish to thank the administrators of the Library of the University of North Carolina, especially Miss Georgia Faison, the Reference Librarian, for aid in securing material.

MARY WATTERS

Jonesboro, Arkansas
January 24, 1933

TABLE OF CONTENTS

A HISTORY OF
THE CHURCH IN VENEZUELA
1810-1930

INTRODUCTION

THE COLONIAL BACKGROUND OF THE CHURCH IN VENEZUELA

THE POSITION of the church in Venezuela may be accounted for in part by the course of its history in the colonial period. This view would seem to have a sufficient justification to warrant a careful, even though summary, survey of the colonial church in a study concerned primarily with the history of the institution from the beginning of the War for Independence.[1]

Any attempt to define the status of the church in Venezuela during the colonial period involves the investigator in contradictions. Apparently the church had much the same preponderance of social power in this country that it had in other divisions of the Spanish Empire in America. Conditions within the institution and contests with the civil authorities along with intellectual currents from Europe and the United States had, indeed, relaxed its control before the end of the eighteenth century. In the writer's opinion, it was, nevertheless, still dominant over the minds of the great majority of the people at the outbreak of the War for Independence. On the other hand, the institution, it is believed, never took such deep roots in Venezuela

[1] In the Archivo Nacional of Caracas there are documents on the colonial church, collected under the title, *Asuntos eclesiásticos.* These are more considerable and valuable for the period after 1786, due to the inclusion of the records of the Audiencia of Venezuela on the institution. The rich archives of the church in the records of the Audiencia of Santo Domingo are to be found only in the Archives of the Indies in Seville. It is the purpose of the Venezuelan government to secure copies of these that have reference to ecclesiastical matters. Although an examination of these documents is necessary to a definitive study of the colonial church, which the writer would like to undertake later, a study of them has not been deemed essential to the present work on the church since 1810.

The archives of the Archbishopric of Caracas contain much documentary material on the church from the beginning of the seventeenth century. That of the sixteenth has been largely lost. The *Libros de edictos* of the bishops and the capitular records of the later centuries are there. Among these documents is the monumental work of Bishop Martí, the records of his visit of 1771 to 1784. A copy of it is found also in the *Asuntos eclesiásticos* in the Archivo Nacional. There has been no publication undertaken of the documents of the Archbishopric of Caracas, such as that of Silva for the diocese of Mérida. The Venezuelan government has recently published, however, the valuable work of Martí.

[3]

as in other parts of the Empire. The church was subject to conditions that weakened all institutional control in this part of Tierra Firme. The long-continued anarchy of the conquest and the reckless individualism of the conquerors left here a greater heritage of disorder and of factionalism, disruptive forces that the isolation of this section and its neglect by Spain left unchecked. Geographic conditions made communication slow and hazardous. The slight advancement of the Venezuelan Indian in social organization defeated efforts toward his conquest and civilization. The noted French traveller, Depons, in his excellent survey of Spanish rule in eastern Tierra Firme, made at the beginning of the nineteenth century, gave eloquent testimony to these baffling difficulties:

Of all the conquests which have been achieved in the New World in the name of the Spanish monarch, that of those parts which we are now treating (Venezuela) was the longest, the most toilsome, and, we may add, the most imperfect. The mountains with which the country is covered, the multitude of rivers whose inundations interrupt the communications for a great part of the year; the lakes, marshes, and deserts opposed difficulties which only those men violently goaded by ambition could brave; but what must have contributed still more to retard the progress of the conquerors in several parts of America was the multiplication of Indian governments, which, not being incorporated so as to form one nation like those of Mexico and Perú, rendered the victories of the Spanish less decisive and their negotiations more difficult. Every cacique waged a separate war, a war of stratagem and ambuscade; the ciciques seldom entered into leagues and seldomer still either offered or received battle in open field. A conquered nation gave sometimes no more than four leagues of additional territory to the conquerors; the country was disputed by inches, and its contest effected by dint of courage, patience, privation, and dangers.[2]

---

[2] Depons, Francois, *Voyage to the Eastern Part of Tierra Firme*, translation by "An American Gentleman," (Washington Irving), 3 vols., (New York, 1806), vol. i, p. 6. This work has recently been translated into Spanish by Dr. Vicente Dávila, under the direction of the Venezuelan Academy of History; *vide*, *Viaje á la parte oriental de Tierra Firme*, (Caracas, 1930). This translation appeared first in the numbers of the *Boletín* of the Academy of History.

And, as Depons suggests, the arduous task was never fully accomplished. Neither ecclesiastical nor political control was successfully achieved in colonial Venezuela.

Within the church itself there prevailed the decentralization and factionalism so characteristic of Venezuelan society. The institution was not able to control its own organization. Throughout the Spanish colonial church there were, indeed, bitter conflicts between the regular and secular clergy, but in Venezuela divisions occurred frequently within the separate orders and between the units of the secular organization. Such dissensions naturally lessened the political and social effectiveness of the institution. The relative neglect of this region by Spain and the poverty of Venezuela affected the church adversely; its personnel was always inadequate and its wealth was never equal to that of the church in Mexico, in Perú, nor even in Colombia. But these conditions did not prevent the church in Venezuela from being the most effective civilizing agent throughout the colonial period. This judgment may be made of its work both among the native peoples, whose nomadic habits made them so difficult to subdue, and in the Spanish towns, where the political ambitions of the creoles and the introduction of rationalistic philosophy in the eighteenth century threatened its control.

In this introductory chapter a survey of the colonial church is presented according to the following divisions: (1) the introduction and evolution of the mission and the mission system as institutions of church and state among the Indians; (2) the organization and functioning of the secular division of the church among the Spanish population and the reduced Indians, with special emphasis on its relations with the civil power and its influence in society; and (3) the status of the church on the eve of emancipation from Spain.

I

BOLTON HAS STATED admirably in his article, "The Mission as a Frontier Institution in the Spanish-American Colonies," the purpose of the mission in the politico-religious program of the Spanish monarchy.[3] Its function in the imperial system was to civilize the fron-

[3] *American Historical Review*, vol. xxiii, pp. 42-61.

tier; it was to instruct the Indians on the edge of settlement in the Catholic faith and to discipline them to the point that they could be turned over to the control of the civil officials and the secular clergy. The mission was thus the main agency for the transmission of Spanish civilization to the New World and for the social salvation of the Indian through it—a program, the generous scope of which was in striking contrast, not only to the English policy of the extermination of the indigenous race, but also to that of the French, which was satisfied with the transmission of the faith alone. That commercial exploitation often attended the execution of this program is recognized; it was a defect to which the system easily lent itself. Desire for profit did not obscure, however, the laudable objectives. In the early centuries, at least, these were predominant. But the Spanish mission was not only to convert and to civilize the frontier; in addition, it was a political and military institution to defend the outposts of empire from the encroachment of foreign powers and to extend them by opening up new lands. To promote the work, the state granted military and financial aid. As a frontier institution, the mission was expected to move continuously into new territory, turning its "reduced" and instructed Indians over to the secular clergy and the civil officers. Due to the difficulties of reduction in Venezuela and to the slowness with which the Spanish entered the interior, particularly the extensive Orinoco region, the mission and the *doctrina,* the stage between it and the Spanish town, remained the predominant institutions of the church among the Indians until the very end of the colonial period.

The work of the missionaries began in Venezuela early in the sixteenth century. With the conquerors there came friars to evangelize the Indians.[4] The mission as a recognized institution of state for the fulfillment of the program outlined above did not begin, however, until the middle of the seventeenth century. The first missionaries came on their own initiative, being given leave merely by the king to undertake the evangelization of the natives. They were granted no aid. With respect to them, the Spanish monarchs pursued a policy similar to that followed in the political sphere:

[4] The story of these early missionaries in Cumaná is told by Arístides Rojas in his *Estudios históricos: Orígenes venezolanos,* (Caracas, 1891), vol. i, pp. 38-71.

namely, to leave the early promotion of colonization to individuals, giving little aid and subjecting the process to little regulation. Both Dominicans and Franciscans attempted to establish monasteries on the eastern coast of Venezuela. Along with the colony of the celebrated Las Casas, they soon reaped, through the complete destruction of their enterprises, the results of Indian hostility to slave traders. The activity of the church shifted then to the west, where the first bishopric in Venezuela was established at Coro in 1531. The evangelical element so prominent in Cumaná from 1513 to 1520 was quickly extinguished, Rojas has observed in his quaint and charming essays on early Venezuela.[5] This civilizing agency was not to reappear for a century, and then in response to political necessity and with the protection of Spanish arms.

Missionaries appeared also in Guayana in the sixteenth century. In his *Noticias historiales de las conquistas de Tierra Firme*, Pedro Simón stated that a Franciscan accompanied Berrío in all his explorations and participated in the foundation of Santo Tomás in 1592. A little later a number of Dominicans came and a monastery was established at this place. Four friars accompanied de Vera in his search of Manoa. But the difficulties encountered took away all thought of founding missions in this country. All the ecclesiastics except those in the monastery at Santo Tomás left Guayana. This establishment itself was soon abandoned.[6] The failure of this enterprise seems to have ended missionary activity on the Orinoco in the sixteenth century.[7] Simón made no mention of other missions up to 1623, the date of the publication of his work. The frustration and defeat of the efforts both in Guayana and in Cumaná are to be attributed rather to the extreme difficulties and dangers of the undertaking than to any lack of zeal on the part of the missionaries.

After a century and a half of valiant, if misdirected effort, the

[5] Rojas, Arístides, *Estudios históricos*, vol. i, p. 88.

[6] Simon, Pedro, *Noticias historiales de las conquistas de Tierra Firme*, 5 vols., (Bogotá, 1882-1892), vol. v, p. 362 *et seq.*

[7] In his famous work, *El Orinoco ilustrado*, Gumilla mentioned Jesuit activity in Guayana in 1576. But the more trustworthy account of Rivero placed the incidents to which the former referred in the year, 1664; *vide* his *Historia de las misiones de los llanos de Casanare y ríos Meta y Orinoco*, 2 vols., (Bogotá, 1883), vol. ii, p. 171 *et seq.* For a criticism of the statements of Gumilla, *vide*, Tavera-Acosta, B., *Anales de Guayana*, 2 vols. (Ciudad Bolívar, 1913-1914), vol. i, pp. 9-21; *passim.*

conquistadores had failed to subdue the Indians in Venezuela. In recognition of this fact, Philip II, in 1652, ordered that armed conquest cease. In a royal *cédula* of the same year, he instituted the mission system. Under the terms of the institution he granted to the Capuchins of Aragon a large part of the province of Cumaná. In 1658, the Capuchins were also established in the Province of Caracas.[8] This division of the Franciscans was to become the predominant religious order in Venezuela; the Observants, usually referred to simply as the Franciscans, were second in importance. Dominicans, Augustinians, Jesuits, Candelarians, and Mercedarians were located later in parts of Venezuela.[9] Besides occupying a part of Cumaná and the larger part of Caracas, the Capuchins founded the important missions of Caroní on the lower Orinoco.[10] In Cumaná the Franciscan Observants were granted the region of Píritu, in which they worked from their center at Barcelona. In the division of Guayana, they were given the central Orinoco region.[11] This

[8] Rionegro, Froilán de, *Relaciones de las misiones de PP. capuchinos en Venezuela, 1650-1817*, 2 vols. (Seville, 1918), vol. i, p. 83 *et seq.*

[9] During the colonial period the distribution of monastic establishments had been the following: Franciscans (Capuchins and Observants), twenty-three; Dominicans, six; Jesuits, three; Augustinians, two; Mercedarians, one; Candelarians, one. There were, in addition, six convents for women. (González Guinán, F., *Historia contemporánea de Venezuela*, 15 vols., Caracas, 1909-1925, vol. ii, p. 34). All these did not remain until the end of the era; those of the Jesuits disappeared with the expulsion of the order in 1767. Martí reported only sixteen monasteries in Caracas in his report of his visit in 1771 to 1784. In his figures on the colonial church taken from the Archives of the Indies in 1829, Torrente listed only twelve establishments in Venezuela in comparison to two hundred fifty-two in Mexico, one hundred fifteen in Perú, forty-five in Chile, sixty-four in Buenos Aires, and sixty-six in New Granada. (Torrente, Mariano, *Historia de la revolución de Hispano-América*, 3 vols., Madrid, 1829, vol. i, pp. 46-49).

[10] Other important documents on the Capuchin missions are found in Blanco, J. F. and Ramón Azpúrua, *Documentos para la historia de la vida pública del Libertador*, 14 vols., (Caracas, 1875-1877) vol. i; Cuervo, Antonio de, *Colección de documentos inéditos sobre la geografía y la historia de Colombia*, 5 vols., (Bogotá, 1893), vol. iii; Altolaguirre y Duvale, Angel de, *Relaciones geográficas de la gobernación de Venezuela, 1767-1768*, (Madrid, 1908); Strickland, Joseph, *Documents and Maps on the Boundary Question between Venezuela and British Guayana from the Capuchin Archives in Rome*, (Rome, 1896), and other collections made in connection with this boundary question; *Relaciones históricas de las misiones de padres capuchinos de Venezuela, Colección de libros raros ó curiosos que tratan de América*, 2nd. series, vol. xxii (Madrid, 1929). Although they must be used with care, the many documents published in connection with the boundary disputes of Venezuela are very valuable for the study of the history of the colonial period, especially for the history of the church. These various collections are listed in the bibliography found at the end of this study.

[11] For the study of the Franciscan missions told by men who participated in the work, *vide*, Ruíz Blanco, Matías, *Conversión en Píritu, Colección de libros raros*, vol. ii (Madrid, 1892), and Caulín, Antonio, *Historia geográfica, natural, y evangélica de la Nueva Andalucía*, (Madrid, 1779), p. 212 *et seq.*

extensive territory had been entered by various orders after 1664—the Franciscans, Augustinians, Jesuits, Dominicans, and Capuchins. All had deserted it by the end of the seventeenth century.[12] The Jesuits had made especially heroic efforts to maintain the work under the direction of Antonio Monteverde, who wished to connect the missions in the *llanos* of the Meta and the Casanare with the lower Orinoco where there was a *presidio*.[13] The endeavor was discouraged from its beginning. Upon their arrival the missionaries found the guard decimated and starving. In attempts to establish themselves in 1664 and 1679, the Jesuits lost some of their best workers. As a result, the field was formally given up to the Capuchin order in 1682.[14] Causes of defeat lay not only in lack of defense, but also in the absence of means of subsistence in this isolated region and in the general unhealthfulness of the country. Because of the scarcity of missionaries, the Capuchins made no attempt to occupy this territory surrendered to them until 1724. In the meantime, but only after long petitioning before hostile officials, the Jesuits had been granted a small guard; and with it they made other attempts to enter Guayana in 1691 and 1695.[15] But the guard deserted, since their salary was not paid. Again the Jesuits were forced to withdraw. But, in 1731, these intrepid missionaries returned, and having overcome finally the material obstacles, they possessed by 1736 six flourishing missions on the upper Orinoco. In an agreement between the superiors of the Franciscans, the Capuchins, and the Jesuits, sanctioned by the governor, the territory was divided in 1736 be-

---

[12] *Counter-case of the United States of Venezuela before the Tribunal of Arbitration*, 3 vols., (New York, 1899), vol. iii, p. 69.

[13] Borda, J. J., *Historia de la Compañia de Jesús en la Nueva Granada*, 2 vols., (Poissy, 1872), vol. i, p. 126 *et seq.*; Rivero, Juan, *Historia de las misiones de los llanos de Casanare y ríos Meta y Orinoco*, (Bogotá, 1883), p. 171 *et seq.* Other accounts of the Jesuit missions on the Orinoco are found in the following: Gumilla, José, *El Orinoco ilustrado, historia natural civil y geográfica de este gran río y sus caudalosas vertientes*, (Madrid, 1741); Gilii, Filippo Salvadore, *Saggio di storia americana; o sia storia naturale, civile, e sacra de regni e delle provincia spagnuole di Tierra Ferme*, 4 vols. (Rome, 1780-1784); Cassani, José, *Historia de la provincia de la Compañía de Jesús en el Nuevo Reino de Granada*, (Madrid, 1741). An excellent secondary account is that of Antonio Astrain in his *Historia de la Compañía de Jesús en la asistencia de España*, 7 vols., (Madrid, 1920), vols. vi and vii.

[14] Strickland, Joseph, *Documents and Maps on the Boundary Question between Venezuelan and British Guayana*, Appendix 1, pp. 1-5.

[15] Rivero, J., *Historia de las misiones de los llanos de Casanare y ríos Meta y Orinoco*, p. 277 *et seq.*

tween these three orders. The Capuchins of Aragon were to occupy the region from the sea to Angostura: the Franciscans, that from Angostura to the entrance of the Cuchivero into the Orinoco; and the Jesuits, the region from this point to the frontiers of New Granada.[16] A little later Governor Solano divided the very considerable region left to the Jesuits, granting the upper Orinoco and the Río Negro valleys to the frontier of Brazil to the Capuchins of Andalucía. They established no missions, and in 1779 Centurión granted to the Franciscans the right to enter this territory and also to occupy the missions of the Jesuits. According to the reports of Governor Marmión to the Spanish government in 1788, the Jesuit missions were without missionaries from the expulsion of the order in 1767 until the Franciscans entered in 1785.[17] Centurión had asked for secular clergymen to put in charge of some of them, but the bishop had none to send. These vigorous missions declined rapidly after the expulsion of their founders; to this fact the viceroys of New Granada, officials in Guayana, the German traveller, Humboldt, and others testify.[18]

There were frequent disputes between the orders over their respective territorial limits. Uncertainty and confusion as to delimitations and consequent disputes over jurisdictions among the regular clergy resembled similar controversies that arose between the civil officials and the secular clergy over the same problems. All contributed to the turbulence of Venezuelan colonial life. Before the institution of the mission system, the Franciscans appealed to the Spanish monarch in 1651 to recall the Capuchins from Cumaná, claiming rights by prior occupation. An order was issued for the recall of the Capuchins, but it was never carried into effect. In 1657 the king divided the territory, assigning the Franciscans the Province of Píritu.[19] The Capuchins of Aragon in the Province of Caracas had complaints of intrusion against all their neighbors, ac-

[16] Documentos relativos a la cuestión de límites de navegación fluvial entre el imperio del Brasil y la república de Venezuela, (Caracas, 1859), p. 109 et seq.
[17] Counter-case of the United States of Venezuela before the Tribunal of Arbitration, vol. iii, p. 122.
[18] Posada, E. and P. M. Ibáñez, (editors), Relaciones de mando, Biblioteca de historia nacional, vol. xiii, (Bogotá, 1910) p. 431; passim.
[19] Relaciones históricas de las misiones de padres capuchinos de Venezuela, p. xxviii.

cording to the reports made in 1758 by Pedro de Ubrique, prefect of the order.[20] The Franciscans in Píritu carried away their Indians, claiming them as fugitives, and those of Guayana even burned Capuchin missions, he declared. But against the Jesuits his charges were still more severe. With this order the Capuchins had a long-continued conflict over the possession of the mission, Cabruta, on the River Meta and over fugitive Indians. Ubrique appeared in arms to undertake the occupation of this mission, but superiors confirmed the Jesuits in possession.[21]

The task of reducing the Indians to the mission régime was never completed. Nature defeated the Franciscans on the upper Orinoco and the Río Negro, Depons observed.[22] The Guaraunos at the mouth of the Orinoco remained gentiles and independent. Others who had been reduced reverted to savagery. The Goajiros and Motilones, fierce Indians of the Maracaibo district, returned to their former manner of life and gave continuous trouble to the governments of Caracas and Bogotá.[23] Humboldt found many Indians in the uplands of Cumaná living as independent groups.[24] Individuals and groups alike fled from the missions and hid in the inaccessible interior back from the rivers.[25] Both the nomadic character of the Indian and the geography of the country made against success in reduction and civilization. Lack of adequate resources and workers also retarded expansion. Venezuelan missions suffered from the general neglect of Spain for this region of Tierra Firme. Carlos de Sucre, governor of Cumaná, declared to the Spanish government in 1736 that he could use five hundred friars on the Orinoco and had not one to offer.[26] Diego Portales, captain-general and governor of

[20] Blanco and Azpurúa, Documentos para la historia de la vida pública del Libertador, vol. i, pp. 444-445.
[21] Astrain, A., Historia de la Compañía de Jesús en la asistencia de España, vol. viii, p. 468.
[22] Depons, Voyage to the Eastern Part of Tierra Firme, vol. i, p. 214 et seq.
[23] Ibid.
[24] Humboldt, A. de and Aimé Bonpland, Personal Narrative of Travels to the Equinoctial Region of the New Continent, 1799-1804, translation by H. M. Williams, 6 vols., (London, 1826), vol. iii, passim.
[25] In answer to those who attacked the Spanish as exterminators of the Indians, Gumilla, long a missionary on the Orinoco, offered the suggestion that the natives had not declined in numbers but were merely hidden; vide, El Orinoco ilustrado, vol. ii, p. 322. Such an idea might easily occur to one who had had experience with Venezuelan Indians.
[26] Counter-case of Venezuela, vol. iii, p. 43.

Venezuela, had made a special plea to the king ten years earlier for religious workers among the Indians.[27] Humboldt deplored the lack of missionaries on the upper Orinoco and the Río Negro at the end of the eighteenth century.[28] Venezuela suffered even more from dearth of missionaries than other parts of Tierra Firme. New Granada with two and one-half times the population had more than six times as many members of the regular clergy as Venezuela.[29] In view of these obstructions and inadequacies, it is remarkable that the majority of the Indians in Venezuela were brought within the mission system.

In spite of the considerable records of the missions, the impermanence and instability of many of them makes impossible any certainty as to their number and location at a given date.[30] Missions frequently had to be abandoned as a result of the sudden flight of the Indians or the lack of sufficient workers. Some were combined; others moved for reasons of health or subsistence; some missions projected were never established; others existed for years without being reported. As a result, both tables and maps are often erroneous. The following figures will give some suggestion of the number and size of the missions in the last half of the eighteenth century. In 1776, the Dominicans had fourteen in the district of Maracaibo according to the report of the viceroy of New Granada.[31] In 1763, the Franciscans had thirty-three in Cumaná and the Capuchins, twenty; in 1799, these contained respectively 21,000 and 18,000 Indians.[32] In 1788, the Capuchins and Franciscans had seventy-two missions in Guayana, Governor Marmión stated.[33] This number included the five Jesuit missions delivered to the Franciscans three years earlier. A memorial from the Capuchin missions

[27] Counter-case of Venezuela, vol. iii, p. 23.
[28] Humboldt, Personal Narrative of Travels to the Equinoctial Region of the New Continent, vol. v, pp. 578-580.
[29] Restrepo, J. M. Historia de la revolución de la república de Colombia, 5 vols., (Besançon, 1858), vol. i, p. xxvii.
[30] United States Senate Document, no. 6, 55th Congress, 2nd Session, Venezuelan Boundary Commission Report, 3 vols. (Washington, 1898), vol. iii, pp. 199-200.
[31] Posada and Ibáñez, Relaciones de mando, p. 224.
[32] Humbert, Jules, Les origines vénézuéliennes: Essai sur la colonization espagnole au Vénézuéle, (Paris, 1905), p. 234.
[33] Counter-case of Venezuela, vol. iii, Report of Marmión, pp. 108-145.

in 1816 reported twenty-nine establishments with 21,246 natives.[34] There were Augustinian missions in the Apure and the Orinoco valleys, but the writer has found no record of their number and size.[35]

In the defense of the frontiers against the encroachment of foreign powers, the missions in Venezuela rendered great service to the state. Those on the north coast had to face attacks of the English and French: indeed, their establishment was sometimes primarily defensive. Governor Castro founded a mission at La Guaira on one occasion solely as a coast guard. But it was in Guayana that the institution served the state most notably as an agency for expansion and defense. In this province the missions had to meet the Dutch, the Portuguese, the French, and the English. The Dutch, who allied themselves with the untamed Caribbean Indians, were their most persistent and most dangerous rival. But in the contest against them the missions possessed advantages. "Since 1734 the missions had been organized into a veritable institution of state; compared to the simple Dutch posts, the villages founded and peopled by missionaries represented a colonizing effort serious and solid," declared Humbert, the French historian of colonial Venezuela.[36]

Reports both from civil officials in Venezuela and from the Dutch on the Orinoco to their home government give testimony to the work of the missionaries in holding and extending the Spanish frontier against the operations of the Dutch West India Company.[37] Fearing the advancement of the Dutch, Governor Sucre urged the need of more missionaries.[38] When Iturriaga was put in charge of the commission on limits with Portugal, he was instructed likewise to study the Dutch encroachment and to determine the extent of the Capuchin settlement. He put a missionary, Father Garriaga, in charge of a special mission to the revolting negroes of Surinam in an effort to bring them under Spanish control.[39] In 1763, Diguja, governor of Cumaná, made an urgent appeal to the Spanish govern-

---

[34] Strickland, *Documents*, pp. 70-71.
[35] Restrepo, J. M., *Historia de la revolución de Colombia*, vol. i, p. 475.
[36] Humbert, Jules, *Les origines vénézuéliennes*, p. 281.
[37] For reports in the Dutch archives, *vide*, *Venezuelan Boundary Commission Report*, vol. ii, *passim*.
[38] *Counter-case of Venezuela*, vol. iii, pp. 42-43.
[39] *Venezuelan Boundary Commission Report*, vol. i, pp. 395-396.

ment for promotion of the missions as a defense against the Dutch West India Company.

By means of the missions, serving as advance posts, the Dutch and their assistants, the Caribbean Indians, have been prevented to a great extent from reaching the interior of the country through the Cuyuní and Mazaruni Rivers. . . . It is self-evident according to that testimony that it is a matter of vital importance to continue these missions southward. There is no other way to check the Dutch and prevent them from making settlements, as they attempt to do in the country aforesaid, which . . . is kept under the vigilant eye of the missionaries, who can report at once to the *presidio* anything which happens. . . . It is notorious that the Dutch, seeking to extend their commerce and especially their traffic in Indian slaves, insisted upon opposing the establishment of Spanish missions, which were insuperable obstacles not only to this inhuman trade, but also to their constant design of extending their territory.[40]

That even the small guard kept in Guayana was entirely dependent on the missions for subsistence, Diguja recognized. Should the mission fail at any time to furnish supplies, the inhabitants of the *presidio* would certainly starve, he reported.[41]

"The spread of the Spanish colonization was slow and confined to the efforts of the Capuchin missionaries, who were the only Spanish and the only colonizers on the spot," Strickland has stated. Without admitting the entire validity of the Venezuelan claims based on these activities, he recognized that the Capuchin documents and maps were the invaluable evidences of whatever claim Venezuela might make to territory in lower Guayana.[42]

Even the severest critics of the mission system recognize its service to Spain and to Venezuela as an institution of territorial expansion and defense. After having passed an unfavorable judgment on the mission as a civilizing agency, the Venezuelan historian, Duarte Level, concludes:

They saved the integrity of the country. In our question of limits with British Guayana the only solid and incontestable arguments that

---

[40] *Case of Venezuela, Documents and Correspondence relating to the Question of Boundary between British Guiana and Venezuela.* (Atlanta, 1896), pp. 104-105; p. 114.
[41] *Documents relating to the Question of Boundary between Venezuela and British Guayana,* 3 vols. (Washington, 1896), vol. i, pp. 48-49.
[42] Strickland, *Documents,* p. xvi; p. xxi.

we were able to present for justifying our rights to Guayana was the work the missionaries did there. . . . In planting the cross they fixed the limits of Venezuela.[43]

At this point a word might be said of the contributions of the missionaries to the knowledge of geography, of natural history, and of Indian cultures. The extensive and always alluring valley of the Orinoco was better known in the seventeenth and eighteenth centuries than it has been since that time. The well-known work of Father Román in the exploration of the Río Negro, or of Carvajal on the Apure, or Gumilla in the Orinoco region are merely notable incidents in a long list of explorations.[44] Missionaries were promoters of the opening of new lands and the extension of commerce, as their representations to the king indicate. For example, the Franciscan, Alvarez de Villanueva sent a long memorial to Charles IV in 1791, in support of the opening of the Amazon to free commerce by a treaty with Portugal.[45] Sometimes they were much too ambitious in their programs to suit Madrid. Plaza in his *Memorias* said the scheme advanced by the Jesuits in 1740 for connecting the commerce of the Meta with the Amazon astonished the Spanish ministry and hastened the expulsion of the order.[46] By pacifying the natives in the Province of Cumaná and checking the Caribbean Indians, the Capuchins opened the way into the *llanos*, establishing contact between that province, Caracas, and Guayana.[47] It might be said in this connection that practically all the towns founded in Venezuela during the colonial period owed their origin to the missionary.[48] The real work of colonization was done by him. Since military and civilian agencies had failed to occupy the country after

[43] Duarte Level, Lino, *Historia patria: Cuadros de la historia militar y civil de Venezuela* (Madrid, without date), p. 162.

[44] Altolaguirre y Duvale, Angel de, *Relaciones geográficas de la gobernación de Venezuela*, pp. xxxviii-xxxix; p. xlii; Humboldt, *Travels*, vol. v, p. 487 *et seq.*; Carvajal, Jacinto de, *Relación de descubrimiento del río Apure hasta su ingreso en el Orinoco*, (León, 1892).

[45] Álvarez de Villanueva, Francisco, *Relación histórica*, p. 33 *et seq.*

[46] Plaza, José Antonio de, *Memorias para la historia de la Nueva Granada desde su descubrimiento hasta el 20 de julio de 1810*, (Bogotá, 1850) pp. 313-314; vide also Cuervo, *Documentos*, vol. iii, p. 175 *et seq.*

[47] *Documents relating to the Question of Boundary between Venezuela and British Guayana*, vol. i, p. 17, *et seq.*

[48] Humboldt and others made note of this fact.

a century's effort, this peculiar frontier institution had to be introduced to accomplish the task.

The researches of missionaries in Indian culture, including linguistics, their studies of geography and natural science, and their civil and ecclesiastical histories, have been left in such celebrated writings as those of Pedro Aguado, Pedro Simón, Ruíz Blanco, Gilii, Rivero, Cassani, Cisneros, Caulín, Gumilla, and others. The value of the writings of Cassani and Gumilla on Guayana and of the map of the region by Father Samuel Fritz was recognized by the commission on boundaries between Spain and Portugal in 1750. These works were chosen by the commission as a basis for their report.[49] According to the statement of Strickland, the map made by Barcellona of the Capuchin missions of Guayana was the best in the Spanish archives on the limits of the Dutch settlement in that region.[50] No man knew the country better than Barcellona, said Strickland.

Up to this point this study has been concerned with the projection and establishment of missions; their distribution among the various orders; the services of the missionaries to the state in exploration, the promotion of new regions, and actual territorial expansions and defense; and their contribution to knowledge through their writings. Attention should now be directed to the methods employed in bringing the Indians within the missions and to the administration of these institutions.

II

THE SPANISH KINGS intended that reduction to the mission régime should be by persuasion, the system being instituted to remove the evils of armed conquest as well as to remedy the failure of that method. Efforts were made to realize this ideal of the monarchs. In 1755, Eugenio de Alvarado, commandant in Guayana, gave the following description of the methods followed by the Capuchins of that province on their *entradas*, or *conquistas de almas:*

Before entering the forest, they prepare . . . girdles of mankin and calico, hatchets, knives, and cutlasses to present to the Indians and beads for their wives. They select from the community of the mission two or three trustworthy Indians of the tribe that inhabits the

---

[49] Altolaguirre y Duvale, *op. cit.*, pp. xxxviii-xxxix.
[50] Strickland, *Documents*, p. xviii.

locality which they go to visit, and these serve as witnesses of the good treatment given to the Indians who establish themselves in missions. They also take one or two soldiers from the garrison of Guayana who serve as a guard in the mission and are well informed as to the road and provided with swords and firearms. Then they enter into the places where the Indian families are gathered into huts . . . and with these presents and kind words they endeavor to win them over and thus gain their good will. Some gather more fruit than others; but the first excursion serves only as a preliminary, and it is necessary to repeat the journey several times according to the character of the tribe.[51]

That a method so mild as this description suggests was not always employed is indicated by reports from other civil officials, from the accounts of the missionaries themselves, and from the observations made by foreign travellers. In a report to Count Aranda on the Jesuit administration in Guayana, Alvarado himself stated that force was used if necessary for success.[52] Humboldt spoke of the use of force by the Jesuits and Capuchins of Guayana.[53] That compulsion was commonly used by the Capuchins of the province of Caracas their own reports indicate. In 1676, Charles II granted to this order the right to recruit citizen-soldiers from Spanish villages to be established near the missions, and to use these forces for capturing the Indians and restraining them within the missions. This same privilege was later extended to the Capuchins in Guayana. Under the grant of 1676, the Capuchins of Caracas began to go out with considerable armed forces, often from two hundred to three hundred men, after the fashion of the *conquistadores*. In 1689, they were again ordered to go alone; but they appealed against this order, and in 1692 the former system of reduction was reëstablished.[54] The small returns from these *entradas* indicate the increasing difficulty of reducing the Indians to the mission régime. From 1707 to 1720, the missionaries used 1,357 soldiers and secured 1,531 men. Results were often less than these totals indicate. In 1726, two missionaries with seventy soldiers spent three months in securing sixteen

[51] *Counter-case of Venezuela*, vol. iii, p. 56.
[52] Cuervo, Antonio B., *Colección de documentos inéditos sobre la geografía y la historia de Colombia*, vol. iii, pp. 151-152.
[53] Humboldt, *Travels*, vol. v, pp. 541-542.
[54] Blanco-Azpurúa, *Documentos*, vol. i, pp. 397-400.

Indians.   In 1733, one friar and ninety-two men worked two months, returning with forty-two Indians; in 1742, a missionary with one hundred five captured only five natives, after losing one man in the encounter and having nine wounded.   With a force of three hundred, two missionaries undertook in 1720 an expedition in search of El Dorado.   Most of the soldiers deserted, and after five months the survivors returned with forty-eight Indians.[55]   It is said that the Capuchins of Guayana often took only the women and children, depending upon attracting thus the men to the mission.[56] The Jesuits used reduced Indians with considerable success in bringing the wild Indians into the mission.   A notable case is that of the Indian, Antonio Calaimi, who brought many of the Betoyes under the rule of the missionaries.[57]   But the Capuchins found that the Indians they sent out for this work never returned.[58]   They came to rely on the armed band as the only effective instrument of reduction.

Modern critics of the mission system find the methods used by the missionaries on *entradas* an easy point of attack on the system. But, after reading the contemporary accounts, one is inclined to accord much sympathy to the missionary.   In the province of Caracas, where force was used most, the Indian had been embittered by continued resistance to the Spanish conquerors.   Their nomadic character made them submit to sedentary life only under compulsion. Thus, the missionary had often no other means of accomplishing the work set for him by church and state, a task which the conquerors had failed to perform.   Force was not always used.   The Jesuits made valiant efforts to reduce by persuasion.   Even when a guard was furnished, men like the redoubtable Gumilla often chose to go alone.   Humboldt said that the Franciscans, Dominicans, and the Augustinians did not use force and that, at the time of his visit, it was prohibited by superiors in other orders and virtually abolished. When force was used, its worst features arose from native antagonism rather than from the severity of the missionary.[59]   A mission-

[55] Blanco-Azpurúa, *Documentos*, vol. i, p. 401 *et seq.*
[56] Baralt, R. M., and Ramón Díaz, *Resumen de la historia de Venezuela*, 3 vols., (Maracaibo, 1914), vol. i, pp. 435-436.
[57] Becker, D. T., and J. M. R. Groot, *El nuevo reino de Granada en el siglo xviii*, (Madrid, 1921), p. 10.
[58] Blanco-Azpurúa, *Documentos*, vol. i, p. 401; *passim.*
[59] Humboldt, *op. cit.*, vol. v, pp. 541-542.

ary told Humboldt that mission Indians taken on *entradas* often turned into murderous savages upon encountering men from hostile tribes.[60]   He observed that the Capuchins of Guayana took advantage of the hostility between the tribes to secure the adherence of the weaker ones. The missionary should probably be relieved in large part of the responsibility for the severe methods of reduction. But it remains that the Indian was antagonized; and thus the influence that the church might have had on him was lost.

Even after they were brought at such cost within the mission settlements, the Indians were yet by no means secured to the rule of the missionary. Olivares, prefect of the Capuchin missions of Caracas, declared they stayed only long enough to receive the tools and trinkets distributed to them; then they escaped at the first opportunity, often burning the church and the mission house before they left.[61] Ubrique, prefect of these missions in 1758, lamented that so few missions remained of those established, a result due to the desertion of the Indians.[62] To check their escape into the *llanos*, the king ordered in 1720 that the missions be moved nearer the coast and that Spanish villages be established between them and the llanos.[63] The missions in Guayana suffered depletion, not only through the desertion of the Indians, but from the attacks of the Dutch and the Caribbean Indians.

The missions were entirely in charge of the regular orders. Each order was independent of the others in its organization and operation. At the head of each there was a provincial, who served under a *vicario-general* resident in Spain. The *vicario-general* and provincial were appointed by the Spanish crown under the royal patronage. The following account given by Alvarado of the Capuchin organization in Guayana describes the system within the separate provinces. The regulars met at Upata every three years to elect a prefect, to whom they pledged obedience. They selected, at the same time, officials who managed the common funds and with them made purchases for the missions or for the fathers of goods not produced in the mis-

---

[60] Humboldt, *op. cit.*, vol. v, pp. 427-428.
[61] Blanco-Azpurúa, *Documentos*, vol. i, p. 390 *et seq.*
[62] *Ibid.*, p. 453.
[63] *Ibid.*, p. 403.

sion. These officials resided at Santo Tomás, the capital of the province.[64]

At the head of each mission there was a missionary. According to the rules there should have been two, but scarcity of workers made this rarely possible. In Venezuela one missionary sometimes served several posts. The Indians within the mission were allowed to choose certain local officials from their number, but the individuals thus selected functioned under the absolute rule of the missionary. The practice was established as a means of training the Indian for civil life.

The primary purpose of the mission in the program of the Spanish monarchs was to instruct the Indian in the Catholic faith. To further the attainment of this objective missionaries were ordered by the Laws of the Indies to learn the language of the Indians with whom they worked. The multiplicity of native languages in Venezuela would have made the attainment of this requirement very difficult, and it seems to have been seldom attempted in the later colonial era, when the zeal of the missionaries had been largely lost. But in the seventeenth century some notable work was done in the study of Indian languages, especially by Jesuit and Franciscan missionaries. At the end of the eighteenth century the Augustinians were attempting to carry on this work of the Jesuits.[65] But teaching in the Capuchin missions in the province of Caracas was done entirely in Spanish. The prefects admitted the defects of this system, since the older Indians did not learn the language. The report of Alvarado on the Guayana missions mentioned some use of the Pariagoto dialect, but instruction was usually in Spanish.[66]

It has been succinctly stated that the religious work of the church among the Indians was four-fold: (1) the destruction of earlier systems of belief and worship; (2) reduction to Christianity; (3) construction of missions and churches; and (4) instruction in the Catholic creed.[67] The larger share of the responsibility for the realization of these ends lay with the missions. Since there was

[64] *Counter-case of Venezuela,* vol. iii, p. 51 *et seq.*
[65] Posada and Ibáñez, *Relaciones de mando,* p. 223.
[66] *Counter-Case of Venezuela,* vol. iii, p. 45 *et seq.*
[67] Pierson, W. W., *Lectures,* University of North Carolina, 1929.

found no highly organized religious system in Venezuela, such as existed among the Indians of Mexico and Perú, the work of destruction was relatively slight. But in this lack of a specialized ecclesiastical control, the missionaries found their chief obstacle. This was, at least, the opinion of Miguel de Olivares, long a prefect of the Capuchins of Caracas. Indians unaccustomed to religious ritual were less impressed by the Catholic ceremonials, he observed. And the absence of both ecclesiastical and political control among them made the achievement of any discipline by the church difficult. The task of the church in reducing the Indians of Venezuela would be far more laborious of performance than the work among the natives of Mexico and Perú; in fact, he doubted that it could ever be accomplished.[68] In general agreement with this view, Arcaya found the primary factor in the institutional evolution of Venezuela to be the tendency of the European, in the presence of this primitive crudeness and apart from the restraints of any institutional tradition, to give way to savage impulses instead of subjecting the Indian to the restraints of organized society; particularly so, when his blood was mixed with that of the Indian and the Negro.[69]

These natives of the "third class," as he designated them, Olivares judged to possess too low intelligence and culture to be instructed; the conquerors had with reason doubted that they were rational. In his phrase they understood "nothing about the eternal." After years of teaching, they returned to savagery at the first opportunity. Not less gloomy was the report of an archbishop-viceroy of New Granada, Córdoba. He was convinced that instruction in civil life should be placed first, on the grounds that religious instruction was futile. "God free a bishop of the Catholic church from preferring anything to the propagation of the gospel; but the interest of religion itself demands that one not cast pearls before swine," he declared.[70] Depons considered these Indians not fit for religion.[71] Humboldt found little difference between the savage and the reduced

[68] Blanco-Azpurúa, *Documentos*, vol. i, p. 396; pp. 417-418.
[69] Arcaya, Pedro M., *Estudios sobre personajes y hechos de la historia venezolana*, p. 253 *et seq; passim*.
[70] Posada and Ibáñez, *Relaciones de mando*, p. 228.
[71] Depons, *op. cit.*, vol. i, pp. 239-242.

Indian; both, "occupied by wants of the moment, discover a marked indifference for religious opinions."[72]

What was true in Venezuela was, of course, more or less true in other parts of the empire; to attract the Indian the church had to tolerate many compromises with Indian customs. And, even after accepting such compromises, its hold on the Indian through the restraints of religion alone was probably slight. But in Venezuela it appears to have been even slighter than among the Indians more advanced in civilization. The mission was far more important as an agency of the state than of the church. It was an educational institution where the Indian learned to speak and sometimes to read Spanish; it gave him some rudimentary training for citizenship; and it was an economic organization for self-support and for training the Indian in industrial life.

The administration of the Capuchins in Guayana may be taken as illustrative of the economic system. There were differences, however, among the orders in the details of administration; also, there were local and regional variations arising from the type of industry followed. General agriculture prevailed in Cumaná; in the llanos of Caracas, cacao was the chief product; in the Andes region, cattle and fruit culture and industrial arts, including lace-making, were engaged in. In the missions controlled by the Jesuits, industrial pursuits, such as weaving, fruit culture, cattle raising, and general agriculture, were all found. In Guayana, cattle was the chief product; they flourished and multiplied with great rapidity, being thus the means by which the Capuchins had been able to establish themselves here where subsistence had been found so difficult.[73] Sugar was produced and other food crops, including grains and cassava. Some crude manufacturing was done; in the late eighteenth century, Humboldt found considerable development of cotton spinning and the tanning of leather.

At the time Alvarado made his famous report, 1755, there were eleven missions all grouped about the central one, Divina Pastora.

[72] Humboldt, *Travels*, vol. ii, p. 211.
[73] There is an interesting story of the bringing of the first cows from Barcelona; Baralt and Díaz, *Resumen*, vol. i, p. 433, gives it in brief; also Depons, *op. cit.*, vol. ii, p. 112.

Each mission had a common farm worked by the Indians and plots that the natives worked for themselves. In addition, there was a central ranch, where cattle were raised for sale in Guayana and Trinidad and, it was said, for contraband trade with the Dutch. Several smaller ranches supplied the missions with fresh meat and milk and another furnished horses and mules. A sugar mill, centrally located, produced sugar, molasses, and rum for all the missions. These common establishments were managed by superintendents and worked with Indian labor, the returns going into a common fund to be used for the purchase of supplies for the churches, for the expense of *entradas*, for the support of the old and infirm, and for other common purposes.

In addition to these communal enterprises, there were individual ones both for the missionaries and for the Indians. The former employed Indian labor on their farms, paying for it in cloth, tools, and trinkets. They often sent the natives into the interior to gather valuable oils, which they sold at a handsome profit; and with the Caribbean Indians, they conducted a flourishing trade in hammocks. The Indians might sell to their own profit the products of their farms or such small manufactures as they made of fibers and horse hair. For the Spanish inhabitants of Guayana they might work for a wage fixed by law.[74] They were reputed to be always impoverished. The missionaries attributed the indigence of the natives to indolence, drunkenness, and improvidence; but enemies of the missions accused the directors of exploiting the natives for their own gain.

In addition to the income from the establishment itself, support for the mission might come from alms. Some missions in the province of Caracas seem to have relied considerably on this source. The missionary received also a small salary, or *sínodo*, from the state, the amount varying regionally from fifty to two hundred fifty *pesos* a year. There were frequent complaints from prefects of arrears in payment. Depons stated that the payment to the Capuchins of Guayana had been stopped on the grounds that they no longer needed support.[75]

[74] *Counter-case of Venezuela*, vol. iii, p. 51 *et seq.*
[75] Depons, *op. cit.*, vol. ii, p. 111.

The early missions in Guayana had found great difficulty in subsisting in this region untouched by any currents of trade; in fact, the lack of means of economic support had been the chief cause of the repeated abandonment of the region by the different orders. But after the introduction of cattle into the Capuchin missions they began to prosper. By the end of the eighteenth century, the Capuchins were directors of a considerable industrial establishment, possessing in 1788 one hundred eighty thousand head of cattle, Governor Marmión stated. These missions, according to the statements of Governors Centurión, Inciarte, Marmión, and other civil officials in the late eighteenth century, were operated to the benefit of the missionaries only, who, they contended, isolated and exploited the Indians. The civil authorities opposed particularly their monopoly of the best lands and of the entire labor supply. To the mission régime Centurión attributed the backwardness of Cumaná, also; it had impoverished both whites and Indians and had not advanced the natives in civilization. Many who had been in missions for forty years were as ignorant and barbarous as ever and as useless to the state as they were when they wandered in the forests as savages, he declared. An advanced advocate of economic reform, representative of the investigative spirit of the reign of Charles III, he saw the possibilities for the promotion of the Orinoco, a region that from the early days of the *conquistadores* never failed to fire the imagination of those who visited it, even though it had defeated, until the Capuchins came, all who attempted its development. To open the region to commerce and promote immigration, Centurión proposed the establishment of towns of Spanish and Indians under civil control. Such an arrangement would be more conducive to the civilization of the latter and to the economic progress of both groups, he insisted. And he actually projected thirty-five such towns along the Orinoco, taking cattle from the Capuchins to distribute among them. The archives of the period are filled with the records of the controversy which he provoked with the missionaries over the initiation of this program. But when he attempted to go further to bring the missions under civil control, he met defeat.[76] The Spanish government took the side of the mis-

---

[76] Strickland, *Documents, passim; Counter-case of Venezuela*, vol. iii, *passim*.

sionaries; in a *cédula* of July 6, 1774, it was ordered that their establishments be left undisturbed.[77]   Although the attack on the missions was renewed by Governor Marmión, he met no better success. Not until the liberal revolution of 1812 in Spain was the monopoly of the Capuchins broken in law.   The immediate absolutist reaction prevented the abolition from being made effective.   When the revolutionary forces entered Guayana in 1816, they found the missionaries still in control.[78]

To the missions in other parts of Venezuela one finds similar, if not so vigorous, opposition.   The long memorial of Olivares mentioned above is an answer to an attack led by the citizens of San Felipe, supported by the governor and bishop, to secure the delivery of this town to the Spanish and the secular clergy.   The missionaries were charged with exploiting the labor of the Indians on their private plantations and engaging in contraband trade.   The latter charge, whether true or not, brought upon them the opposition of the powerful Guipúzçoa Company.   But, according to reports in 1758, no change had been made in the control of the village; the missionary had apparently gained the ear of the king.   There were similar conflicts with the Capuchins in Trinidad.[79]

In the districts of Maracaibo and Mérida the administration of both Capuchins and Dominicans was attacked as negligent and ineffective in keeping the unruly Goajiros and Motilones in control. In 1776, while the region was still under New Granada, the viceroy, Manuel de Guirior, proposed to substitute a civil régime and make religious instruction secondary to reduction to civil life, a plan similar to that outlined by Centurión for Guayana.[80]   He placed a commandant, Guillen, over the Motilones, subordinating the missionaries

---

[77] Blanco-Azpurúa, *Documentos,* vol. i, p. 458; Duarte Level, *op. cit.,* p. 160.

[78] José de Olazarra, commissioned by the Spanish Cortés in 1813 to investigate the Capuchins mission of Guayana, reported that they had 17,892 people in their charge, with whose "persons and goods they did as they pleased"; that "their wealth and trading were notorious"; that, although these missions had been in charge of the Capuchins for eighty-eight years, none of the Indians could read or write.   In the same year the Cortés decreed that they should pass to the secular clergy, "in virtue of the evil the inhabitants suffer in the moral as well as in the political sphere," (Duarte Level, *op. cit.,* p. 160).

[79] Blanco-Azpurúa, *Documentos,* vol. i, p. 388, *et seq.*

[80] Posada and Ibáñez, *Relaciones de mando,* p. 126; Plaza, *Memorias,* p. 319.

to his rule. But Guillen was soon removed, and no attempt appears to have been made to continue his work.

The Franciscan Observants did not receive the criticism accorded the Capuchins. Humboldt and Depons commended their establishments in Píritu. But the observations of these travellers were concerned with the intellectual interests, the tolerance, and the hospitality of these missionaries rather than with their management of the mission. The administration was admitted to be negligent, although not oppressive. Humboldt was inclined to be more severe in his judgment of the Franciscans on the Orinoco because of their failure to achieve the material success that the Capuchins had attained. The missions of the Jesuits, placed in charge of the Franciscans, had declined rapidly; as he pointed out, however, they had been demoralized by the various attempts of Solano and Centurión to administer them before they were delivered to the Franciscans.[81]

A statement of the causes of the contemporary criticism of and attack on the mission system and the monastic orders may be set forth more explicitly, even though summarily, at this point. Opposition may be attributed to the jealousy of civilians, who desired the lands, the trade, and the labor supply monopolized by the missions; and of the secular clergy, who opposed the exclusive rule of the regulars in the missions. It was encouraged by the philosophy of rationalism and utilitarianism, which early found a welcome in Venezuela along with other contraband goods. There were, moreover, weaknesses and evils in the administration of the missions which might be made a basis for criticism by impartial judges. As to the jealousy of the civilians and civil authorities, Humboldt was no doubt correct in his judgment that it was not so much the actual goods of the missions that was desired; it was rather the opposition to the principle of monopoly, to "the right which one caste or branch of a community arrogates to itself of bringing up youth or of governing, not to say civilizing, the savage."[82] The attacks of the governors in Guayana were directed against the impoverished Franciscan missions as well as against the more flourishing establishments of the Capuchins.

This sentiment of equalitarianism, which aimed at the abolition

[81] Humboldt, *Travels*, vol. v, pp. 73-76.
[82] *Ibid.*, vol. v, pp. 73-74.

of all special privileges, and the civilist spirit, which sought to reduce all jurisdictions to the political power, are especially significant. They were to remain chief sources of later attacks on the church under the Republic. Although these tendencies were intensified in the War for Independence, they were already apparent in the criticism of these institutions, regarded as absolutist and obscurantist, as opposed to the "*luces del siglo*," which this generation of Venezuelans so eagerly sought.

Through defects of administration as well as through weaknesses inherent in the system, some missions were laid open to attack. Like all institutions, they were inclined to abuse the practically unlimited power they possessed. Humboldt observed that the Indians, kept in a state of villainage, were excited to hatred against the monks.[83] Depons remarked that it was not rare to see deputations of Indians seeking relief from the civil authorities against the friars; that the latter overworked the Indians and exploited them in the sale of rosaries and images. Although he expressed great admiration for the zeal of the early missionaries, he was convinced that at the end of the eighteenth century they preferred a life of ease and that "neither the cause of religion nor of national sovereignty was advanced by them."[84] But it should be noted that both Humboldt and Depons offer in the course of their narratives many exceptions and qualifications, even contradictions, to these generalizations; which fact suggests that the mission system was individualized, that no generalizations can correctly describe it. If one takes a balance of the criticisms of these men, it appears that they were more impressed by the evil inherent in the system, which forced the nomadic Indian to a mode of life contrary to his nature, than by any oppressiveness in its administration. Humboldt admitted and gave figures to prove that the mission régime conserved the life of the Indian.[85]

Other European travellers gave appraisals of the system more favorable than those of these two famous critics of Venezuelan society. Lavaysse had only praise for "those worthy Spanish missionaries," and said that it was an agreeable duty "to refute the calumnies

[83] Humboldt, *op. cit.*, vol. v. pp. 532-536.
[84] Depons, *op. cit.*, vol. ii, pp. 109-111.
[85] Humboldt, *op. cit.*, vol. v, p. 23.

of which they have been the object both in America and Europe."[86]
Pondenx and Mayer attributed to the missionaries the Spanish civilization in Venezuela and the increase of Spanish possessions. · "They
have proved that mildness is a means more efficacious than the force
of arms. Imbued with evangelical principles, they have treated these
people as their brothers and have rendered, in civilizing them, a
service essential to humanity."[87]

Criticisms from the local documents of the period are even more
inconclusive than these if one seeks an absolute judgment on the
merits of the mission system. The severe criticism of Centurión can
be balanced by the very favorable report of Alvarado, made only a
decade and a half earlier, or that of Diguja, appearing only eight
years prior to Centurión's. Modern Venezuelan historians, Gil Fortoul, Eloy González, Tavera-Acosta, Duarte Level, Salas, Michelena
y Rojas, and others, lean heavily in the formation of their judgments
on the reports of Centurión and unfavorable statements selected from
Humboldt and Depons. One is inclined to accept as more just the
estimate of the earlier Colombian historian, Restrepo. Although he
admitted that the system was not perfect, he commended the zeal of
the missionaries and their conservation of the life of the Indian, in
contrast to the policy of extermination followed in the English colonies in North America, and deplored the abolition of the system by
the new republic.[88] The judgments of the French historians, Humbert and Desdevises du Dezert, who based their opinions on studies
in the Spanish archives, are even more favorable than that of Restrepo. The latter praised the administration of the Capuchins in
Guayana as more admirable than that of the Jesuits in Paraguay,
an administration which has been regarded generally as the ideal of
benevolent paternalism.[89]

The search for substitutes for the mission system indicates the
wide-spread criticism of it in the eighteenth century; but the failure

---

[86] Lavaysse, Dauxion, *A Statistical, Commercial and Political Description of Venezuela, Trinidad, Margarita and Tobago*, (London, 1820), p. 411.

[87] Pondenx, H. and F. Mayer, *Mémoire pour servir a l'histoire de la revolution de
la capitainerie générale de Caracas, depuis l'abdication de Charles IV jusqu' au mois
d'aôut 1814*, (Paris, 1815), p. 19.

[88] Restrepo, *op. cit.*, vol. i, pp. 475-476. But he gives a different opinion in the
appendix, p. xxxiii.

[89] Humbert, *op. cit.*, p. 307, quotes the opinion of Desdevises du Dezert.

to find satisfactory agencies to replace it suggests the difficulty of handling the Indian problem in any other way. Centurión's ambitious project was a lamentable failure. Humboldt ridiculed the "towns" of Spaniards and Indians that the governor had designated as *villas* to impress the ministry at Madrid.[90] And even Centurión did not propose to remove the missionaries in places where they were already established. Such action he feared would lead to the desertion of the Indians.[91] There were, moreover, no secular clergy to put in charge. He had tried to secure priests for the Jesuit missions without success. Even the churches in Angostura had to be served by missionaries. The desertion of the Indians delivered to the secular clergy in other provinces often made necessary a new reduction by the regulars. This fact suggests both a strength and a weakness of the mission system. Although it was devised to prepare the Indian for civil life, its advantages were to be realized only by its permanence. Released from it, the Indian reverted to a primitive mode of life with the loss of the virtues proper to such an existence.

In concluding this survey of the mission system the following summary judgment might be offered. The missionaries had been the most effective institution of state in the colonization of Venezuela; they had accomplished its pacification where the conquerors had failed; in doing so, they had conserved the life of the Indian, so that today he forms the base of the population of the republic. They had opened up the interior; explored the country, leaving in their records of this work valuable geographic, scientific, and historical documents; they had established towns and defended the frontiers. They had reduced a large part of the Indian population to the mission; within it, they had given the native an introduction at least to Spanish civilization, including some valuable industrial training and preparation for civil life.

If this work was incomplete and not wholly effective, such a result may be attributed in large part to factors beyond the control of the missionaries: to the physical and material difficulties, to the nomadic character of the Indians, to the lack of workers and funds, and

[90] Humboldt, *op. cit.*, vol. v, pp. 404-405.
[91] Blanco-Azpurúa, *op. cit.*, vol. i, pp. 456-458.

to the opposition of the civil officials.   On the other hand, the failure to achieve the permanent social salvation of the Indian may be attributed in part to the relaxation of discipline in the orders in the eighteenth century and local dissensions and rebellions against superiors and, in some instances, to the exploitation of the Indian by the missionary.   Whatever the cause, the result was significant for the future of the church under the Republic.   With the abolition of the missions in the revolutionary epoch, the control of the church over the Indian was lost.   He became either hostile because of hatred toward the missionary, or indifferent through the failure of the church to make a permanent impression on his mind.   The civilizing effect of the missions disappeared with them.

Reference has been made above to local dissensions in the orders and rebellions against the authority of the provincials.   One finds in these institutions excellent illustrations of the individualism and decentralization of Venezuelan society.   The Franciscans in Guayana opposed control by the provincial and college in Píritu.   Humboldt heard the story of their seizing the provincial on a visit to them, imprisoning him, and choosing a substitute from their own number. But discord within the rebellious group led to the discovery of their action.   At Esmeralda he observed a "lively interest" in this "sedition of the monks."[92]   During the bitter conflict between the civil officials and the missionaries in Guayana, when one might expect to find unity in resistance, monks appealed to the commandant over their prefect.   The commandant eagerly seized the opportunity to intervene, and the prefect had to appeal to Spain to maintain his authority.[93]   Instances of internal dissension could be multiplied.   In view of this lack of unity, one can understand the division of the clergy in the War for Independence, itself a civil war.

But local resistance to superiors should not be taken to suggest resistance to royal authority or to the royal patronage in principle. The regular clergy like the secular was, indeed, regarded as a primary support of that power in America.   It was a chief defense of

[92] Humboldt, *op. cit.*, vol. v, pp. 508-510.
[93] Strickland, *Documents*, p. xvii.

the territorial integrity.[94]   Although the missionaries probably engaged in contraband trade with the Dutch, they resisted any extension of political jurisdiction by foreign power.   Opposed by the civil
officials as a power too independent of the state, the missionaries
found protection in the Spanish monarchy.   The regular orders furnished one of those numerous balances of power preserved in the
Spanish system.   In view of this relationship existing between the
regular orders and the Spanish kings, they might be expected to
unite in support of the royal authority upon the outbreak of the
revolution in 1810.   That they did not do this is indicated in Chapter I of this study.

III

THE REMAINING part of this introductory study will be concerned
with the secular division of the ecclesiastical organization in colonial
Venezuela and with some general considerations of the status of the
church at the end of the colonial period.   In its territorial organization the church presents a complexity similar to that of the political
and judicial powers; and its delimitations were different from those
of either of these, a fact which exaggerates further the lack of unity
throughout the administration.   Only in 1803 was the ecclesiastical
jurisdiction unified under the archbishopric of Caracas, created in
that year.   Even then it did not become coincident with the political
division.   The British Island of Trinidad remained within the archbishopric of Caracas until 1819, and the districts of Pamplona and
Cúcuta in New Granada continued to be administered by the Bishop
of Mérida until 1832.   The ecclesiastical organization in Venezuela,
as well as the political, furnished a most intriguing instance of that
characteristic decentralization in Spanish colonial administration; in
no other division of the Empire, it is thought, could such a lack of
integration be found.[95]   The completion of unification only at the

---

[94] The Jesuits were suspected of disloyalty in their dealings with the Portuguese in
Brazil. For a report by Alvarado, Commandant in Guayana to Count Aranda with
reference to the question, vide, Cuervo, Documentos, vol. iii, pp. 111-225, especially
p. 175 et seq. Alvarado, who had highest praise for the internal administration of the
Jesuits, regretted that he could not report so favorably as to their external policy.
[95] This is the conclusion of Dr. Pierson, who has made a special study of the
colonial political organization and administration.

very close of the colonial period left its heritage of division and factionalism to the national church as well as to the state.

The secular clergy served the Spanish population and the reduced Indians. Hence, its prominence in a province varied inversely with that of the regulars in the missions. Caracas early became the center of the secular organization. But the first bishopric in Venezuela was erected at Coro in 1531, its incumbent being made a suffragan of the Archbishop of Santo Domingo. This city remained the legal residence of the bishopric until 1636, when it was transferred to Caracas. Exposure of Coro to attacks by foreigners was given as a reason for removal in the royal *cédula* that formalized the transfer; the cathedral itself had been sacked by the English in 1567 and later by the Dutch. Another basis for the location of the ecclesiastical authority at Caracas was the fact that this city had become the center of political jurisdiction and of the Spanish population, containing thus a larger number of priests.[96] As a matter of fact, Caracas had been the *de facto* seat of the bishopric, or at least of the residence of the bishop, since the administration of Bishop Manzanillo, 1581-1591, who, according to Terrero, resided in that city most of the time.[97] After his time the custom became fixed that the bishop should reside there.[98] In 1613, Bishop Bohorques attempted to effect a legal transfer to Caracas on the grounds of the impoverished condition of Coro, where the church had suffered from narrowness of resources ever since its establishment. He petitioned the king for the removal, writing in the meantime to the dean and chapter at Coro to come to Caracas to await the royal decision. Only the dean obeyed his injunction; the rest of the chapter, supported by the secular *cabildo*, petitioned against the removal. The king rejected the petition of this

[96] Blanco-Azpurúa, *Documentos*, vol. i, p. 44.

[97] Terrero, Blas José, *Teatro de Venezuela y Caracas*, (Caracas, 1926) pp. 15-16. This quaint history of the church, written by Father Terrero in the latter part of the eighteenth century, forms the chief basis for the charming studies of Arístides Rojas on the church. Some errors of Terrero and Rojas are corrected by Monseñor Navarro in his recent excellent history, *Anales eclesiásticos venezolanos*, (Caracas, 1929). Another source for the study of the secular church is the work of Mariano Talavera y Garcés, published serially in his *Crónica eclesiástica*, 1856-1857, and recently collected and republished by Navarro under the title, *Apuntes de historia eclesiástica de Venezuela* (Caracas, 1929); also Gil Dávila, González, *Teatro eclesiástico de las primeras iglesias de las indias occidentales*, 2 vols. (Madrid, 1649).

[98] Sucre, Luis A., *Gobernadores y capitanes generales de Venezuela*, (Caracas, 1928), p. 79.

bishop.[99] In 1635, Bishop Agurto de la Mata succeeded in getting
the support of the governor, Ruíz Fernández de Fuenmayor, who
was in conflict with the *cabildo* over a matter of *regalias*, and effected
a transfer. In 1636, the king sanctioned the removal as a *fait
accompli*.[100] This controversy of fifty years over the location of the
episcopal see is but one of the interesting conflicts within the church
organization and between the civil and ecclesiastical powers that fill
the history of colonial Venezuela.[101]

The provinces of Margarita and Cumaná were incorporated in
the bishopric of Porto Rico in 1558; in 1624, the city of Santo
Tomás was added to this bishopric; and, in 1625, all Guayana.[102]
In 1790, the bishopric of Guayana was created with its incumbent a
suffragan of the archbishop of Santo Domingo. Under its jurisdiction were placed the islands of Trinidad and Margarita and the
provinces of Cumaná and Guayana. In spite of its occupation by the
British in 1797, Trinidad remained a part of this ecclesiastical organization until 1819.[103] The bishopric of Mérida was erected in
1777, its occupant being a suffragan of the archbishop of Santa Fé.
According to the law, it included territory within both the captaincy-
general of Caracas and the vice-royalty of New Granada. Another
long controversy arose over this erection. Caracas opposed the
separation of Coro from her episcopal control, and the cities of
Pamplona, San Cristóbal, and Cúcuta protested against their separation from the archbishopric of Santa Fé. But in 1790 the king, in
answer to these communications, reaffirmed the boundaries established
in 1777. That this did not end the dispute the documents of the
diocese of Mérida indicate. Petitions, protests, and commissions to
fix boundaries followed, until the king in 1806 again confirmed the
delimitations of 1777.[104] But over the clergy in the rebellious districts the Bishop of Mérida only with difficulty effected any control.

[99] Talavera y Garcés, *Apuntes*, p. 63; Depons, *op. cit.*, vol. iii, p. 65.

[100] Terrero, *op. cit.*, pp. 29-31.

[101] Incidentally, it indicates, too, the intense municipal rivalry.

[102] Gil Fortoul, *Historia constitucional de Venezuela*, 2 vols., 2nd edition (Caracas,
1930), vol. i, p. 86.

[103] Blanco-Azpurúa, *Documentos*, vol. i, p. 225.

[104] Silva, Antonio Ramón, *Documentos para la historia de la diócesis de Mérida*, 6
vols., (vols. i, ii, iii, iv, vi, Mérida, 1908-1922; vol. v, Caracas, 1927), vol. i, pp.
329 *et seq; passim.*

Following the occupation of Santo Domingo by the French in 1795, Caracas and Guayana were for eight years without a metropolitan. In 1803, the archbishopric of Caracas was created and the bishoprics of Guayana and Mérida were placed under its administration. This act completed the ecclesiastical consolidation of Venezuela.

As suggested above, the lack of administrative unity in the Venezuelan church gave rise to diversity in practice, to lack of discipline, and to a failure to achieve anything approaching an institutional spirit and tradition within the organization. The bishop of Caracas, in attempting to extend the discipline established in his diocese in the celebrated *Constituciones sinodales* of 1687 to the diocese of Guayana, encountered difficulties due to the custom of those churches of following the rules of bishopric of Porto Rico.[105] Not only did there exist the problem of such formal differences; there was the more significant difficulty of bringing the clergy under the moral power of the church through provincial or diocesan councils or through the visits of bishops. During the time that Cumaná and Guayana were included in the bishopric of Porto Rico, they were probably visited very seldom. At least there are few records of such visits. Martí was the first to go to the new capital, Angostura.[106] The western region under Santa Fé suffered a similar lack of supervision. Even in the province of Caracas the undertaking of a general visit was a notable endeavor. The difficulties that Bishop Martí experienced in his visit in the last quarter of the eighteenth century suggest what must have been the almost insurmountable obstacles at an earlier period. This physical problem exaggerated the personal one, the individualism of the clergy, which made it difficult for the bishop to control even the local clergy.

The activity of the secular clergy was concentrated in the province of Caracas. Bishop Martí reported a visit to two hundred twenty-eight churches, sixteen convents, and one hundred eighty-eight *cofradías* in the diocese of Caracas in the years, 1771 to 1784. There was, however, considerable expansion in Mérida in the late eighteenth century. The following facts indicate roughly the relative

[105] Talavera, *Apuntes*, p. 103. The *Constituciones sinodales del obispado de Venezuela*, 3 vols., (Madrid, 1761), were followed by the Venezuelan church until 1904.
[106] Talavera, *Apuntes*, p. 101; Tavera-Acosta, *Anales de Guayana*, vol. i, p. 101-102.

strength of the secular organization in the three jurisdictions at the time of the Revolution. The diocese of Caracas was served by two hundred forty-seven priests, with an income from the tithe of 316,215 pesos; the diocese of Mérida by one hundred sixty-four, with an income of 74,000 pesos; and the diocese of Guayana by forty-five, with an income of 24,000 pesos, the latter paid from the royal treasury, into which the tithe collected from the province went.[107] In comparison, New Granada, with two and one-half times the population, had about four times the number of priests.[108] But the diocese of Caracas was the wealthiest in Tierra Firme measured by the income from the tithe alone. Although that of Santa Fé had more than twice the number of priests, it had an income of only 286,000 pesos. In some years the archbishop of Caracas alone received an income of 70,000 pesos; the bishop of Mérida had about one-fourth as much; the bishop of Guayana was paid a salary of 4,000 pesos.[109] The bishop and chapter of the last named diocese were, according to Lavaysse, the most poorly paid ecclesiastics in America.[110] The number of higher clergy varied in proportion to the importance of the jurisdiction. Depons recorded in 1801 seventy prebendaries in the cathedral at Caracas in addition to the official canons; the number was much smaller in Mérida, he said, and in Guayana there were only two canons, not a sufficient number to constitute a chapter. Before the creation of the bishopric, the churches in Santo Tomás were served by regulars from the missions.[111] Even after the establishment of the bishopric, Depons observed that services were conducted in a mere hovel. Not until some time after the Revolution was a cathedral built. All this indicates that the activity of the secular clergy was practically non-existent in the province of Guayana.

[107] Restrepo, *op. cit.*, vol. i, appendix, p. xxvii.

[108] The following figures given by Torrente indicate the relative extent of the church establishment in the several divisions of the Spanish Empire: Mexico had five bishoprics, eighty-four canons, two hundred fifty-two convents; Perú had six bishoprics, forty-five canons; one hundred fifteen convents; Chile, two bishoprics, seventeen canons, forty-five convents; Buenos Aires, seven bishoprics, forty-six canons, sixty-four convents; New Granada, eight bishoprics, sixty canons, sixty-six convents; Caracas, three bishoprics, seventeen canons; twelve convents; *Historia de la revolución hispano-americana*, 3 vols. (Madrid, 1829) vol. i, pp. 46-49.

[109] Depons, *op. cit.*, vol. ii, p. 88.

[110] Lavaysse, *op. cit.*, p. 128.

[111] Tavera-Acosta, *Anales de Guayana*, vol. i, p. 101.

Many curacies and *doctrinas* in other parts of Venezuela were served by regulars. This practice produced much friction between the regular and secular organizations. Regulars holding curacies were placed under secular control, but managed to escape often from regulations by either jurisdiction. Trouble from this source led the king in 1757 to limit the number of curacies in a province that might be held by regulars, and finally to forbid the practice altogether. But the law was not executed in Venezuela.[112] Indeed, it would have been impossible to execute it, since secular priests could not be secured or induced to take these places. Centurión had found this true in his endeavor to restrict the rule of the regulars.

Accounts of contemporaries as well as of later historians point to the great wealth of the church in Venezuela. Depons declared that the riches of the country were swallowed up in pious foundations.[113] Restrepo made a similar observation. Ségur, Lavaysse, Humboldt, Pondenx, and Mayer spoke of the clergy as wealthy and the churches as imposing, even magnificent. Later Samper deplored the concentration of wealth in the hands of the church.[114] Salas said that the colonial church had the best lands and that the regular orders alone possessed more wealth than the state.[115] Without doubt the church was comparatively wealthy, at least in the province of Caracas. Yet the general poverty of the captaincy-general until the late eighteenth century would make such relative wealth appear small when compared to that of the church in the richer divisions of the Empire. Even Salas admitted this fact. And when wealth began to increase in Venezuela, enthusiasm for pious donations had declined. Depons's descriptions of the material condition of the church, which are the most complete outside the notable work of Bishop Martí, indicate that churches in centers of Spanish population were adequate and substantial, but not magnificent, even in Caracas. In most places outside Caracas he found only a single church. These were in most instances described as good. The observations of Cisneros are sim-

---

[112] Baralt and Díaz,, *op. cit.*, vol. i, p. 463; Posada and Ibáñez, *Relaciones de mando*, pp. 291-292; Plaza, *Memorias*, p. 319.

[113] Depons, *op. cit.*, vol. ii, p. 116.

[114] Samper, J. M., *Ensayo sobre las revoluciones politicas y la condición social de las repúblicas colombianas*, (Paris, 1861), p. 49; p. 203.

[115] Salas, Julio, *Civilización y barbarie*, (Barcelona, 1908), pp. 76 *et seq.*

ilar.[116] From the extensive ecclesiastical survey of Bishop Martí made on his visit in the diocese from 1771 to 1784, one gets no picture of a church whose material establishment was impressive.[117]

In this survey of the church organization it remains to say something of the operation of the Inquisition in Venezuela. The jurisdiction of the Holy Office of Cartagena extended to Venezuela, being represented in the leading cities by commissaries. Here, as elsewhere in the colonies, it was concerned largely with preventing the introduction and sale of prohibited books. And its activity was observed to be slighter in Venezuela than in New Granada.[118] According to Lea, a considerable flurry occurred in 1660 over the introduction of some Calvinistic writings by the Dutch in the Orinoco regions.[119] But books found by travellers in some private libraries in Venezuela would indicate that the work of the Inquisition, even in this limited field of activity, was not very effective. It had been effective enough, however, to make it one of the most hated institutions of the Spanish régime. Its representatives also appear to have been sources of disturbance, political and ecclesiastical, outside their regular jurisdiction.

Mention should be made of the place of the church in colonial education.[120] Primary schools were organized in Caracas soon after the foundation of the city in 1567. The first schools were private. But through the activity of the colonial agent, Simón Bolívar, before the Spanish government, a seminary and a school of grammar were established in 1592. Decrees of 1608 and 1614 gave securer economic foundation and, hence, permanence to the public schools.

The clergy were primary agents in the promotion of public education. Moreover, three conventual schools were established in the

---

[116] Cisneros, J. L., *Descripción exacta de la provincia de Venezuela*, Colección de libros raros ó curiosos, vol. xxi, (Madrid, 1912).

[117] Martí, Mariano, *Relación de la visita general que en la diócesis de Caracas y Venezuela hizo el . . .* 3 vols., (Caracas, 1928).

[118] Restrepo, *op. cit.*, vol. i, pp. 512-513.

[119] Lea, H. C., *The Inquisition in the Spanish Dependencies*, (New York, 1908).

[120] Notable studies of colonial education are: Caracciolo Parra, *La instrucción en Caracas, 1567-1725*, (Caracas, 1932) and Juan de Díos Méndez y Mendoza, *Historia de la Universidad Central*, (Caracas, 1911). Together these constitute a most important contribution to the institutional history of Venezuela. Vicente Dávila's *Próceres merideños* contains material on education in Mérida. Arístides Rojas has a chapter in his *Orígines venezolanos* on colonial education. Gil Fortoul gives a good brief survey in his *Historia constitucional*, vol. i, p. 111 et seq.

seventeenth century with chairs of theology, ethics, and philosophy. The Seminary of Santa Rosa, opened only in 1692, was entirely under the direction of the episcopate; within it a primary school was later established. Other primary schools were likewise under the direction of priests. The first school for girls was established in Caracas by Father Malpica. The Royal and Pontifical University of Caracas, founded in 1721, was, until 1775, joined in its direction with the seminary and until the close of the colonial era was controlled by ecclesiastics. In his recent *La instrucción en Caracas*, Parra gives merited emphasis to the valiant labors of the bishops, Alcega, Angulo, Baños y Sotomayor, and Escalona y Calatayud, in the interest of education.

Admitting that education in the Spanish dominions in America was narrowly theological in content and scholastic in method, Parra recognizes this condition as the fault of the age, of the stage of European civilization, and not of Spain nor the church. That Venezuela did not have educational accommodations equal to those of Mexico and Perú he attributes to the fact that her population and resources did not justify and could not support so large an establishment. Moreover, educational expansion was retarded often by causes purely local in nature, the controversies between the civil and ecclesiastical authorities. *Competencias* characterized in particular the episcopal administrations of Bohorques and Tovar; in the first case, the secure establishment of the grammar schools was prevented; in the second, the foundation of the seminary.

Against the monopoly of the clergy in education the republican governments from their beginning directed their efforts. The church, it was contended, had allied herself with the monarchy to keep the colony in ignorance of new currents of thought. Priests were prominent, however, in the small beginnings in scientific studies in the eighteenth century. Father Andújar was one of the first teachers of mathematics; in 1798, he began instruction in this science in his home. Simón Bolívar and Andrés Bello, later celebrated in all Hispanic-America, were among his pupils. Humboldt found Father Puerto of the Franciscan convent in Caracas the only man in the colony acquainted with astronomy. In Mérida, where schools began to be founded much later than in Caracas, there seems to have been from the beginning an enthusiasm for scientific investigation. The clergy led in the promotion of this endeavor, but without any success. A seminary was established in 1790, but the petition for a university to be supported by the income of the former Jesuit college, the king rejected. The University of Mérida was founded in 1810 by the revolutionary government of the province. Bishop Milanés and Canon Uzcátegui were leaders in its establishment; and scientific studies were included from its foundation. As Rivas, Vallenilla Lanz, Parra, and others have suggested, the emergence of such men as Bolívar and Bello must indicate that colonial culture under the direction of the clergy was not wholly lacking. It is gratifying to see the increasing appreciation among Hispanic-American historians of Spain's phenominal colonial effort and her remarkable achievement.

IV

AMONG THE secular clergy in colonial Venezuela, particularly in the episcopate, there was a notable group of ecclesiastical statesmen. Sons of the families of highest social rank sought places in the church. Among the higher clergy, as Navarro asserts, were men of learning and of austere lives. While the bishops were usually Spanish, many of the higher clergy were creoles. The first archbishop, Ibarra, who had also been the first bishop of Guayana, was a native Venezuelan. Favoritism, Depons thought, never influenced the appointment of these higher churchmen; all seemed eminently qualified for their work.[121] Men of remarkable personality, they shaped the ecclesiastical office instead of being shaped by it. Hence, to analyze the episcopate one must seek its character in the individual administrations of the bishops, not in established policies of the office. Contrasts, like Rodrigo de Bastidas and Gonzalo de Angulo, or Mauro de Tovar and Diego Antonio Díez Madroñero, will be disconcerting to one who expects to find that the office was controlled by inflexible rules made in Madrid.

Yet one generalization may be made. The episcopate was distinguished on the whole by the secular aspiration of its incumbents, their desire to secure the dominance of society and even the civil

[121] Depons, op. cit., vol. ii, p. 85.

control of the country in competition with the political authorities.[122] Distinction in civil office was, to be sure, common in the ranks of Spanish colonial churchmen. Monarchs entrusted to them many political functions; indeed, they often filled the highest places in the government as viceroys, judges of the *audiencias*, and governors of provinces. Ecclesiastics, it is true, did not hold civil office in Venezuela so frequently as the clergy did in other divisions of the Empire.[123] But they attained, through their ecclesiastical position alone, a political power as well as a social influence comparable to that exercised in any other jurisdiction. Indeed, they are equalled in their individuality, their unique character, and their remarkable statesmanship, only by the interesting group of churchmen found in colonial Chile.[124]

Arcaya has given the following excellent appraisal of the place of the episcopate in colonial Venezuela:

In the sixteenth century and almost as late as the middle of the seventeenth, the royal power was less effective for maintaining order than that of the church. The former depended very much on the actual force which supported it; and that force was not in evidence to any great degree in the colony. European troops seldom appeared there; and, indeed, the territory was too large for the armies and fleets at the king's disposal. It was, therefore, almost exclusively through the influence of the church that the habits of civilized life could be implanted in the country. . . . To this work . . . the Venezuelan bishops applied themselves with extraordinary energy. They encountered great resistance; and to accomplish their civilizing mission, they not only had to use persuasion and gentleness, but in fact to assume a sort of dictatorship in order to break up abuses, protect the weak, chastise iniquity, and, finally, to lay the foundations of a society inspired by justice and not by brute force. They made great progress in this direction; and if the work was not after all solidly accomplished, it was not through the lack of any effort on their part, but because conditions were extremely difficult. Thus, then, the quasi-dictatorship of our first bishops was just and beneficent. Venezuelan society was in the medieval stage; the same phenomenon was reproduced which had appeared in Europe when the bishops and

---

[122] There were, it is true, bishops of great piety who gave chief attention to the spiritual and pastoral functions of their offices.

[123] Only one bishop, Bastidas, held the highest civil office.

[124] Pierson, W. W., *Lectures,* University of North Carolina, 1930.

the abbots were the only persons capable of protecting the masses against the excesses of chieftains and warrior bands.[125]

The quaint *Teatro* of Blas José Terrero and the equally charming studies of Arístides Rojas as well as the studies of Talavera and Navarro and chapters of Arcaya indicate the pronounced diversity in personality among the churchmen that individualized their administrations. The *conquistador* spirit of the Bishop-governor, Bastidas; Angulo's defense of the Indians against *encomenderos* and *ayuntamientos*; Bohorques's initiation of those celebrated conflicts with the civil power, the *competencias*, carried to a climax by Mauro de Tovar; the defense of the imperial integrity by Valverde in his opposition to contraband trade, the administrative reform of the church by Diego y Baños Sotomayor in the *Constituciones sinodales* in 1687; the reform of customs in Caracas by the beloved Madroñero; the practical effort toward diocesan reforms, material and moral, undertaken by Martí in the making and recording of his memorable visit: these suggest merely the variety of emphases in the various episcopal administrations. Some bishops magnified the beneficent functions of the office; others seemed to forget or neglect them in their efforts to maintain their prerogatives and formal *regalias*. An attempt is made only to indicate the character of the episcopate as it was exemplified in the lives and policies of a few of the many notable men who filled it.

From its institution, the episcopate developed an interesting history peculiar to Venezuelan soil. According to the story that has come down from Pedro Aguado through Simón, Oviedo y Baños, Baralt, and others, the first bishop, Bastidas, fell under the contagion of the *conquistador* spirit and sanctioned the expedition of Limpias and Hutten in search of El Dorado, an expedition to be financed by the sale of slaves taken in war.[126] Later historians, it is true, have relieved Bastidas from any responsibility for the severe treatment of the In-

[125] Arcaya, Pedro, *Estudios de sociología venezolano*, (Madrid, without date), pp. 89-90.
[126] Aguado, Pedro, *Historia de Venezuela*, 2 vols., (Madrid, 1918-1919) vol. i, p. 254 *et seq.*; Simón, *Historiales*, vol. v, pp. 198-199; Oviedo y Baños, José de, *Historia de la conquista y población de la Nueva Granada*, (Madrid, 1885), vol. i, pp. 149 *et seq.*

dians taken on this expedition.[127]   In his *Historia del Estado Falcón*, Arcaya admitted that Bastidas, in his rôle of protector of the Indians, did not succeed in stopping the enslavement of natives taken in war nor in checking the *encomienda* system; but he pointed out that this bishop did secure the freedom of that very superior group of Indians, the Caquetíos, who regarded him always with great affection as their deliverer.[128]   In a special study of Bastidas, Rojas declared that his first years were given to creating a society where none existed; that, although as governor he was a victim of the epidemic of El Dorado, he should be judged as a constructive statesman and as just and charitable.[129]   The very severity of his earlier critics, who were all churchmen, indicate the rigid criteria of the church in regard to the treatment of the Indians.

Ballesteros, the successor of Bastidas, also was active in matters of state.   In a long memorial to the king in 1550 he suggests something of the place of these early bishops as advisers in political affairs. He recommended steps for the reform of both church and state, attributing the corruption of society and the deplorable state of the Indians to the misconduct of these institutions.   He advised that the number of *regidores* be increased and suggested individuals for the places; and he outlined an elaborate plan for economic expansion.[130]

Bohorques, bishop from 1612 to 1618, initiated that series of struggles with the civil authorities, the *competencias*.[131]   This intransigent prelate entered into bitter conflict with the governors, Girón and Berrío, and the *cabildo;* he used censures and excommunications to such an extent, even during a severe drought and famine, that the terrified people appealed to the governor against him; and the civil

---

[127] These base their reinterpretation on the account of Juan de Castellaños, *Elegías de varones ilustres de Indias*, Biblioteca de autores españoles, 3rd. edition, vol. iv, (Madrid, 1874), Oviedo y Valdés, and other early narratives.

[128] Arcaya, Pedro, *Historia del Estado Falcón*, (Caracas, 1920), p. 231, *et seq.* For other criticism on this very interesting question of Bastidas, *vide*, Sucre, *Gobernadores y capitanes generales*, p. 22, note 2, and Talavera, *Apuntes*, pp. 126-129, the latter a discussion by Navarro.

[129] Rojas, *Orígenes venezolanos*, pp. 91-122.

[130] Aguado, *op. cit.*, vol. i, appendix vii, pp. 767-803. Although he deplored, in the memorial, the state of the Indians, Ballesteros showed a less commendable spirit in certain personal dealings; *vide*, Arcaya, *Historia del Estado Falcón*, p. 278.

[131] Rojas declared that he was not worthy of his office—that he was fitted for the rôle of a *conquistador*, not of a bishop; (*Leyendas históricas*, pp. 75-76).

authorities secured his promotion. Although Terrero deplored the extravagant measures of this prelate, he held that much of the responsibility for the conduct of the office belonged to his vicar, Gabriel de Mendoza, the commissary of the Inquisition.[132]

Over Angulo, the successor of Bohorques, Mendoza also gained influence; and the *competencias* continued. In this administration they centered around the question of the defense of the Indians from exploitation by the *encomenderos*. Angulo became, in fact, distinguished in his office as the protector of the Indians. In 1619, the king had charged the governor along with the bishop to break up the *encomiendas;* Angulo made this the special concern of his episcopal visitation in 1623. Arcaya gives in his *Estudios de sociología venezolana* a detailed account of his visit to Coro and his conflict with the *encomendero*, Francisco de Arteaga. Finding the evidence against Arteaga convincing, the bishop ordered that the *alcaldes* put the force of the city at his disposal for proceeding against him, citing in support of his demand precedents of aid given to Bishop Alcega, 1607 to 1610, and to Bishop Bohorques, 1619, for a similar purpose. Admitting that Angulo's action seems extreme, Arcaya defends his dictatorship on the grounds that "only churchmen speaking in the name of religion were able to secure justice." But the secular cabildo opposed the bishop in the name of the royal prerogatives and charged one of its *alcaldes* to represent it before the *audiencia* in Santo Domingo, a contestation in which the bishop's power received a check and his influence was reduced.[133] With these triumphs, the governor and the *cabildo* lost that respect, veneration, and holy terror with which they had regarded the prelates and assumed toward them an attitude of audacity and insolence, Terrero observed.[134] Although there were vigorous efforts made by later bishops, especially Mauro de Tovar, 1646, and González de Acuña, 1676, to protect the natives, the defeat of Angulo marked the end of this phase of the beneficent power of the bishop.

The *competencias* continued, however, arising most often over

[132] Terrero, *op. cit.*, pp. 21-25.
[133] Arcaya, *Estudios de sociología venezolano*, pp. 92-100.
[134] Terrero, *op. cit.*, pp. 29-31.

points of prerogatives and formal regalias. In the isolation of colonial
society and with the formalism characteristic of the people, such matters of official and social precedence received an exaggerated emphasis. Often these conflicts brought divisions within the ecclesiastical
body, indicating the lack of unity and control. Sometimes the bishop
joined the governor to oppose the chapter; for example, Bishop
Agurto de la Mata supported the governor, Ruíz Fernández de
Fuenmayor, in his demands that two of the three dignitaries in the
choir should receive the governor and that one of them should offer
him the holy water. This was contrary to the king's *cédula,* which
stated that a deacon or subdeacon was sufficient for both purposes.
The governor, in turn, favored the bishop's petition for the removal
of the seat of the bishopric to Caracas against the opposition of the
ecclesiastical *cabildo.*[135] On the other hand, the bishop at times took
the side of the governor in his contests with the municipal *cabildo;*
Bishop Escalona y Calatayud thus undertook the defense of Diego
Portales in his long-continued struggle with the *ayuntamiento* of
Caracas. In this case, to be sure, he acted at the instance of the
king.[136]

More often, however, the contests were between the *ayuntamiento,* ever jealous of its prerogatives, and the bishop, provisor, or
entire ecclesiastical *cabildo.* The following incidents will illustrate
the character of these celebrated contests of *regalías.* In 1623, while
Bishop Angulo was away on his famous visit in the interest of the
Indians, the Vicar Mendoza took occasion to lower the pride of the
ayuntamiento. It was the custom on the Sundays of Minerva for
the governor and all the members of the *ayuntamiento* to go in the
procession to the cathedral. But Mendoza instructed the canons to
come early on that day, and when the civil officials arrived, the procession had been formed. In an appeal to the Audiencia of Santo
Domingo, the *ayuntamiento* won the support of that body. The
bishop was ordered to restore to the council its accustomed seats in
the cathedral. The latter refused, however, to return to the cathedral for some time, attending instead the church of San Francisco.[137]

[135] Terrero, *op. cit.,* pp. 29-31.
[136] Rojas, *Leyendas históricas,* 2nd series, (Caracas, 1891) pp. 167 *et seq.*
[137] Terrero, *op. cit.,* p. 26.

On one occasion, the bishop appeared in the procession with a great number of pages in attendance. The governor, Nuñez Melean, appealed to the *audiencia* against such display.[138]   The court in this instance upheld the bishop, declaring that he should have all the attendants he wished when he appeared in public.   But, in a similar gesture of display on the part of the clergy later, the court was not so generous to the churchmen.   In a procession in honor of Saint Rosalie in 1728, the canons, once in the streets, raised beautiful purple parasols with gold handles and marched, "full of satisfaction, while members of the *ayuntamiento* flushed with anger."   Complaint being made, the *audiencia* declared that upon occasions so solemn, and particularly in marching with the *ayuntamiento*, the canons ought not to carry parasols![139]

Often the social consequences of the *competencias* were more serious, leading to veritable revolutions within the capital.   The severity of Bishop Bohorques has already been mentioned.   But the administration most disturbed by the *competencias* was the episcopate of Mauro de Tovar, 1639-1653.   This prelate never spoke except through censures or excommunications, Terrero declared.[140]   He is referred to as a Hildebrand, who wished to subordinate the civil authorities completely to his will, and as a puritanical censor of private conduct.   Yet this same bishop is noted as one of the outstanding defenders of the Indians, and is spoken of as just and charitable.   His errors were "offspring of his disposition and his time rather than of his heart," Rojas admitted.   "In this epoch of social conflict, of armed conquest, the most humble characters were converted into gloomy tyrants," he concluded.[141]   It seems probable that much of the beneficent work of the church was overshadowed by the bitterness of these *competencias*.

[138] This same governor had made extravagant demands for recognition for himself and his wife.

[139] Rojas, *Leyendas*, pp. 220-230.

[140] Terrero, *op. cit.*, pp. 31-36.

[141] Rojas, *Leyendas históricas*, p. 76; p. 220 *et seq*.   Rojas declared that the scandals of Mauro de Tovar's administration were such that the members of his family mutilated the registers of two chapters to destroy the records and that the second volume of Oviedo y Baños disappeared through being too severe on the bishop.   For a criticism of this statement *vide*, Navarro, *Anales eclesiásticos*, pp. 76-77, note.

V

THE POLITICAL and social significance of these conflicts in colonial life and their implications for the future relations of church and state should be stressed. Their importance is not to be measured by the apparent weight of the immediate issues, which may appear trivial, but rather by the bearing of these matters of form on the larger questions of political and social status. It was a battle of powers, civil and ecclesiastical, in which the civil gained predominance. The relentless struggle of the church for political place left attitudes of determined resistance on the part of the civil authorities, especially in the creole *cabildo,* such that the church was to suffer a complete subordination when it could no longer look to the king for the protection of its prerogatives. That the conflict was more severely drawn in Venezuela than in other jurisdictions is indicated by the fact that more elaborate rules were formulated in Madrid to govern the relations of church and state in this captaincy-general. And for the provocation of these disputes, Rojas has pointed out, the creole *cabildo* was more responsible than the clergy. The exaggerated "will to political power" is a characteristic of this interesting people that has been observed by other students of Venezuelan society. It early made its appearance in the resistance of the *cabildo* in the celebrated *competencias.*

Yet the social power of the church was not soon broken as other incidents indicate; nor did all bishops attempt to assert it, like Bohorques and Mauro de Tovar, through censures. In striking contrast to these men were such bishops as the devout Alonzo Briceño, 1661-1668; or Antonio González de Acuña, 1671-1682. But the most beloved of all the bishops was Diego Antonio Díez de Madroñero, 1757-1769. Allying himself with the governor, Solano, he sought to check the *competencias;* he won even the *ayuntamiento* to support his religious reforms. No ecclesiastic had exercised such an influence over the society of Caracas; he converted the city into a convent, it has been said. His prestige became such that he could destroy the cherished carnival with its crude games and pagan dances and substitute for it a procession of the rosary. Although absorption in religious rites reached its height in this episcopate, Rojas's pictures of colonial life, the records of Terrero, and the observations of Depons, Ségur, and others indicate the prominence of religious activities throughout the colonial period.[142]

In view of this fact, one will encounter some difficulty in explaining the lack of popular defense of the church in the attacks made on it under the Republic. Some suggestions may be made at this point that will help to answer this question. Reference should be made also to observations made above concerning the opposition to the mission system in the eighteenth century.

In the first place, absorption in religious ceremonials should not be taken as an indication of a deep-rooted or fanatical hold of the church on society.[143] The extreme religiosity of the people may be attributed to a considerable extent to a desire for distractions on the part of an isolated group and to a love for the display and ceremony to be enjoyed in processions, baptisms, burials, and other rites. The French traveller, Pondenx, observed that religious ceremonies among this vivacious and volatile people were objects of recreation.[144] When other forms for such expression were offered, the influence of the church declined. Madroñero dead, Caracas forgot the procession of the rosary; the pagan carnival was restored.

Vallenilla Lanz gives considerable weight to the interpretation of Venezuelan character made by the Spanish historian, Torrente, as an explanation of the loss of power in the church. Torrente emphasized the unique character of the Venezuelans among Hispanic-American peoples—their extreme vivacity, volatility, and intellectual precocity; their political-mindedness and concern for secular advancement—all of which would encourage them to accept new currents of thought, however incongruous such might be with the social environment.[145] Whatever value might be given to this interpretation as an explanation, it would apply with more force to Caracas than to Mérida, for instance. In the latter district, the character is more

[142] Rojas, *Leyendas*, pp. 76-140; the chapter entitled "Caracas fué un convento" is a charming picture of the administration of Madroñero.

[143] Although the religion of the people was sufficiently superstitious, there are few indications of extreme fanaticism. Exception should be made, however, of the flagellants of the Maracaibo district; Rojas, *Leyendas*, p. 53 *et seq.*

[144] Pondenx and Mayer, *Mémoire*, p. 21.

[145] Vallenilla Lanz, Laureano, *Críticas de sinceridad y exactitude*, (Caracas, 1921), p. 434.

serious and morose; but, to be sure, the church has retained a much
greater influence in Mérida.

Another source of the popularity of the church in the colonial
epoch was the opportunity offered for the expression of class sentiment in its processions and other forms of social distinction and in its
religious brotherhoods and sisterhoods. Every class, even the slaves,
had their special organizations, and the various castes in Caracas their
special churches. The levelling influences of the Revolution thus
weakened one great support of the ecclesiastical institution.

The instability of the position of the church was accentuated in
the late eighteenth and early nineteenth century through the influence of the liberal philosophy of Europe, so eagerly accepted by the
remarkable group of men which appeared in that generation. The
influx of radical thought began to undermine the intellectual predominance of the church much before the end of the colonial period.
Contacts with foreigners were always imminent on this coast. These
the church feared and attempted to guard against; some bishops were
leaders in opposing contraband trade.[146] Their opposition was made,
to be sure, in defense of the royal power, to which the church was
ever loyal; but it was motivated also by a desire to maintain their
own institutional monopoly. The monopoly of the Catholic church
was not shaken so far as formal adherence was concerned, but such
associations tended toward the development of a spirit of tolerance
and religious indifference. Humboldt commented often on the tolerance even of members of the clergy in the eastern section of Venezuela. He found the Franciscan friars liberal in their attitude to
foreigners and eager for knowledge of scientific developments in
Europe. Restrepo observed that the influence of religion varied inversely in Tierra Firme with associations with foreigners, being
slightest in Venezuela.[147]

But such contacts in the earlier centuries were slight compared
to those which followed the liberal reforms in the Spanish imperial
system in the latter part of the eighteenth century. The increasing
fear of the church is indicated by a comparison of the report of
Bishop Martí, 1771-1784, and the documents of the diocese of

[146] Valverde's administration was notable for this.
[147] Restrepo, *op. cit.*, vol i, p. xxxii.

Mérida around the turn of the century. Martí spoke occasionally of heterodoxy in the church; but of a heterodoxy attributed to ignorance and to mixture of Catholic ceremonial with Indian customs. It was the Indianization of the church, existing especially in the interior and in isolated places, which he would correct. But the Bishop of Mérida, Milanés, 1802, was disturbed by the introduction of foreign ideas; he expressed particular uneasiness over the English influence. This fear developed into a panic with the expedition of Miranda to Coro, but it had existed before his appearance. One finds no reference to such disturbing factors in Martí's long survey of the condition of the church.

With the liberalization of Spain's commercial policy, contacts had multiplied; foreign travel increased, and foreign books brought not only the science but the rationalistic philosophy of Europe. Its influence, according to the observation of foreigners, was greatest in Venezuela. Humboldt declared that, outside Havana, civilization had assumed a more European physiognomy in Venezuela than in any part of America.[148] Ségur found copies of Rousseau's *Social Contract* and the writings of Raynal in La Victoria, and the works of Paine were circulated in Cumaná. Depons, Ségur, Lavaysse, and others comment on the tolerance, the intellectual curiosity, and the sophistication of the society of Caracas; it had, Ségur observed, the appearance of a European capital. There is, no doubt, some exaggeration in these opinions; but they suggest the relative intellectual liberalism of Venezuela. Depons remarked that these people recognized their backwardness and were eager to correct it. Although social and intellectual life had formerly centered around the church, the appearance of literary circles such as that of Uztáriz indicate intellectual expansion outside this institution.

With the increase of wealth in the late colonial period and the expansion of secular interests, the church was considerably weakened before the Revolution. Depons observed many evidences of a decline: the ecclesiastical courts had lost in the contests with the civil; there were not half so many friars in the convents as fifty years before; no convent had the required number of inmates; no new

[148] Humboldt, *op. cit.*, vol. iii, p. 472.

convents were being established; and there were relatively fewer priests than earlier.[149] Pious donations, he declared, had swallowed up the wealth of the country, but he found that things were beginning to change and that people gave their wealth less frequently to the church. "The inhabitants," he said, "are devout enough to preserve the convents already established without being willing to augment their number."[150] Ségur found opposition to the wealth and the power of the clergy a reason for the revolutionary changes in the status of the church.[151]

The forces mentioned above operated from without to reduce the influence of the church. There was also decline within the institution. Although superior men were found in the ranks of the higher clergy to the end of the colonial period, some to remain its leaders for several decades after the establishment of the Republic, there was a noticeable decline in personnel in the lower ranks. Since the priesthood was not closed to the lower classes, many sought places in it as a means of social advancement. Terrero deplored the decay of standards and the inferior character of the priesthood. He made a division in his history, calling the period after 1800 the second ecclesiastical era because of the moral decline in the ranks of both the regular and secular clergy. The better classes began to send their sons into the army or the profession of law; the priesthood, he declared, had come to be filled "with men of no note and of obscure birth," who took the places "to make their fortune and clothe themselves with an authority superior to their merit." Instead of displaying qualities of spirit, zeal, and integrity in office, they were servile, seeking merely to retain place.[152]

Other documents of the church give evidence of the decline. Bishop Martí regretted the relaxation from the reforms of Madroñero.[153] In the documents published at the end of the century, the

---

[149] Depons, *op. cit.*, vol. ii, p. 116 *et seq.*

[150] *Ibid.*, p. 118.

[151] Ségur, *Mémoire*, vol. i, p. 234.

[152] Terrero, *op. cit.*, p. 69 *et seq.*

[153] Martí, *Visita, passim.* A word might be added about this remarkable document referred to several times in the course of this chapter. On this visit covering twelve years, the bishop visited and made detailed records of the religious establishments in twelve cities, one hundred eighty-nine towns, and nine villages, all of which contained two hundred eighty-eight churches, sixteen convents, four hospitals, and one hundred eighty-eight *cofradías*. In addition to ecclesiastical statistics, he gave facts concerning

bishops of Mérida showed even greater disturbance over the abuses of the clergy. The first bishop, Lora, found serious need to correct the treatment of the Indians; he urged that they be regarded as sons, not as slaves, and took steps to prevent collusion between the priests and the *corregidores* in the exploitation of the Indians. Such conduct he declared was leading the Indians to hate the priests.[154] Complaints on this ground might have been issued against some members of the clergy at any time during the colonial epoch; but such conditions were recognized in these reports as being more general and worse. As the new intellectual currents weakened the hold of the church in the upper circles of society, it was losing predominance over the lower by the abuses of the priests. Yet in spite of the operation of these forces, it retained a considerable degree of control over the popular mind as developments in the course of the revolution were to indicate.

The church maintained its political prerogatives through the protection of the monarchy.[155] It was the chief bulwark of the royal power in a period when revolutionary ferment was beginning to appear.[156] There appears to have been no ultramontane sentiment in the church and no opposition to the absolute control that the Spanish kings exercised through the patronage.[157] In view of this fact, the support of the Revolution by a large part of the clergy, as set forth in the following chapter, will require explanation. That the introduction of liberal thought had not left the clergy unaffected has

the foundation and subsequent history of the places visited and of existing economic and social conditions. Sánchez considers it the best source of information on Venezuelan social history. There is probably no work on social history of equal value to be found in the records of any of the Spanish colonies. It is indeed a monumental work —one of the many contributions to history made by the colonial clergy. The Venezuelan government has recently published it in three volumes.

[154] Silva, *Documentos*, vol. i, pp. 171 *et seq; passim.*

[155] In the period of Bourbon absolutism, some restrictions were, however, placed on the church. These are discussed in more detail in Chapter II. The reïssuance of the law against the inheritance of property by the priest who heard the final confession of a deceased person and the increasing lay control of the tenth are instances of such restrictions.

[156] An interesting instance of the royal dependence on the church in the execution of its policy is to be found in the communications of Godoy with the Bishop of Mérida with regard to proposed plans of the Spanish cabinet for the promotion of agricultural education in Venezuela; *vide*, Silva, *Documentos*, vol. ii, pp. 46-49; *passim.*

[157] The loyalty of the clergy to the Spanish policy gave occasion for attack by the liberals. They were held responsible for the exclusion of ideas through the Inquisition and for the restricted educational system.

been pointed out. Many of the higher clergy were creoles and hence were more easily impressed by local interests. The individualism and decentralization in the Venezuelan church made, moreover, against unity on any general principle; extraneous factors entered to influence attitudes and conduct. These will be discussed more fully below.

CHAPTER I

THE CHURCH IN THE WAR FOR INDEPENDENCE

THE POLITICAL significance of the church in the Spanish imperial system gives special interest to its attitude to the revolution against that system. No fact better indicates the civil war character of that movement than the division within this institution, regarded by the Spanish kings as the surest support of the royal power and prerogatives.[1] In no division of the empire was the clergy united in defense of the sovereignty of the monarchy. But conflicts within the church, friction between it and the local civil authorities, and factors entirely personal often determined the alignment of the clergy on the revolutionary side rather than opposition to the monarchy *per se*.

The division of the clergy in Venezuela on the question of the acceptance or support of the revolution followed, moreover, no such clearly defined lines as it did in Mexico, for example.[2] Indeed, no general rule can be applied to describe the division in Venezuela. It cut through both high and lower clergy and the regular orders. There were native-born members of the clergy who adhered to the side of the king, while some foreign-born, and possibly Spanish, supported independence.[3] In his *Vida de Don Francisco Miranda*, Becerra held that as a directing force the clergy through its diocesan organization followed an opportunist policy, although individuals among the priesthood were influenced by personal motives or disposition to refuse to follow the directing power.[4] This judgment appears to be true as applied to the archdiocese of Caracas, but it does not fit the situation in the diocese of Mérida; nor does it quite cor-

---

[1] The interpretation of the Revolution as a civil war has been ably defended by Vallenilla Lanz; *vide*, for example, his *Caesarismo democrático-Estudios sobre las bases sociológicas de la constitución de Venezuela*, 2nd edition, (Caracas, 1929).

[2] In the early stages of the Revolution in Mexico, the higher clergy supported the cause of the monarchy; members of the lower led the movement for independence.

[3] Urquinaona speaks of a European monk who was influential in promoting the movement for independence in Cumaná; *vide* his *Memorias*, p. 58.

[4] Becerra, Ricardo, *Vida de Don Francisco Miranda*, 2 vols. (Madrid, without date), vol. ii, p. 129.

rectly describe that in Guayana. In Mérida, the chapter, in charge of the government of the diocese in the vacancy existing in the bishopric in 1812, split over the issue, the division being facilitated by a long-standing controversy in the church over the matter of moving the seat of the cathedral to Maracaibo. Both groups claimed the directing power. The members who had favored the transfer of the see went to Maracaibo, securing finally in 1813 the approval of the king for its temporary removal and location at that place; those remaining in Mérida chose a new *vicario-capitular*, seeking sanction for the action and advice from the archbishop of Caracas, who at the time was supporting the revolution.[5] Even the convent of nuns in Mérida divided, thirteen of the thirty members going with the secessionist group to Maracaibo. This incident furnishes an excellent illustration of the influence of local issues in determining the alignment of the clergy in the revolutionary movement in Venezuela.

In fact, there is a peculiar sectionalism that characterized more correctly than any other principle the division of the clergy in Venezuela on the revolution. It is not strange that such a condition should be found, since no part of the Spanish empire had exemplified so fully the decentralizing tendency of the imperial system as the captaincy-general of Venezuela. As indicated above, neither church nor state was unified administratively until the eve of emancipation. There was little, if any, cohesive force in either. The clergy of Coro and Maracaibo and of Guayana were zealous loyalists, a fact attributable in part to the larger percentage of Spanish priests in those places, in part to the local sentiment of the sections. Maracaibo, the only district that rivalled Caracas in wealth, and Coro, the former center of the political and ecclesiastical establishments, were jealous of Caracas. When Caracas accepted the revolution, these cities became the strongholds of the Spanish power. Priests became leaders in support of the rights of the king. The Capuchin missionaries in Guayana had particular reason for devotion to the royal rule: the monarchy had defended them from the attacks made on their control by Centurión, Marmión, and other governors for half a century. It might be said as a tribute to their loyalty that they perished in the

_____
[5] Silva, *Documentos de la diócesis de Mérida,* vol. iii, pp. 277-285; vol. v, p. 286.

war on the side of the king or emigrated; they refused to embrace the revolution. On the other hand, the clergy of Mérida and Barinas were predominantly for independence and in many cases, at least, from a point of principle; a number remained revolutionists through the changing fortunes of the national cause, and some rendered very valuable service to it. In Cumaná, Barcelona, and Caracas, the clergy was more divided, and its alignment less stable. In the province of Caracas, Valencia was the outstanding center of clerical influence, and it was strongly royalist. Municipal rivalry with Caracas had led to an agitation for a new province, of which Valencia should be the center. Local feeling toward Caracas thus encouraged royalist sentiment in Valencia, and the clergy led in its promotion. In Caracas the directing force of the archdiocese changed its policy with the fluctuating course of the revolution. It was entirely opportunist. But there were priests who remained loyal or revolutionist throughout the course of the war, suffering exile or persecution for their perseverance in the one or the other cause. In the Oriente, especially in Cumaná and Barcelona, there was considerable support of the revolutionary cause, although it was less general and less determined than in Mérida.[6]

Considerations entirely personal, in some cases, determined the course followed by members of the clergy, indicating still further the absence of cohesive power in the church. Individualism as well as sectionalism weakened the central control. Torrente mentioned in several places *curas* who deserted the royalist side, because they had not been rewarded for their services by ecclesiastical and social advancement.[7] Ramón Ignacio Méndez, later prominent as archbishop of Caracas, complained to Heredia, member of the royal *audiencia*, that in spite of his having opposed Miranda and having refused to sign the Declaration of Independence, he had been imprisoned by Monteverde. He left the horrors of his imprisonment, he declared, to seek the ranks of the revolutionist, Páez, in Apure.[8] Urquinaona and others tell the story of a *cura* of Caracas, José

[6] Duarte Level, *op. cit.*, pp. 244-245.
[7] Torrente, *Historia de la revolución hispano-americana,* vol. iii, p. 107; pp. 352-353.
[8] Duarte Level, *op. cit.*, p. 277, quotes his letter.

Antonio Rojas Queipo, who went over to the royalist side after active support of the revolution, because he had been removed from his place in the University of Caracas for undue severity in the punishment of a student. He became notorious as one of the spiritual advisers of Monteverde and a member of his committee on composing the proscriptions of the revolutionists.[9] Cases such as these, and they might be multiplied, suggest the strongly individualistic character of the whole movement.

The influence of the clergy in the Revolution in Venezuela can probably best be indicated by a brief survey of its activity in the successive stages of the struggle for independence. Although the clergy as a class had been staunch defenders of the royal power in the colonial epoch, individuals had not been untouched by liberal, even revolutionary, thought. Several priests had had an active part in the premature revolution of Gual and España in 1797, and others had been sympathetic with that movement.[10] But Miranda met a different reception from the clergy in his ill-fated expedition of 1806, a fact attributable in part to his choice of Coro, the most decidedly royalist section, as a landing place. He found, indeed, no active support; but the clergy were especially hostile. In his account of the expedition, Biggs attributed its failure largely to this factor. Miranda tried by special communications to draw out the clergy, but the priests fled, taking their parishioners with them.

It is very evident, from this and other circumstances, that the inhabitants of this country will never listen to the proposals of our commander-in-chief, unless they are led on and countenanced by their priests; and without the concurrence of the priests, his cause could not succeed. These ecclesiastics have too much wisdom to give up a certainty for an uncertainty; to espouse an adventurer and revolutionist against the reigning government, which protects their endowments and immunities and builds up their influence; and they have probably, as a body, too much loyalty of feeling and principle to be seduced by ordinary prospects into a renunciation of their allegiance.[11]

[9] Urquinaona, *Memorias*, pp. 140-141, note.

[10] Landaeta Rosales, Manuel, *Sacerdotes que sirvieron la causa de independencia de Venezuela*, (Caracas, 1911), p. 10; Depons, *op. cit.*, vol. i, p. 152.

[11] Biggs, James, *The History of Don Francisco de Miranda's Attempt to Effect a Revolution in South America*, 2nd edition, (Boston, 1810), p. 135. Captain Biggs was a citizen of the United States, whom Miranda enlisted in his enterprise.

But the cautious policy of the church toward possible political changes appears even in this preliminary stage of the revolution; the bishop was evasive rather than condemnatory in his reply to Miranda's letter, so that the king saw fit to censure him for not properly emphasizing the union of throne and altar.[12]   In his pastorals, however, Miranda was pronounced a heretic in league with Jews and Protestants, and all were declared subject to excommunication who dealt with him.[13]

In the movements of 1810 and 1811 some notable liberal leaders appeared among the clergy of Caracas and Mérida. Contemporary and later historians recognized that the famous *canónigo de Chile*, José Cortés Madariaga, was foremost in the overthrow of the government of the Spanish captain-general, Emparán, in 1810 and in the creation of the Supreme Junta under local control. José Domingo Díaz, the royalist official, in his *Recuerdos* described him as one "born for revolution."[14]   Not only was he a revolutionist, but an ardent republican, as later activities indicate. He was more a tribune of the people than a pastor, Rojas declared.[15]   Even the more liberal members of the clergy held him in question for his extreme views.[16] Having promoted the establishment of the new republic, proclaimed in the Declaration of Independence on July 5, 1811, Madariaga became its first diplomatic representative, being sent to New Granada to promote the union of the two countries in the war against Spain.

Along with Madariaga, Francisco José Ribas also represented "the clergy and the people," as it was said, in the Supreme Junta of 1810. Upon the request of the *ayuntamiento* that it choose representatives, the ecclesiastical *cabildo* had named M. V. Maya and Juan Nepumuceno Quintana. Both were very reactionary, and were refused admittance.[17]   Madariaga and Ribas were then selected by the republican leaders as deputies of "the clergy and the people." It is interesting to note that this first political body of Venezuela, a

[12] Becerra, *Vida de Miranda*, vol. ii, p. 162.

[13] Silva, *Documentos*, vol. ii, p. 89 *et seq.*

[14] Díaz, José Domingo, *Recuerdos sobre la rebelión de Caracas*, (Madrid, 1829), p. 17.

[15] Rojas, Arístides, *Estudios históricos*, vol. i, p. 177 *et seq.*

[16] Blanco-Azpurúa, *Documentos*, vol. iv, p. 71.

[17] Ponte, Andrés F., *La revolución de Caracas y sus próceres*, (Caracas, 1918), p. 103.

state soon to attack all special civil and political privileges, recognized the class as a distinct political group. Although there was a persistent purpose to restrict the secular activities of the clergy throughout the revolutionary epoch, the political authorities showed, nevertheless, a certain cautiousness in not breaking too completely nor too soon with the past. At the same time, the civil authority made its own selection of priests, who were hence in no sense representative of the clergy. As has been mentioned, Madariaga was questioned even by its more liberal members.

José Félix Blanco, later prominent in the army of Bolívar, was also involved in the movement of 1810.[18] Like Madariaga, Blanco seemed better fitted for a civil career than for the priesthood; he admitted that he took orders *"inconsulta."* The day of ecclesiastical statesmanship in the Spanish Empire had reached and passed its height, but it had not ended; hence, it is not strange that men such as these should still be found in the church.

In Mérida the clergy had a more prominent part in the movements of 1810 and 1811 than they had in Caracas. In the former city they were the intellectual leaders, while Caracas had a notable group of non-clerical educated men schooled by travel and study in Europe. The Spanish-born bishop of Mérida, Santiago de Milanés, hesitated to support the new movement. He was persuaded to it by Talavera and Uzcátegui, members of his *cabildo*, and Ortiz and Villate, priors respectively of the Dominican and Augustinian convents of Mérida, but over the protests of the intransigent royalist canons, Yrastorza and Mas y Rubí.[20] Although he took the oath to support the Republic and attempted to mediate between Coro and Caracas to end the civil discord, he expressed to Talavera his fear that the revolution was premature. And he feared especially the fate of the church under the Republic. "I foresee and regret the wounds that the Catholic religion will receive from the multitude of impious works that will be imported from France to Venezuela under

[18] Ponte, *La revolución de Caracas*, p. 93.

[19] "Reseña autobiográfica" published in *Tres próceres de la independencia*, (Caracas, 896), p. 101.

[20] Silva, Antonio R., *Patriotismo del clero de la diócesis de Mérida*, (Mérida, 1911), p. 5 *et seq*.

the pretext of free intercourse," he declared.[21]   But Milanés favored civil peace and followed an opportunist policy.[22]

A notable group of priests appeared in the revolutionary *juntas* and in the constituent assemblies of 1811 in Mérida, Barinas, and Trujillo. A number of them were members of the higher clergy, men of liberal opinion, possessing real statesmanship, political as well as ecclesiastical.[23] In his two studies, *Próceres trujillanos* and *Próceres merideños*, Vicente Dávila gives high praise to their contributions to independence and to the organization of the new state, praise that the documents of the period indicate to be wholly merited. From this group of ecclesiastics came the leaders in the Venezuelan church for a generation following the establishment of the Republic. At a time when the profession of law and the army were tending to overshadow the ecclesiastical career in Caracas, Mérida was experiencing an intellectual awakening that found its chief support in the clergy.[24] Prominent in these first revolutionary activities were Ignacio Fernández Peña of Barinas, an outstanding liberal, deputy to the constituent congresses of 1811 and 1821 and later archbishop of Venezuela, 1840-1849; Mariano Talavera y Garcés, a member of the chapter of the cathedral of Mérida, later bishop of Trícala and *vicario apostólico* of Guayana and the celebrated historian of the church;[25] Buenaventura Arias, also of the cathedral chapter, subsequently bishop of Jericho and *vicario apostólico* of Mérida; Luis Ignacio Mendoza of Barinas, deputy to the Congress of Cúcuta, a man whose liberal political opinions General O'Leary approved as agreeing entirely with his own;[26] Francisco Uzcátegui, canon of the cathedral of Mérida, known as the Madariaga of Mérida, a man of generous mind, chief promoter of the pre-revolutionary intellectual

[21] Silva, *Documentos,* vol. iii, p. 264.

[22] He was killed in the earthquake of 1812.

[23] For records of the activity of the clergy of Mérida, *vide* the collection of documents, *Patriotismo del clero* by Silva, especially pp. 114-117.

[24] Excellent biographical sketches of these leaders are found in Vicente Dávila's *Próceres trujillanos,* (Caracas, 1921), and *Próceres merideños,* (Caracas, 1918).

[25] Juan Vicente González has called him "the sacred orator of the revolution." His "Manifesto of the Junta of Mérida to the People" drawn by him as vice-president of the junta is a celebrated revolutionary document; *vide* Silva, *Patriotismo del clero,* p. 60 *et seq.*

[26] O'Leary, Simón B., *Memorias del General O'Leary,* 32 vols., (Caracas, 1879-1888), vol. xiii, p. 89; vol. xxvi, p. 301.

movement in Mérida, and, according to Dávila, the leader of the revolution in this metropolis of the Andes;[27] and Ignacio Alvarez, called the Madariaga of Trujillo, celebrated for his brilliant pronouncements in defense of the sovereignty of the Venezuelan nation.[28]   The clergy were so prominent as leaders of the revolution in Mérida that objection was raised in the Congress of 1811 to the separation of this section from the province of Caracas on the ground that it would fall under the political domination of the clergy.   In answer, a lay member from Mérida admitted the clerical leadership, but praised its patriotism and liberalism, declaring that these ecclesiastics had studied the political philosophy of Europe and America in order to be able to instruct the people.[29]

In Cumaná and Barcelona the clergy had some part in these first steps toward independence in 1810 and 1811.   In his recent *Historia de Carúpano*, Tavera-Acosta mentions priests who participated in the revolutionary *juntas*.   Generally they favored the revolution and fled from or were imprisoned by Monteverde.[30]   Duarte Level and Becerra stated that the clergy in this section were as a group for independence.[31]   Urquinaona referred to a European friar who overcame the resistance to the publication of the Declaration of Independence in Cumaná.   But the clergy did not appear so prominently as directors of the movement as in the province of Mérida.   Upon the persuasion of the archbishop, they were easily won over to reaction in 1812, according to the statement of Heredia.[32]

Nine priests were members of the Congress of 1811, which drew up and issued the Declaration of Independence.   Of this group, M. V. Maya of the *cabildo* of Caracas, and Ramón Ignacio Méndez, deputy from Barinas, opposed it.   Maya refused to sign it, insisting

---

[27] Dávila, *Próceres merideños*, p. 97.

[28] Dávila, *Próceres trujillanos*, p. 197.   He took the jewels of the church to sustain the revolutionary army when he emigrated with Urdaneta to New Granada in 1813; Uzcátegui did the same in Mérida, and José Ignacio Briceño and Cristóbal Mendoza in Caracas.

[29] Silva, *Patriotismo del clero*, pp. 90-100.

[30] Tavera-Acosta, *Historia de Carúpano*, vol. i, p. 125, p. 134; *passim; vide*, also, Landaeta Rosales, *Sacerdotes que sirvieron la causa de independencia, passim.*

[31] Duarte Level, *Cuadros militar y civil*, pp. 244-245; Becerra, *Vida de Miranda*, vol. ii, p. 129.

[32] Heredia, J. F., *Memorias del regente Heredia* (Madrid, without date) p. 75.

that his constituents had instructed him to defend the rights of Ferdinand VII, appealing thus to the "imperative mandate"; Méndez objected because of his oath to conserve the rights of the monarchy.[33] Miranda pronounced their arguments "sophistical." The Congress was particularly hostile to the opposition of Maya, which was persistent. Duarte Level declared it saw in him, not a man merely, but a power that had to be met and overcome. "The voice of Maya was a battle-cry between the state and the church. . . . He was not a man, but a force planted in the face of the revolution."[34] The other priests voted with the majority for independence. But in the assembly they adhered to the conservatives led by Felipe Fermín Paúl, who sought to check the radicalism of Miranda and Coto Paúl. They feared the influence of the French philosophy brought in by Miranda.

Although the clergy had an interesting and a not unimportant part in these early developments of the revolution in Venezuela, it could hardly be said that its influence as a group was decisive, certainly not outside the province of Mérida. Even there the priests served probably more significantly as an efficient instrument for the organization and expression of liberal opinion than for its creation. Hence, the chief interest of the historian in these activities of the church lies in their indication of the philosophy and attitude of the clergy rather than in any great practical value for the success of the Revolution. Active protagonists of independence among the clergy were probably a very small minority of the group. Many acquiesced in the early success of the Revolution, and for a short time its opponents were silenced. These opponents were soon heard, however, in the reaction already well under way before the earthquake of 1812 made it general.

The clergy were more influential in this reaction, which led to the success of Monteverde in 1812, than certain of its members had been in promoting the Revolution. The war against the "impious government of Caracas," as it was called, became a sort of religious crusade under the preaching and leadership of the priests. The abolition of the Inquisition and of ecclesiastical privileges by the Con-

[33] Duarte Level, *op. cit.*, p. 274.
[34] *Ibid.*, pp. 270-271.

stituent Congress consolidated the opposition of the clergy. Added
to this was the fact that the government had sanctioned the publication of the articles of the Irishman, William Burke, on religious
toleration and allowed them to appear in the official *Gaceta*. The
publication of these articles defined the irreconcilable conflict between
the old ideas and the new, as Baralt observed. Many priests who
had advocated, or at least acquiesced in, the Revolution turned now
to active support of the royalist cause.[35] The earthquake of March
26, 1812, gave the final justification to the devout for the reaction
already begun. That it struck more severely Caracas and Mérida,
the centers of the revolutionary sentiment, was regarded as a special
sign of divine disfavor. The priests found it easy to make general
the resistance developing since 1811 in Valencia, Guayana, and the
Occidente. In Coro and Maracaibo, sections which had resisted successfully the revolution of 1810, there began early in 1811 a movement for the reconquest of the country for Ferdinand VII. Andrés
Torrellas, a priest of the interior, led in the organization of the reconquest. Going up to Coro, he urged the civil authorities to undertake an expedition against Caracas; along with Pedro Guzmán a
priest of Coro, he helped to finance it. He stirred his parishioners to
zeal for the undertaking, so that they wrote the captain-general and
governor, offering their services to make war on Caracas in defense
of the Christian religion.[36] Torrellas won over the Indian chief,
Reyes Vargas, and the two were, until 1820, important factors in
the royalists ranks. They joined the forces of Monteverde in his
march to Valencia and Caracas in 1812.

In Valencia the reaction, which became effective in 1811, was
led by a group of priests and friars, the chief of whom was Pedro
Hernández, a Franciscan, who joined Queipo Rojas and Torrellas
as a constant companion and adviser of Monteverde, according to the
Memorias of Urquinaona and statements of Restrepo and others. In
the region of Valencia, where the reaction reached its height, one
saw, Restrepo observed, an almost continuous religious procession.
People went into battle bearing their sacred images, with banners on
which were representations of Ferdinand VII and the Virgin of

[35] Baralt and Díaz, *op. cit.*, vol. ii, p. 71.
[36] Urquinaona, *Memorias*, pp. 71-72.

Rosario. Caracas had destroyed the Christian religion, it was proclaimed; the Congress and the greater part of the inhabitants were atheists; the churches were closed and the sacraments suspended.[37] A Venezuelan contemporary complained:

The sacred cause of freedom was neglected for a blind, puerile, fearful, and extravagant devotion. Multitudes thronged the churches day and night; public prayer and penance were the occupation of the people; agriculture, commerce and the arts stood still; he who did not surrender himself to the ridiculous mania of living in penance was regarded as a dissolute libertine who provoked the anger of heaven. This dismal contagion extended to the people of the interior; so that Venezuela was suddenly converted into a vast camp, presenting to the eyes of the philosopher nothing but caravans of pilgrims trooping to Mecca or hordes of inhabitants in religious frenzy.[38]

The archbishop of Venezuela, Narciso Coll y Prat, had arrived in Caracas after the establishment of the Supreme Junta in 1810. Up to the time of the earthquake he had given at least formal support to the Revolution. But he had protested with the clergy of Caracas against the ecclesiastical reforms of the Congress and was suspected of directing from his retirement the reaction in Valencia and other cities of the diocese, according to an *informe* of Múñoz Tébar, the secretary of Miranda, on May 12, 1812.[39] Two members of his cathedral chapter, Maya and Quintana, had been first to welcome the forces of Monteverde into Valencia. After the disastrous earthquake of March 26, 1812, which priests pronounced an expression of the wrath of heaven against the sin of rebellion, the government ordered the archbishop to issue a pastoral to offset this preaching. He delayed response, finally issuing a pastoral whose circulation the government forbade, pronouncing it subversive. His exile was decreed by Miranda. For this action Madariaga has been held largely responsible. But through the influence of Yanes, serving with Roscio and Madariaga on the commission appointed to execute the decree, it was not carried out.[40] With the success of the reaction, the arch-

[37] Restrepo, *op. cit.*, vol. ii, p. 11 *et seq.*
[38] Quoted in W. S. Robertson, *Life of Miranda*, 2 vols. (Chapel Hill, N. C., 1930) vol. ii, p. 148.
[39] Blanco-Azpurúa, *Documentos*, vol. iii, p. 620.
[40] *Ibid.*, vol. v, pp. 500-539.

bishop became royalist, and stayed in Venezuela supporting the government in power. Finally he was recalled to Spain in 1816 upon the recommendation of Morillo, who doubted his loyalty to the monarchy, as Miranda and Bolívar had questioned his support of the revolution. He proceeded throughout, as Gil Fortoul has observed, "with the most diligent opportunism"; but at heart he was always royalist one may easily conjecture.[41]

In his famous Address from Cartagena to the People of New Granada, issued in 1813, Bolívar attributed the failure of the revolution in Venezuela in large measure to the active hostility of the clergy.[42] But there is evidence of contrary action. For example, the *cabildo* of Caracas complained in the same year of some "ignorant or corrupt priests, who convert the pulpit into a sanguinary tribunal where they declare against the king and for the excellencies of the Venezuelan system instead of preaching the gospel."[43]

In an attempt to check the reaction, the government of Miranda resorted to extreme measures. But such were applied with some hesitancy to the clergy, even though they were recognized as its leaders. The treatment accorded the archbishop is proof of this fact. Even the extreme royalist, José Domingo Díaz, commended the treatment of Pedro Hernández, the chief promoter of the reaction in Valencia, as the one act of generosity shown by either side in that epoch; and Restrepo criticized it as the beginning of a fatal policy of clemency followed by the Republic.[44] Both sides recognized the influence of the clergy and sought to control it; in fact, to exploit it. In 1814, Bolívar sent Coll y Prat and a considerable group of ecclesiastics on a special commission to Valencia with the hope that they might win over this center of royalism.[45] On the other hand, many

[41] During the controversy of Guzmán Blanco with the church, *La opinión nacional* of Caracas published a series of articles on Coll y Prat, occasioned by an article of Arístides Rojas. Rojas presented the archbishop as royalist in spirit throughout his administration, publishing some interesting correspondence that indicates the distrust of the archbishop by civil and military leaders and the basis for this in the greater warmth of Coll y Prat toward the royalist government. His support of the revolution appears to have been merely formal. These articles from *La opinión nacional* are found also in Blanco-Azpurúa, *Documentos*, vol. v, pp. 500-539.

[42] Blanco-Azpurúa, *Documentos*, vol. iv, p. 122.

[43] *Ibid.*, vol. iv, p. 604 *et seq.*

[44] Díaz, *Recuerdos*, p. 36.

[45] The expedition failed; the archbishop turned back before he reached his destination, and the priests were taken by Boves; Urdaneta, Rafael, *Memorias*, (Madrid, 1916), p. 57.

priests were exiled; according to Groot, Morillo deported eighty-six from La Guaira on one occasion.[46]   He appeared to be particularly suspicious of the clergy, even of those supposedly loyal.   And priests were shot, both by orders of Miranda and Bolívar.[47]

In this connection one might mention the execution of the twenty-two Capuchin missionaries who survived Piar's conquest of Guayana in 1817.   This act of the government of Bolívar has been variously interpreted as to the source of responsibility for it and much deplored by national historians.   The Capuchin missionaries had held Guayana for the monarchy up to 1817—a fact which suggests the continued influence of the friars over the Indians.[48]   After the occupation by the revolutionary forces, an order was given that the twenty-two missionaries be sent into the interior; instead, they were shot.   Baralt placed the responsibility on Bolívar, who, he declared, asked when told that the friars had been captured why they had not been killed.[49]   Larrazábal pronounced this account of Baralt an excellent Thomas of Canterbury story, but not good history.[50]   He and O'Leary attributed the execution to an error on the part of an officer sent to remove the missionaries to Divina Pastora.   Ignorant of the local geographical designations, he inferred from the order that he was to kill them.[51]

It might be noted that these missions, which had been so continuously attacked by the civil authorities and whose administration has been almost unanimously condemned by Venezuelan historians, proved very valuable to the patriot cause.   From them were drawn almost all the resources for the armies for the years 1817 to 1819. Blanco stated that more than twelve thousand head of cattle and large amounts of other supplies were secured from them in the nine months of his administration as director of the missions in 1817 and 1818.[52]   Eloy González in his study of the financing of the Rev-

[46] Quoted in Blanco-Azpurúa, *Documentos*, vol. iii, p. 306.

[47] Díaz, *Recuerdos*, p. 41; Heredia, *Memorias*, p. 72.

[48] The loyalty of the Indians to the king in other sections of the country, especially in Coro, Arcaya has pointed out as an indication of the influence of the church; *vide* his *Estudios sobre personajes y hechos*, p. 164.

[49] Baralt and Díaz, *op. cit.*, vol. ii, p. 368.

[50] Larrazábal, Felipe, *Vida del Libertador Simón Bolívar*, 2 vols., (Madrid, 1918), vol. ii, pp. 76-77.

[51] O'Leary, *Memorias*, vol. i, p. 376.

[52] Blanco-Azpurúa, *Documentos*, vol. xiii, p. 462.

olution, *La ración del boa*, attests to their great usefulness as the granary of the revolutionary forces. It is interesting to note that the Indian regiment, *Rifles*, which took part in the famous battle of Ayacucho was recruited from the natives that these missionaries had held in reduction. Their immediate acceptance of the revolutionary cause upon the destruction of the mission is regarded by the Venezuelan writers as an indication that they hated the missionaries.[53]

Upon the advancement of the revolutionary cause after 1819, the clergy came generally to its support. In 1818, Morillo was already reporting to Spain that the priests were particularly disaffected, declaring that he had requested Spanish lawyers and missionaries and that he must now have Spanish priests.[54] A report of the ecclesiastical court of Mérida, May 23, 1817, is interesting as a clerical and royalist statement concerning those absent from their places in the parishes for service in the Revolution. This *expediente*, signed by Carlos Mas y Rubí, declared that the following were suspended from their places, assigning the reasons listed: José Antonio Mendoza, a violent revolutionary; Santiago León, violent revolutionary; Luis Ovalle, a pronounced insurgent, but not so radical as the former; Ramón Ignacio Méndez, systematic insurgent, but moderate and a defender of the church; Joaquín Durán, a pronounced insurgent; Ignacio Briceño, a partisan by blood and simplicity; Pablo Ignacio Quintero, insurgent through ignorance; Angel María Briceño, seduced and intimidated, of good character; Manuel González, a moderate insurgent; Enrique Salas, seduced, of good character; Antonio María Briceño, an insurgent, repented, but emigrated through fear; Diego Guerra, partisan through ignorance and timidity; Juan José Mendoza, insurgent, pronounced, systematic, somewhat extreme; Luis Mendoza, systematic insurgent; Mariano Talavera, extreme insurgent; Benancio Becerra, pronounced and extreme insurgent; Juan Bautista Ardilla, emigrated because of annoyance; Francisco Jácome, pronounced and extreme insurgent; Francisco Martas, moderate partisan; Juan de Díos Picón, only known that he followed his father.[55]

[53] Duarte Level, *op. cit.*, pp. 155-156.
[54] *Correo del Orinoco*, July 25, 1818.
[55] Silva, *Patriotismo del clero*, pp. 108-109.

On the battle field priests do not appear so often as leaders as they did in the early years of the Revolution in Mexico.[56] On the royalist side,. Andrés Torrellas is the outstanding example of a soldier-priest. With the Indian, Reyes Vargas, he was a most enthusiastic defender of the rights of Ferdinand VII. Dávila in his *Acciones de guerra* lists several engagements in which he appeared as leader of the royalist forces. Lasso de la Vega, Bishop of Mérida, who occupied in 1814 the see left vacant by the death of Milanés in 1812, led his parishioners in battle for the cause of the monarchy. Although there were many priests in the armies of the revolutionists, few seem to have achieved any military distinction.[57] José Félix Blanco was an exception; he rendered important service in the army of Bolívar, rising to the rank of general. Several others are listed by Dávila and Landaeta Rosales as attaining some military distinction. Páez considered Blanco and Méndez as the outstanding patriots among the clergy. The latter was his constant companion on the Apure.[58]

In 1820, the Bishop of Mérida took the oath of allegiance to the Republic, after having considered emigration as an alternative. In his famous apology, *Conducta del Obispo de Mérida,* he defended his action on the grounds that :(1) he was convinced now that the republican government represented the will of the people; (2) Ferdinand VII had lost all claim to the allegiance of America in recognizing the sovereignty of the Spanish people in his oath to support the constitution of 1820; and (3) Venezuela owed no allegiance to the Spanish people.[59] Like the higher clergy of Mexico, the Bishop found reason for withdrawing support from the Spanish cause in the anti-clericalism of the constitution of 1820. As a new convert, he became a most ardent defender of the independence of the Republic, rendering important service to it in securing contact with the Papacy.

After 1821 the resistance of the clergy to the new Republic was

---

[56] Bancroft, H. H., *History of Mexico,* (San Francisco, 1885), vol. iv, pp. 423-424.

[57] There were thirty at one time with Páez in Apure.

[58] Páez, José Antonio, *Autobiografía,* 2 vols., (New York, 1867-1869), vol. ii, p. 118.

[59] Silva, *Documentos,* vol. vi, pp. 145-191.

confined to a few obscure priests and friars who figured in local uprisings.[60] The directing forces of the clergy accepted the political transformation. With its acceptance, the new government was inclined to praise, perhaps somewhat extravagantly, the patriotism of the clergy.[61] Its contributions in money, its influence in securing support for the Revolution, as well as its military aid were commended. But no doubt much of the commendation was merited. The religiosity of the masses of the people gave the clergy predominant influence, which the revolutionary government sought to capitalize. Reference has been made to Bolívar's attempt to use Coll y Prat and his priests in Valencia in 1814. Later he used the Bishops of Popayán and of Mérida to much better effect in putting down the remaining resistance to the Republic and in quelling local uprisings. The Bishop of Popayán was especially useful in checking his intransigent royalist flock in Pasto. When a French attack was feared in 1825, Bolívar wrote Santander from Lima: "Do not forget to declare a crusade against the atheistic French. . . . The Bishop of Mérida and all other fanatics will be able to serve in this case in the churches, in the pulpits, and in the streets."[62]

It has been suggested above that it is difficult to make any satisfactory generalizations as to the attitude of the Venezuelan clergy toward the Revolution against the Spanish monarchy. Nor is it easy to estimate its services either to the cause of the king or to that of independence. The very fact that the church did not act as a body, that it was sectionalized and individualized, makes it difficult to isolate it sufficiently to treat it as a class apart. Only in the reaction following the earthquake in 1812 did the clergy act with any degree of unanimity until it came generally to Bolívar's support following the success of his armies after 1819. The Bishops of Mérida and Popayán, royalist until 1821, led finally their even more reactionary parishioners to accept the new government. But some on both sides refused to follow an opportunist policy, preferring death or exile to acquiescence. Because of the regard for the office, the clergy were

---

[60] For a discussion of the participation of churchmen in these uprisings, vide below, Chapter II.

[61] For example, vide the report of the Secretary of the Interior of Gran Colombia in 1821, Archivo Santander (Bogotá, 1913-1920), 17 vols., vol. vii, pp. 345 et seq.

[62] Ibid., vol. xii, pp. 284-285.

able to exercise an influence much beyond their numerical strength. Nevertheless, such influence could not be considered a decisive factor in the Revolution.

The status of the church did not become a definite issue in the Revolution in Venezuela, as it did Mexico after 1820. Through the diplomatic skill of Bolívar any definition of its position in the new state was evaded until independence was won. Hence, the clergy could still anticipate favorable treatment at the hands of the new government and were encouraged to support the Revolution.

A word should be said in the conclusion of this chapter about the contribution of the revolutionary period to the development of anti-clerical sentiment and the conflict between the church and the state, which followed immediately the close of the Revolution. In view of the attack on the privileges of the church in Gran Colombia and the even more extreme steps taken by Venezuela after her separation from the union in 1830, one might be inclined to seek the source of the opposition in the attitude of the clergy toward the struggle for independence. But there appears to be slight support for such a view. The most irreconcilable of the priests had been killed or deported or had emigrated; of those left the ones who had held out longest against the Revolution were as new converts the most enthusiastic protagonists of the new order. It is true that certain obscure priests were charged with prolonging the civil discord, endangering the stability of the Republic, and delaying international recognition. Such activities, exaggerated by the opposition of the Masons, produced a bitterness that the war itself had not engendered, and had much to do with the intensification of anti-clericalism. As a matter of fact, the churchmen who contended most vigorously for the rights of the church in the new state, arousing all the forces of anti-clericalism, were the outstanding patriots among the clergy: Méndez, Talavera, and Arias. The patriotism of Méndez, the most intransigent defender of the privileges of the church, was cited by his opponents as his one redeeming character. And the new state was not inclined to criticize harshly the opportunism of men like Coll y Prat and Lasso de la Vega. The former was soon to be redeemed as one outstanding for his pastoral virtues and held up as the ideal type of ecclesiastic, the bishop submissive to the government in power. The Revolution *per se* had apparently left little, if any, hostility or bitterness toward the church. But such was to develop in the civil discord that followed and will be discussed in the following chapters.

CHAPTER II

CHURCH AND STATE IN THE BOLIVARIAN ERA

THE DEFINITION of the status of the church in the new political and civil order in Venezuela was a question of concern to her statesmen from the beginning of the revolution against Spain; in fact, it was a question second only in importance to the determination of the fundamental character to be given the political organization. And because of its political and ecclesiastical bearings and its international implications, no problem required more judicious handling than this. Legislators, deistic in philosophy and tolerant toward all religions, had to consider nevertheless the colonial inheritance of an exclusive Catholic church protected by the Spanish kings; a church that, through the favor of the monarchs, had indeed often won precedence over the civil power in the *competencias,* more bitterly fought in Venezuela, it seems, than in any part of the Spanish Empire. In the eighteenth century, it is true, there had been some decline in the political status of the church in Spain; Bourbon rulers, dominated by extravagant notions of secular absolutism, discouraged clerical pretensions. But the civil and political position of the church in the colonies had not been seriously affected; kings still regarded the institution as the surest support of the royal power and protected it accordingly from any encroachment other than their own.

The colonial inheritance of ecclesiastical pretensions and power both increased the desire of the civil authorities to subordinate and control the church and, at the same time, indicated the difficulties that might be incurred in any attempt to lower its status. The revolutionary governments had to deal with an institution that had possessed influence over the minds of the people to such an extent that interference with its exclusive privileges might, it was feared, produce revolt against the political power. Although it was declared in the discussion of clerical questions that the people of Venezuela had made no opposition to such ecclesiastical reforms as were proposed, those making such judgments would have had to admit the possibility of revolt. And the possibility of popular support of the church had been realized in the reaction of 1812. Throughout the decade of the twenties there was a continuous uneasiness that a repetition of such an uprising might occur and embarrass the new state in its attempt to achieve stability and to secure international recognition. On the other hand, there was also the positive advantage that might be gained in securing the active support of the institution for the defense of the new order. No one apparently appreciated the potential value of this support so well as Bolívar, since none foresaw so clearly as he the social problems to be met by the new Hispanic-American Republics. In a famous statement made in a letter to Pedro Gual, he declared that he feared peace more than war; he feared the social disorder and the possible anarchy that would follow the disbanding of armies long accustomed to military life. And none of the revolting peoples faced such stupendous problems of recovery and reorganization, political and social, as his own; for none had suffered such overwhelming economic and social losses.

For assistance in the social reconstruction Bolívar looked to the church. A practical political purpose is apparent in his *rapprochement* with the two remaining bishops in 1820; he sought their support for and positive defense of the new order in the state, as well as their assistance in his approach to the Papacy. "A bishop is a useful person," he observed to the vice-president, Santander, in informing him that the Bishop of Popayán had agreed to remain in Gran Colombia and to take the oath to support the new state.[1] By his policy of accommodation he was able to secure the services of the royalist bishop of Mérida, Lasso de la Vega, who had supported the resistance of Coro and Maracaibo to the revolutionists even to the point of leading their armies in battle. And he won also the Spanish bishop of Popayán, the only Spanish bishop in the revolting colonies who did not emigrate; a cleric, moreover, whose edicts and excommunications against the revolutionists had already become a legend and whose

[1] *Archivo Santander*, vol. viii, p. 260.

diocese, including Pasto, aptly called by Mitre, "the La Vendée of America," was the most reactionary district of Gran Colombia.

The dependence on the church for aid in the achievement of social stability led Bolívar to issue, in the midst of the disorders in the late twenties, certain reactionary decrees, enhancing the position of the church. These decrees brought upon him the severe criticism of liberals and gave rise even to the thesis, set forth by Monsalve and accepted by others, that Bolívar was a devout Catholic rather than a deist and that his personal opinion on clerical matters was conservative.[2] But Bolívar's clerical policy was only the expression of his realistic conception of politics; he sought in the ecclesiastical as well as in the political constitution to reconcile his liberal philosophic ideals with the facts of Venezuelan social life.

During the continuance of the war Bolívar's policy of accommodation with the church was expressed not only in his *rapprochement* with the royalist bishops, but also in the Constitutions of Angostura and Cúcuta. Although there was no provision in either of these for an exclusive Catholic church, nor even for state aid to the church, there was, through his influence primarily, no specific denial of such exclusiveness in a definite grant of freedom of worship. And there was no attack on the privileges of the church nor positive claim by the state of the right of patronage. As Bolívar explained later to an American friend, the omission from the constitution of a grant of religious toleration was a concession to the sentiment of the country. It represented no illiberalism in his philosophy, but a temporizing with circumstances. The definition of the place of the church in the state was merely delayed for a more convenient day. The delay and the apparent concession of its former privileges

[2] Monsalve, J. D., *El ideal político del Libertador*, 2 vols., (Madrid, 1916). For a similar interpretation of Bolívar's policy on ecclesiastical questions, *vide*, Groot, J. M., *Historia eclesiástica y civil de Nueva Granada*, 5 vols., (Bogotá, 1891); and Navarro, N. E., *La masonería y la independencia*, (Caracas, 1928). A different conception is presented by Gil Fortoul, *Historia constitucional;* Parra Pérez, C., *Bolívar: contribución al estudio de sus ideas políticas*, (Paris, 1928); also his "Les idées religieuses et philosophiques de Bolívar," *Bulletin de l'amérique latine*, vol. 8, (1918-1919), pp. 257-271; Ponte, Andrés, F., *Bolívar y otros ensayos*, (Caracas, 1918); Mancini, Jules, *Bolívar et l'emancipation de colonies espagnoles*, (Paris, 1912); Leturia, Pedro, *La acción diplomática de Bolívar ante Pío VII, 1820-1823*, (Madrid, 1925); Villanueva, Carlos A., "Bolívar et l'église en amérique," *Bulletin de la bibliothéque americaine*, vol. ii, (1912), pp. 161-175; 272-281.

gave the church hope, however, of retaining and even of augmenting those privileges under the republican régime.

I

THIS BRIEF INTRODUCTORY statement, points of which will be elaborated later, should suggest something of the difficulty of reconciling colonial traditions, military and diplomatic necessities, and social facts with the anti-clericalism of statesmen who sought to make Venezuela a new-world France and who were, many of them, too impatient to adhere to the temporizing program of Bolívar. It is the purpose now to trace the evolution of the relations of church and state in Venezuela and Gran Colombia in the period of constitutional beginnings from 1811 to 1830. A statement of Miranda's plans for ecclesiastical reform might well precede this analysis.

Miranda's constitution for the church is an interesting feature of his plan for the political reorganization of Venezuela presented to William Pitt in 1808.[3] Incomplete though it is and of historical interest only, since it was never enacted into law, it is suggestive of the attitude of liberal leaders toward the church in the pre-revolutionary period. According to his plan, the Inquisition was to be abolished at once. The prohibition of this court was to be a primary feature of all later ecclesiastical reforms, indicating the deep-rooted resentment of colonials toward an institution which they held responsible for their intellectual isolation.[4] Religious toleration was declared to be a natural right.[5] This feature was likewise to be a fundamental consideration in all later reforms, although for practical political reasons it was not always specifically provided for in law. During the war the clergy were to be controlled by a *vicario-general* appointed by the assembly; pastors were to be elected by the people. The hierarchical order was to be determined by a provincial council called by the assembly. Ministers were not to be molested in the

[3] For a copy of this Project of Miranda, *vide*, Gil Fortoul, *Historia constitucional*, vol. ii, appendix pp. 315-323; for an analysis of his political philosophy and an evaluation of European influences on his thought, *vide*, Robertson, W. S. *Life of Miranda*.
[4] The presence of many proscribed books in private libraries in Venezuela and the general acquaintance of the revolutionary leaders with European liberal thought indicate that intellectual isolation was far from complete; *vide*, above, Introduction.
[5] Religious liberty he should have said, it seems.

performance of their religious offices, but they were to be excluded from all civil and military functions. This plan seemed to look to the complete reorganization of the church by the state without reference to papal authority. It did state, however, that the Catholic church, as the one recognized by all Venezuelans, would be upheld by the state. But in its proposal of hierarchical reorganization by the state and the election of the clergy by the people, provisions made in complete disregard of canon law, it suggests more strongly the civil constitution of the clergy of France of 1791 than any of the national constitutions that followed.[6] Its restrictions on the clergy in the form of denial of rights to hold civil and military office go further even than this radical French constitution.

Miranda's constitution for the church embodies, in fact, a more radical break with the past than any that followed in this period. His long-continued contact with European liberal philosophy is reflected here as it is in his political ideology. Regarded askance by many of his countrymen as a sort of alien, he was especially feared by the church as a most dangerous protagonist not only of French deistic philosophy, but, what it feared more, of the English policy of religious toleration. Probably no other revolutionary leader provoked such antagonism on the part of the church as Miranda.[7]

In spite of its decidedly liberal features derived from the French Declaration of Rights and the Constitution of the United States, the Constitution of 1811 was conservative of the colonial régime in pronouncing the Catholic religion exclusive. Article I of the Constitution declared:

The Catholic, apostolic, Roman religion shall be that of the state and the only and exclusive one of the inhabitants of Venezuela. Its protection, conservation, purity, and inviolability shall be one of the first duties of the national assembly, which shall never permit in any of the territory of the confederation any other worship, public or private, nor any teaching contrary to that of Jesus Christ.[8]

[6] In his recent study, *La acción diplomática de Bolívar ante Pío VII*, Leturia holds that the French civil constitution of the clergy was of fundamental influence in the ecclesiastical reforms in Venezuela. Without doubt the French influence was prominent in the development of the anti-clerical attitude. As far as the formal law was concerned, however, it seems the Spanish tradition was more closely followed.

[7] *Vide*, Silva, *Documentos*, vol. ii, p. 85 *et seq; passim.*

[8] This constitution is included in the *Prólogo de los anales de Venezuela*, published by the Academia Nacional de la Historia (Caracas, 1903).

As the preceding discussion indicates, this provision did not represent the views of Miranda, nor·did it express those of many others in the constituent assembly.[9] It may be explained rather as a dictate of political necessity, as Gil Fortoul has suggested. Although a majority of the members of the Congress were of the most advanced school of liberal philosophy, on this question they were regardful of public opinion, which was already reacting against the Revolution and even more strongly against the Republican government. To this reaction the clergy were contributing, particularly by their protests against an article on religious toleration which had appeared in the official *Gaceta de Caracas*.[10] This article, written by the Irish resident, William Burke, attempted to set forth the practical advantages to be obtained from toleration of all religions. The clergy were given the privilege of answering it in the same publication. Their replies, coming from the Franciscans of Valencia, from Antonio Gómez of the University of Caracas, and from the entire governing body of the University of Caracas, indicated clearly what would be the attitude of the church toward any liberalization in ecclesiastical policy.[11] Admitting the possible material advantages in increase of wealth and population to be gained from religious toleration, it was contended that the social and moral unity to be secured only by religious unity were more to be desired. Appeal was made especially to Rousseau's opinion of the contribution of religious unity toward the achievement of social solidarity. Gómez warned the people that religious toleration would destroy the unity of the "social will" and hence endanger the stability

[9] *El libro nacional de los venezolanos—Actas del congreso constituyente en 1811* (Caracas, 1911); *Libro 4° de actas del supremo congreso de Venezuela en 1812: Orígenes de república*, (Caracas, 1926). These give in part the records of this congress. For notes on the recent discovery of these records, *vide*, Gil Fortoul, *Historia constitucional*, vol. ii, p. 199, note. The debates on the constitution itself have not been found.

[10] *La gaceta de Caracas*, February 18, 1811.

[11] These were published also in pamphlet form as follows: *Apología de la intolerancia religiosa contra las máximas del irlandés D. Guillermo Burke*, (Valencia, 1811); Gómez, Antonio, *Ensayo político contra las reflexiones del S. William Burke sobre el tolerantismo* (Caracas, 1811); La Universidad Real y Pontifical de Caracas, *La intolerancia político-religiosa vindicada, ó refutación del discurso que en favor de la tolerancia religiosa público el D. Guillermo Burke*, (Caracas, 1812).

of the political order.[12]   Toleration was contrary to the spirit, the genius of the Spanish people, the Franciscans declared.[13]   And the University of Caracas cautioned against imitation of the United States, which was compared to a great Masonic lodge wherein toleration had produced religious indifference.[14]   These writers not only opposed any ecclesiastical change, but were entirely reactionary in politics, defending the divine right of kings and the inviolability of their persons.[15]   It is interesting to note, however, that the clergy sought support for their theses in Montesquieu and Rousseau more frequently than in the church fathers.   Archbishop Méndez later declared that he quoted Montesquieu rather than the ecclesiastical authorities because of the greater weight of the former's opinion with his audience.   There could be, in fact, no more decided evidence of the popularity of the *Spirit of the Laws* than the frequency with which churchmen used it, or misused it, in support of their policies. Too much emphasis can hardly be placed on the writing of Burke and these protests upon it.   They went far toward defining the opposing attitudes upon the constitutional reorganization of the church.   The civil authority might temporize, but its liberal leaders were not likely to surrender to a force that represented what they considered the obscurantism of the colonial epoch.   In the clergy they found a force opposed to what they eulogized as the *"luces del siglo"* and sought for at great social risks.

Even in the face of the increasing reaction, the Congress abolished the Inquisition and all ecclesiastical *fueros,* or privileges. Liberal though he was in religious opinion, Restrepo declared the abolition of the *fueros* to have been extremely unwise.[16]   It became the center of attack on the Republican government.   This provision of the constitution, Article 180, was the subject of much discussion in the Congress, and was opposed to the last by eight of the nine clergymen who were members of the body, although some of these were liberal

[12] Gómez, *op. cit.,* p. 6 *et seq.*
[13] The articles of Burke had thrown Valencia into convulsions, it was declared; *vide, Apología,* p. 5.
[14] Universidad de Caracas, *op. cit.,* p. 87 *et seq.*
[15] *Ibid.,* pp. 17-18.
[16] Restrepo, *op. cit.,* vol. ii, p. 65.

in politics on other questions. Luis José Cazorla, a *cura* of Caracas, set forth in a long speech the practical danger of such an attack on the privileges of the clergy, in view of the fact that the people "confounded their pastors with Jesus Christ" and would revolt at any attack on ecclesiastical *fueros*. As grounds for his fears, he pointed to the reaction already developing into mutiny in Valencia, in opposition to the writings of Burke, and to the devotion of the people of Coro and Maracaibo, who would prefer to surrender their liberty rather than to endanger their religion.[17] With one exception, the priests signed the Constitution with protests on Article 180, and there were long protests from the Archbishop and the clergy of Caracas.[18] But the equalitarian sentiment of the Congress sought to wipe out all distinction of class existing in law; it could not be discouraged by the practical danger, which was recognized.[19] It is to the strength and persistence of this spirit of equalitarianism that Vallenilla Lanz attributes in large measure the continued hostility of the state to the church in Venezuela and its relentless determination to keep the church in complete subordination.[20] The protests from the clergy on the abolition of the *fueros* and the Inquisition, added to their answers to Burke's article on toleration, confirmed the belief that the clergy would oppose all liberal reforms.

As to the patronage, the Constituent Congress of 1811 declared that it "had ceased."[21] This expression was cited later by the clergy as an admission on the part of the state that it did not possess the right. That the government did not put that interpretation on the provision is indicated, however, in a statement of the executive in

---

[17] *Actas del congreso constituyente en 1811*, pp. 364-365; also protests of others, p. 335 *et seq.*
[18] *Exposición que hace el clero de Caracas al supremo congreso de Venezuela reclamado contra el artículo 180 de la constitución federal*, (Caracas, 1812). One priest, Peña of Mérida, a member who was absent from the Congress at the time the article was discussed, wrote supporting it and criticizing the opposition of other members of the clergy. His letter was read in the Congress (*Actas*, p. 357). Beginning with this Congress, there were found in the various assemblies some members of the clergy whose views equalled those of any laymen in liberalism.
[19] *Actas*, p. 335 *et seq.* In view of the circumstances, it was decided, however, that this article not be put into immediate execution.
[20] Vallenilla Lanz, *Críticas de sinceridad y exactitud*, p. 401 *et seq.*
[21] *Actas*, session of October 21.

1812. He objected to a stipulation of a provisional rule for providing for the churches, which had been worked out by a commission headed by the archbishop, on the grounds that it "restricted the natural faculty that governments possess to reject priests who are not believed to be conducive to the security of the state."[22]   The Constitution of 1811 provided in Article I that the Confederation should have the power to conclude a concordat with the Papacy, and the Congress appointed a commission to present a project for such an agreement. Although the work of this commission was discussed several times, the details of its reports do not appear in the published *Actas*, nor is there evidence that a project was accepted.[23] That the thinking on the matter of the patronage was not fully clarified is suggested by the interpretations placed on Article II of the Constitution, which provided that agreements be made with the local clergy until a concordat could be secured with the Papacy. Yanes understood that such agreements should be formal pacts in the nature of concordats, an interpretation that would have accorded the clergy a political position not recognized certainly by the majority of the members.[24]   This interpretation was welcomed by the ecclesiastics, Maya and Méndez. In the statements of the latter there were to be found later further declarations of the desirability of concordats and suggestions of the establishment of a permanent national patronage under the control of a national church rather than of the state. Except for a few advocates of the civil patronage the Venezuelan clergy were probably ultramontane; but what they demanded at this time was that the civil patronage should not be exercised without a grant of the right from the Papacy.

In view of the liberal thought of Miranda, the Briceños, Tovar, Uztáriz, Roscio, Peñalver, and other members of the assembly, the work of this Congress seems curiously conservative in matters of religion. Such conservatism can only represent a temporary con-

---

[22] *Actas de Congreso en 1812*, p. 36.
[23] *Actas de Congreso de 1811*, pp. 284-285; p. 294. On October 31, it was recorded that the matter was discussed at length, all the lawyers and canonists being heard. Peñalver objected to having clergymen on the commission, p. 297.
[24] *Actas de Congreso de 1811*, pp. 284-285.

cession to circumstances.[25]   And in the abolition of the *fueros* of the clergy, there was disregard even of the danger of armed opposition.[26]

The constitution of the province of Barcelona, drawn by an outstanding liberal, Francisco Espejo, represented the anti-clerical sentiment more fully than the Federal Constitution.[27]   Like the Project of Miranda, it suggested the influence of French thought in its nationalism and equalitarianism.[28]   The Catholic religion was to be the only public worship permitted.   Bishops as well as other ecclesiastics were to be elected by the people and confirmed by a neighboring bishop.   All *fueros* and all religious orders were declared abolished on the ground that there should be no class distinctions among citizens.

II

IT IS INTERESTING to note in passing that religious toleration was a feature of the political program of the so-called "Congress" of Cariaco in 1817, of which Madariaga was the leader.[29]   But in the Congress of Angostura in 1819 Bolívar's recommendation that there should be no article on religion was followed.   Public opinion was not yet ready to accept toleration, he feared.   By making no provision for an ecclesiastical establishment, he thought the state might

[25] The formula of the oath drawn by the leader of the conservatives, Felipe Fermín Paúl, is a curious relic of the colonial tradition.   Those taking oath were to swear to support "the mysteries of the Christian religion."   A paper of the day declared that if mysteries were to be maintained, the divine right of Ferdinand VII might as well be defended.   But the religious significance of the oath was such that innovations in matters apparently more essential would have been tolerated more readily than in this formula.

[26] This is the opinion of Restrepo referred to above.   On the other hand, Vallenilla Lanz holds that there was never any danger of popular opposition; he quotes the statement of Roscio that the Inquisition was suppressed without criticism; (*Críticas*, p. 405).   Statements to the same effect were made in the Congress of Cúcuta.

[27] It is interesting to note that both the constitutions of Mérida and of Trujillo were drawn by priests.   That of Mérida was the work of Talavera y Garcés, whom Gil Fortoul esteems a man of "vast political learning," (*Historia constitucional*, vol. i, p. 244, note).   Francisco Álvarez, a man equally able, was the author of the constitution of Trujillo.   But neither constitution contained any provision on religion except a declaration that the Catholic religion should be exclusive; (Gil Fortoul, *op. cit.*, vol. i, pp. 242-245).   Maracaibo and Guayana, both in the control of royalists, did not accept the Federal Constitution nor draw up provincial ones.

[28] Only recently this interesting document was found by Vicente Dávila, Director of the National Archives in Caracas, among the *Documentos de causas de infidencia*. It is published in Gil Fortoul, *op. cit.*, vol. i, pp. 245-249.

[29] Gil Fortoul, *op. cit.*, vol. i, pp. 345-346.

secure for its people toleration in fact, even though not in law.[30] That this interpretation of the failure to make any provision with reference to religion or the church was generally accepted is evidenced by the statements of others. James Hamilton, a British officer in Guayana, wrote the Duke of Sussex in July, 1819, that the constitution extended privileges of civil and religious liberty similar to those enjoyed in Great Britain.[31]

A unique feature of Bolívar's project presented to the Congress at Angostura was its provision for the establishment of a fourth power, the "moral power." Apparently Bolívar foresaw the decline of the social dominance of the church and sought to create in this body an instrument for social control and moral censorship.[32] Otherwise, it is difficult to reconcile this reactionary feature with his accustomed liberalism. The "moral power" was to be exercised by an Areopagus composed of life members organized into two chambers. The powers of the Areopagus extended to surveillance over civic morals, with the right to accord appropriate penalties and rewards; to the censorship of publications; and to the supervision of education. The assembly objected to this feature of Bolívar's plan on the grounds that it would be equivalent to the reëstablishment of the Inquisition and further that it would be difficult to constitute. But it was not rejected outright; it was added as an appendix to the constitution and recommended for later consideration.

In spite of the liberalism of its members the Constitution of Angostura marked a backward step in admitting bishops as honorary members of the Senate.[33] This provision was enacted upon the

[30] Concerning the failure to make provisions for religious toleration in the Constitution of Cúcuta, Bolívar observed to an American friend: "Knowing that the toleration of no religion except the Catholic would be admitted, I took care that nothing be said upon religion when the Constitution of Colombia was established; so that, since there is no clause that prescribes the form of worship, foreigners may worship God as they please. The people of Colombia are not yet prepared for any change in matters of religion. The priests have great influence with the ignorant people. Religious liberty should follow free institutions and a system of general education"; quoted in Gil Fortoul, *op. cit.*, vol. i, p. 436.

[31] O'Leary, *Memorias*, vol. xii, pp. 302-305.

[32] In the introduction to his Project, Bolívar recognized the difficulty of preparing a constitution for Venezuelan society in view of the racial and social conditions. "We are not Europeans, we are not Indians, but a people half way between the aborigines and the Spanish," he declared, . . . "and our situation is thus very extraordinary and complicated."

[33] Copies of Bolívar's Project and of the Constitution of Angostura are found in Gil Fortoul, *op. cit.*, vol. ii, Appendix, pp. 507-550.

recommendation of Ramón Ignacio Méndez, later to be the first
archbishop of Venezuela.[34]   Like the Congress of 1811, this Congress made some gestures toward a concordat with Rome.   Also
some efforts were made toward the establishment of provisional
rules for filling vacancies in the church through agreements with the
local clergy.   These are discussed below.

The radical anti-clerical reforms which attended the revolution
of 1820 in Spain strained relations between that country and the
Papacy.   The government at Angostura, and later the Constituent
Congress at Cúcuta, took advantage of this opportunity to approach
Rome.   The desire to secure recognition by the Pope and the in-
security of military fortunes were no doubt responsible for the cautious policy on ecclesiastical matters in these years.   In spite of the
fact that he was a pronounced liberal, Juan Germán Roscio, president of the Congress, favored moderation.   Writing to Bolívar in
August, 1820, he stated that he had just written Zea, the vice-
president, that advantage should be taken of this occasion for approaching Rome, since Spain's influence would be weakened by the
anti-clerical revolution.[35]   And in a letter in September of the same
year, he deplored the establishment of a Masonic lodge at Angostura
on the grounds that it might embarrass the government in its efforts
to take advantage of the Spanish revolution.[36]   The government at
Angostura named the first commission to treat with Rome.   After
Bolívar's agreement with the Bishop of Mérida, direct communications with Rome were opened through the agency of the church.
And the Bishop made the religiosity of Gran Colombia, in contrast
to the impiety of Spain, his leading argument for the recognition of
the former by the Papacy.[37]

But the desire to secure such recognition did not prevent agitation for radical advancement in religious policy.   Bolívar realized
the danger of such agitation by the ultra-liberals; but, as he wrote
Santander, he feared to oppose the lawyers more than to oppose the

---

[34] For his famous speech on the constitution of the Senate, vide, Correo del Orinoco,
issue of August 7, 1819, and succeeding issues.

[35] O'Leary, Memorias, vol. viii, p. 498; and to Santander he wrote to the same
effect; Archivo Santander, vol. v, p. 215.

[36] O'Leary, Memorias, vol. viii, pp. 504-505.   The lodge was established through
the efforts of the Englishman, James Hamilton.

[37] Silva, Documentos, vol. vi, p. 17 et seq., letter of October 20, 1821.

priests.[38] The published debates of the Congress of Cúcuta, which give much more detailed discussion on ecclesiastical matters than those of the earlier congresses, show the pronounced anti-clerical spirit that existed in that body.[39] This Congress was made notable, too, by the presence of the Bishop of Mérida as deputy from Maracaibo. In this body and later in the Congress of Cúcuta, he was the foremost protagonist of the privileges of the church.[40] His admittance to the assembly was the subject of prolonged dispute. Before he had arrived in Cúcuta or had taken the oath to support the government, he was sending protests to the assembly against the abolition of the Inquisition, which had been one of its first acts.[41] Opposition was raised on the floor of the Congress even to the reading of a petition in favor of an institution so contrary to the "enlightenment of the age." Even his conversion to the national cause was criticized on the grounds that it came only as a result of the liberal revolution in Spain—in other words a royalist was to be preferred to a reactionary nationalist.[42] The most radical spirit was shown by the Briceños, Miguel Tovar, and Diego Fernández Gómez of Venezuela, and by Vicente Azuero and Santamaría of Colombia. These debates on the admittance of the Bishop and the reception of his petition indicate the progress of the radical sentiment that found expression later in opposition to monastic orders and in the enactment of liberal laws on the press and public education.

Curiously enough, it was through the influence of the Bishop of Mérida that Bolívar's policy of making no provision for a state church was followed in this Congress. Restrepo wrote Santander on June 6 that the priests were aroused by the failure of the Congress to recognize the Catholic church as exclusive and that he feared they would yet secure such a provision.[43] But on August 6, Osorio, a member of the Congress, wrote the vice-president:

[38] Lecuna, Vicente, *Cartas del Libertador*, 10 vols. (Caracas, 1929-1930), vol. ii, pp. 170-171.

[39] Cortazar, Roberto and Luis Augusto Cuervo, *Congreso de Cúcuta, Libro de actas*, (Bogotá, 1923).

[40] For his speeches, *vide*, Silva, *Documentos*, vol. vi.

[41] The Inquisition had not existed since 1811 in Venezuela and had been abolished in a part of New Granada.

[42] Cortazar and Cuervo, *Congreso de Cúcuta*, p. 274, p. 300; *passim*.

[43] *Archivo Santander*, vol. vi, p. 301.

The most serious question which, it seemed, was going to divide us was the article on religion that should be placed in the constitution and the terms; you will be surprised . . . the unprejudiced opinion of the Bishop decided the point, in spite of Baños, Otero, Cacerés, Hinestrosa, etc.[44]

Osorio went on to indicate that this omission from the constitution would be interpreted in practice as a recognition of religious toleration, as it had been under the Constitution of Angostura.

This action on the part of the Bishop has given rise to much misconception as to his politico-religious opinions and policy. Gil Fortoul, for example, has commended his liberalism suggesting that his ecclesiastical policy was similar to that of Bolívar.[45] But the primary concern of the Bishop, as he wrote Pius VII and explained at great length later in published writings, was to secure the recognition by the state that the exercise of the patronage should belong to the church.[46] By opposing a "religion of state," he hoped to bring about the abolition of state control over the Catholic church, not to establish liberty of worship. He expected the state to uphold the exclusiveness of the Catholic church without exercising any tuition over it. As a member of the Congress he opposed religious toleration, the extinction of the convents, restrictions on the privileges of the clergy, and even the abolition of the Inquisition. After he had realized his failure to free the church from state control, he urged, as a member of the Congress at Bogotá, that the allocution to the Constitution, which recognized the Catholic church as that of Colombia, be made a part of the first volume of the laws.[47] It is true the Bishop had been extravagant in his enthusiasm for the Republic. He was more patriotic than Bolívar, Santander declared. He had been very useful in consolidating opinion for the Republic in 1820 and 1821. And in diplomatic matters he proved to be a distinct asset to Gran Colombia, securing the first direct contact with the Papacy.

[44] *Ibid.*, vol. vii, pp. 57-58.
[45] Gil Fortoul, *op. cit.*, vol. i, p. 518.
[46] Silva, *Documentos*, vol. vi, p. 164 *et seq.*
[47] *Congreso de 1823: Actas*, Biblioteca de Historia Nacional, vol. xxxvii, (Bogotá, 1926), pp. 85-86. His petition was not granted. For the allocution to the Constitution of Cúcuta, *vide* Cortazar and Cuervo, *op. cit.*, p. 524. It states that all laws shall be made conformable to the Roman Catholic religion, which "has been the religion of our fathers and is and shall be the religion of state."

But in ecclesiastical policy he was decidedly ultramontane and reactionary. His published writings, his debates in the congresses of Colombia, of which he continued to be a member until 1826 and a protagonist throughout for the privileges of the church, and his correspondence with Pius VII and Leo XII and with the Colombian statesmen are overwhelming proof of his conservatism. And the fervor of his patriotism cooled as he came to see that the Republic would not be tender to the immunities of the church; his ultramontanism caused his loyalty even to be questioned later by the government at Bogotá.[48] Bolívar himself reproved him on the grounds that his activities in Maracaibo were too favorable to the Spanish faction.[49]

The Congress of Cúcuta declared the Inquisition abolished and its property confiscated.[50] This institution had indeed exercised no jurisdiction in Venezuela since 1811. It is interesting to note that this law was pronounced to be in the interest of the ecclesiastical courts, whose jurisdiction, it was held, had been usurped by the Inquisition. Only causes of faith were to be subjects for the consideration of the ecclesiastical courts; even in these cases recourse to the civil courts was granted. The power of the ecclesiastical courts should not extend to foreigners nor to those not on the parish register. All matters of external discipline and of censorship were declared to be prerogatives belonging to the civil power alone.

In a law of July 26, 1826, this same Congress declared monasteries with less than eight members subject to extinction and their

[48] Santander wrote to a friend in 1825 that the Intendant in Apure had ordered seized two bulls against the Masons which the Bishop was circulating without the sanction of the government. (*Archivo Santander*, vol. xiii, p. 108). He attempted to circulate them also in the diocese of Caracas. He was accused later of being involved in secret negotiations between a part of the Colombian clergy and the Papacy; *vide*, below.

[49] Lacroix, L. Perú de, *Diario de Bucaramanga*, edited by Cornelio Hispano, (Paris, 1912), p. 177. Lacroix commented (pp. 212-214) on Bolívar's views on the church: his policy of protecting the Catholic religion on the grounds that it was universal in Colombia, his criticism of the clergy, and his opinion of the Bishop of Mérida. The Archbishop of Bogotá he considered a worthy man; Méndez, then Archbishop of Caracas, he praised as valiant, patriotic, and learned in theological matters. But, as Lacroix reported his opinions, he thought the bishops of Mérida and Popayán quite different. The latter had been the cause of much bloodshed; the former not such a great criminal, but delinquent toward the government of the Republic; both were "hypocrites and without faith."

[50] *Leyes de Colombia*, (1821), pp. 79-80, law of August 22, 1821.

goods confiscated to the service of public instruction.[51] Some delegates wished to extinguish all convents for both men and women on
the grounds that they were obscurantist, crude in social customs, lax
in discipline, and corrupt in morals. No education, it was protested,
was to be preferred to that given in these religious establishments.[52]
The new nation was eager for enlightenment that would give its
citizens recognition among the savants of Europe. Keen interest in
the newest books and periodicals from Europe was expressed in the
letters of Bolívar, Roscio, Gual, Santander, Restrepo, the Cuervos,
and others. Groot attributed what he held to be these ill-considered
reforms in the church to this desire to secure the approval of the
European intellectuals.[53] The liberal law on public education, which
provided for primary and normal schools throughout Gran Colombia, and the liberal law of the press expressed well the faith in these
remedies for the intellectual backwardness under the Spanish régime.
The eagerness for intellectual expansion appears, indeed, to have
been the primary reason for the extinction of the convents and for
other restrictions on the privileges of the church. The institution
was regarded as the bulwark of Spanish opposition to the introduction
of new ideas. The possession of their property had no doubt some
weight with those who wished the convents abolished, but it could
hardly be regarded as a leading factor, it seems. Some who favored
extinction on other grounds objected to the confiscation of their
property.[54] These smaller convents were as a rule poor; Depons
had noted the complete impoverishment of some convents in Venezuela.[55] Indeed, an argument advanced for the extinction of these
smaller establishments was that their poverty made them dependent
on public support. Reports indicate that the armies had carried
away from both churches and monasteries any movable property
that might be used in financing the war.[56] Only their lands and
buildings were left. Such popular resistance to the extinction as

[51] *Ibid.*, pp. 67-68.
[52] Cortazar and Cuervo, *Congreso de Cúcuta*, p. 338 *et seq; passim.*
[53] Groot, *op. cit.*, vol. iii, pp. 319-320.
[54] Cortazar and Cuervo, *Congreso de Cúcuta*, p. 375 *et seq.*
[55] Depons, *op. cit.*, vol. iii, p. 150.
[56] *Vide*, for example, O'Leary, *Memorias*, vol. xxii, p. 94, for the report by Bolívar
of jewels taken from the churches. There are many such notices in the public documents of the period.

developed in Spain was declared unlikely. There the extinction was opposed as unjust confiscation; in Gran Colombia the pension granted the ex-cloistered friars would provide for them more adequately than they were cared for in the convents.[57]

The clergy contended that the collection and control of the tithe also reverted to the church with the overthrow of the royal power in America. In some instances it ventured to grant the former royal ninth to the government as a contribution toward the support of the war.[58] The Bishop of Mérida recommended, however, that the colonial practice on this subject be continued with the exception that the royal ninth be used to send ecclesiastical representations to Rome.[59] By a law of October 14, 1821, the government declared the Spanish law with regard to the collection and distribution of the tenth in force until a concordat could be made with the Papacy. To promote agriculture, a law was passed May 19, 1824, exempting from the burden of the tithe all new plantations of cacao, coffee, and indigo, for ten, seven, and four years respectively.[60]

Thus, in the years from 1821 to 1823, the Congresses of Cúcuta and Bogotá had sanctioned religious toleration by failing to declare the Catholic church exclusive or to establish a constitution of a state church; they had abolished the Inquisition and with it all surveillance of the church over the introduction, publication, and circulation of books and periodicals; they had restricted the jurisdiction of the church courts to causes of faith only and granted recourse to civil courts in such cases; moreover, they had entirely exempted foreigners from the ecclesiastical jurisdiction. They had taken the first steps toward the extinction of convents for men and established a high minimum age limit for the entrance of both men and women into the religious life; and they had declared in force the Spanish law on the tithe and restricted its service in the interest of agricultural promotion.

These reforms were in most instances not extreme, some being intended, indeed, as only partial or provisional solutions. Neverthe-

[57] Cortazar and Cuervo, *Congreso de Cúcuta*, p. 375 *et seq.*
[58] For example, the ecclesiastical *cabildo* of Bogotá made such a grant. Groot, *op. cit.*, vol. iv, pp. 44-45.
[59] Blanco-Azpurúa, *Documentos*, vol. viii, p. 53.
[60] *Colección de leyes de Colombia, 1824-1825*, p. 138.

less, they indicate the state's progressive consolidation of its control over the church. But all constituent assemblies, congresses, and executives had avoided a definitive assertion of the right of patronage, even though they took some steps toward the establishment of provisional rules regulating its exercises, from which their intention to assert ultimately the right might be implied. Only in 1823 was the resolution of this delicate question undertaken. The result achieved was the famous Law of Patronage of July 28, 1824, that famous civil constitution of the church declared in force in Venezuela after the dissolution of Gran Colombia in 1830, and, with merely nominal changes, still the basis of the relations of church and state in that republic. It is the purpose of the writer at this point to state briefly the problem of the patronage arising from the colonial revolution against Spain, the temporary rules devised for meeting it, the theories held as to the nature of this right in law, and a brief analysis of the law itself, of the possible influences that determined its form, and its execution under the government of Gran Colombia.

III

THE PECULIAR RELATIONS of the Spanish monarchy to the Papacy with regard to the patronage in its overseas dominions left as a legacy to the new states and to the Papacy as well a most difficult and delicate ecclesiastico-political problem. By the bulls of Alexander VI, May 4, 1493, the first of which granted to the Catholic kings the dominion over the lands in America and the right to Christianize the natives; the second, the same patronal rights granted to Portugal in her colonial possessions, including the important right of presentation; by the bull of November 16, 1501, which conceded the right to the tithe and to first fruits; and by the very important bull of Julius II, July 28, 1508, which conceded the universal right of patronage in America, the Spanish monarchs enjoyed a civil control over the church that was virtually unlimited. Ribadeneyra, a leading Spanish authority on the patronage, declared that no Catholic monarch enjoyed such unrestricted exercise of the patronage as the Spanish kings in America possessed through these bulls.[61]   And in

---

[61] Ribadeneyra, Antonio Joachím, *Manuel compendio del regio patronato indiano*, (Madrid, 1763). There were, to be sure, many other papal actions on the patronage.

the bulls of Benedict XIV, January 11, and June 9, 1753, these rights were confirmed and given an even more secure foundation in law. As long as there was a probability of the restoration of the Spanish power in America, the Papacy would hesitate, of course, to disregard the rights of the Spanish monarchy under these grants. On the other hand, the new states naturally refused to accept any longer the patronage of the king. But, through considerations of policy, they hesitated to declare a national patronage independent of any agreement with the Papacy. In the meantime, the ecclesiastical organization, completely demoralized by the war, was demanding attention. There were vacancies to be filled. Changes in territorial delimitations made necessary some reorganization of the dioceses; and there were many questions of discipline to be defined, among them the control of the regular orders, formerly under the supervision of the Spanish vicario-general.[62] How to meet these needs without doing too great violence to the principles of canon law and hence to the consciences of clergymen and, at the same time, without sacrificing the national control over the church was a problem the new states had to face.

Some statistics on the church will indicate the demoralization of its organization arising from the Revolution. According to Torrente, the Spanish historian of the Revolution, only ten of the thirty-eight bishoprics in Hispanic-America were occupied in 1826; three of these ten incumbents were incapacitated and two emigrated in that same year, leaving only five in active service.[63] The fact that the episcopate had continued in the later years of the imperial régime to be largely Spanish in personnel is sufficient explanation of the vacancies. Only Bolívar was able to retain the services of a Spanish bishop. Argentina, Chile, Perú, and Bolivia had no bishops at the close of the Wars for Independence. In comparison, Gran Colombia might be considered fortunate in possessing two, the Spanish Bishop of Popayán and the creole Bishop of Mérida. But the latter was old and of uncertain health, so that there was danger that the department of Venezuela would be left without any. There had

---

[62] The territorial problem arose from the political separation of Cuenca, Quito, Panamá, and Mainas from the metropolitan centers.

[63] Torrente, op. cit., vol. i, pp. 46-48.

been, too, such depletion in the ranks of the higher clergy that chapters lacked the official canons required by law for the transaction of business left in their hands in the vacant sees. Guayana had no canons left; and the bishop-elect, who had served since 1804 without canonical institution, departed with the royalist armies in 1817. In 1822, there was only one priest remaining in this extensive province, according to the statement of Vergara, Secretary of the Interior, to the Colombian representative to the Papacy.[64] Bolívar was especially alarmed by the almost total lack of priests in the llanos of the Apure, where they were needed to prevent a complete social retrogression among the unruly *llaneros*.[65] Although other regions did not suffer so serious a lack of priests as Guayana, the reduction from deaths, exile, and emigration was everywhere disturbing, producing a deficiency in personnel from which Venezuela had not recovered by the middle of the century. As late as 1847, Venezuela had two hundred less priests than she possessed at the end of the colonial period. In a letter to Pius VII on March 19, 1823, Lasso de la Vega declared that vacancies were general both in the offices of the higher clergy and in the curacies, that churches often passed to transient priests, who occupied them without the approval of the bishop or chapter, that all semblance of discipline in the church had disappeared, and that no contact existed between the archbishoprics and outlying regions like Guayana and Mainas. He confessed his own grant of extraordinary faculties to vicars.[66] Governments asserted power to fill vacancies in ecclesiastical cabildos and, for the time being, priests acquiesced in such irregular procedure, confessing the uneasiness of their consciences to the pope or to their bishops. In such acquiescence in gross violation of canon law, Groot observed a foremost cause of the decline of the church—a fatal subordination and even servility to the civil power.[67] Beyond a doubt the depletion in the ranks of the clergy, the demoralization of the organization, and the almost complete loss of institutional discipline and control, never very effective in Venezuela, are factors to be considered in

[64] *El ministro de relaciones exteriores de Colombia en 1826*, reprinted in pamphlet, (Caracas, 1851).
[65] O'Leary, *Memorias*, vol. xxv, p. 231.
[66] Silva, *Documentos*, vol. vi, pp. 59-69.
[67] Groot, *op. cit.*, vol. iv, p. 233; p. 314; *passim*.

explaining the decline of the church in this country. And its loss of prestige made it difficult to overcome these embarrassments arising from the long and devastating war.

The clergy hoped to solve the ecclesiastical problem by the establishment of immediate and direct contacts with Rome, thus freeing itself from the civil patronage. The statement in the Venezuelan Constitution of 1811 that the patronage had ceased to exist, the fact that the authors of the Constitution of Cundinamarca and the acts of the United Provinces of New Granada had left the question undefined, awaiting an agreement with the Papacy, and the fact that rules made under the Constitutions of 1811, 1819, and 1821 were provisional only and seemed to give the church more independent control over its organization than the Spanish law, gave the institution some grounds for the contention that the state had admitted that it did not possess the right of patronage. Bolívar's attitude might easily be interpreted as favorable to a free church; and the omission of any provisions on religion and the church from the Constitutions of Angostura and Cúcuta were considered by the clergy to have that significance. These facts formed the basis for the arguments of Lasso de la Vega and later of Méndez, Talavera, and Arias against the exercise of the national patronage. They protested particularly against its exercise independent of concession.

But the secular directors of the new republic had no intention of giving up the control of the church. This prerogative was considered essential to the maintenance of independence and the consolidation of the state. And there was in the insistence on this right a sort of glorious gesture of patriotism—a declaration that Gran Colombia would not accept a position inferior to that of the Spanish monarchy in its relations with the ecclesiastical power and an expression of intense nationalism that rejected any subordination to a foreign power. Azuero, a liberal priest, went so far as to declare that the national church need not regard the decisions of the Council of Trent, since they were laws made by Italians.[68] Like the Spanish kings, these new states regarded the patronage as "the most interesting and precious prerogative of the civil power."[69] The political

[68] Groot, *op. cit.*, vol. iv, p. 382.
[69] *A vosotros cualesquiera que seais, salud etc.*, (Caracas, 1851).

writings of this period abound in such pronouncements, indicating the high importance attached to the question of the status of the church in the new régime and the jealous regard for the civil control. In his *Memorias* as Secretary of the Interior under Gran Colombia, Restrepo insisted constantly on this precious right; admitting that its full exercise had been interrupted in the war, he contended that the government had never abandoned it and that no political leader had ever questioned its possession by the civil power.[70] Castillo, Secretary of the Interior in 1824, declared that only political prudence had kept the Congress of Cúcuta from declaring its possession of the right in its plentitude.[71] Later Archbishop Méndez suggested the significance attached to the question when he exclaimed in exasperated irony in one of his protests to Bolívar against the exercise: "Perhaps Colombia exists by reason of the Law of the Patronage!"[72] And in an anonymous pamphlet of the period, the writer declared that "the government regards the law as a pillar such as those seen in Cairo; as one of those laws of the Medes that caused Saint John to lose his head; in a word, as a supernatural law against which neither reason nor circumstances nor the considerations that legislators, past and present, have been accustomed to regard avail nothing."[73] This opinion, it may be observed, exaggerates little the importance attached by Venezuelan statesmen to this constitution of the church, a constitution that the present dictator, Gómez, refers to as "classic."

The insistence on the strict surveillance of the church by the state which found expression in the ample law of 1824 is inconsistent with the philosophy of Bolívar, Santander, Pedro Gual, Restrepo, and other national leaders. In political philosophy these men were liberals, some of them advanced liberals. But none of them advocated the separation of church and state—the chief feature of most liberal programs on the church. Although Bolívar's famous statement to the constituent assembly of Bolivia in 1825, that religion was a matter of conscience, that to legislate upon it was to destroy

<hr />

[70] *Archivo Santander*, vol. x, p. 79; *passim*.

[71] *Ibid.*, vol. xii, p. 71.

[72] *Contestación dada por disposición del consejo de ministros de Bogotá al Arzobispo de Caracas*, (Caracas, 1829), p. 21.

[73] *Venezuela al congreso*, (Caracas, 1833).

it, is a beautiful expression of a policy of religious freedom, the project for a constitution that he presented to this same assembly contained provisions for the civil control of the church. The liberal or, better said, the anti-clerical sentiment expressed itself in the subordination of the church to the state. Inheriting from the colonial régime the tradition of the state's tuition of the church, legislators changed fundamentally the spirit and objective of this tradition. Instead of making their chief aim the protection of the exclusiveness and the privileges of the church as the Spanish monarchs had done, they sought to restrain the institution from any presumptions of power and from any interference with the religious freedom of people of other beliefs. This was, at least, the attitude in Venezuela. Under the Colombian Union the anti-clerical sentiment was much stronger and more radical in the district of Venezuela than in the other divisions of the state. After the separation from the Colombian Union in 1830, this sentiment found expression in further reductions in the status of the church in Venezuela; in reforms the successful institution and maintenance of which, without a religious war or even the development of a clerical party in opposition, constitute a unique feature of the history of this people.

A brief statement might be made here of the action of the government upon the patronage that preceded the introduction of the Law of Patronage. The gestures of the Congress of 1811 toward the establishment of provisional rules, worked out in agreement with the clergy, have been mentioned above. Méndez asserted later that this Congress allowed the Archbishop Coll y Prat to fill vacancies on the Apure.[74] When Bolívar occupied Guayana in 1817, he issued a decree for a *junta* of ecclesiastics to advise the government on problems of the church.[75] To correct the complete lack of government in the bishopric of Guayana brought about by the emigration of the bishop and the two canons, he called upon the clergy to elect a governor for the church.[76] He cited as a precedent for this action the customs of the early Christian church. As a temporary

[74] Méndez, Ramón Ignacio, *Exposición 2° sobre el patronato eclesiástico dirigida al Excmo. Sr. Libertador Presidente*, (Caracas, 1830).
[75] Restrepo, *op. cit.*, vol. ii, p. 428. The decree was not executed.
[76] O'Leary, *Memorias*, vol. xv, p. 452.

expedient for filling vacancies, the Congress of Angostura provided on January 3, 1820, that the vice-president and other high civil officials should approve those named by the ecclesiastical authorities until a concordat could be arranged with the Papacy.[77]   Although acquiescing in the rule, the Bishop of Mérida insisted on the merits of allowing the ecclesiastical authorities, whether prelate or chapter, to act independently of the civil government.   He gave as grounds for his petition the fact that the overlapping of civil and ecclesiastical deliminations would make it necessary to submit nominees to more than one jurisdiction for approval.[78]   His petition, made in a letter to Santander on August 21, 1821, was sent to the Congress with a recommendation from Castillo, then Secretary of the Interior, that the Congress law down a general rule, "so that there be no nullity in these delicate matters" and "so that the government not have to deal separately with each prelate."[79]   There was fear of ultramontane sentiment among the clergy.   The ecclesiastics feared the Vatican more than he feared Morillo, Santander declared.[80]   And the anti-clerical lawyers were hard to hold in check.   They were becoming insistent that power over the church be consolidated.   Bolívar wrote Santander in 1820 that he feared them more than he did the ecclesiastics.[81]   Although Santander was in sympathy with the anti-clerical projects of the lawyers, he wrote Bolívar that he was encouraging the Bishop in his defense of the church in order to secure the aid of the institution in destroying the *godos* and consolidating the Republic.[82]

The temporizing policy of the government with reference to the church was becoming more difficult to maintain.   In view of the communication of Castillo, the Congress authorized the executive in an order of October 12, 1821, to convoke representatives from all the episcopal sees in the free provinces of Gran Colombia to make provisional rules for providing benefices.   These representatives from the church were to act with a commission from the government.[83]

[77] Silva, *Documentos,* vol. vi, pp. 4-5.
[78] *Ibid.,* vol. vi, pp. 4-5.
[79] *Ibid.,* vol. vi, pp. 6-9.
[80] *Archivo Santander,* vol. iv, p. 34.
[81] Lecuna, *Cartas de Bolívar,* vol. ii. pp. 170-171.
[82] O'Leary, *Memorias,* vol. iii, p. 113.
[83] *Archivo Santander,* vol. xii, p. 59.

There was delay on the part of the ecclesiastics and considerable impatience on the part of the government, but the *junta* was finally assembled in Bogotá early in 1823. In it the contrary views of the government and the church were represented. The Bishop of Mérida contended that the patronage had ceased, Castillo and Restrepo that it belonged to the government, which should have sole exercise of it until a concordat with the Papacy could be concluded. Neither of these extreme positions was accepted by the *junta*. It recommended continuing the policy established by the Congress of Angostura: that elections be made by the church and submitted for the sanction of the government.[84]

Some further elaboration of the conflicting theories of the patronage might be made at this point. In his report to the *junta* and in an earlier statement to the Congress on September 1, 1821, Castillo declared that the right of the patronage existed in the nation without any limit. He contended that the kings of Spain had exercised it only in the name of the people; and that upon the establishment of a popular government the right passed directly to the people to be exercised by their representatives. The patronage in America did not rest upon a concordat with the Papacy, he insisted; the king enjoyed it through the foundation and endowment of churches and the conversion of the Indians. And this work was actually performed by the people in America and not by the king; hence the right was theirs. He urged that more satisfactory provisional rules be established to calm disturbed consciences, but that it be made clear that such action involved no renunciation of the patronage by the government. To silence "pretensions that are able to disturb the public peace and embarrass the prosperity which her absolute independence in all her relations ought to assure Colombia," he proposed that legates be sent to Rome to secure a concordat recognizing not only the right of the patronage, but the control of the state over the erection of bishoprics, the reservation of bulls and other papal communications, and the discipline of the church.[85]

In reply, the Bishop attacked the bases of the royal patronage as laid down by Castillo. He insisted that the right rested upon con-

[84] Silva, *Documentos*, vol. vi, p. 29, *et seq.*
[85] *Ibid.*, vol. vi, pp. 8-9; pp. 32-34.

cession alone and that, as a special concession, it could not pass as an inheritance to the Republic. "We have won our independence, but we are not the kings of Castile," he protested.[86] He objected to the idea of the extension of popular sovereignty over the church. The patronage could not be exercised by the people. And, in answer to the glorification of the "sovereign people," he contended that the church was more important to the state than they.

In brief, the church held that the exercise of the patronage was not an inherent prerogative of the political power, that the right enjoyed by the kings of Spain rested solely on the concessions granted them by Alexander VI and Julius II; that these concessions were unilateral grants made through the grace of the Pope and revocable at his will; that such concession could not pass by inheritance to a new sovereign who was not the immediate heir to the throne of the Catholic kings.[87] This conception of the theory of the royal patronage had been defended by the canonist school of lawyers in Spain. It was well set forth by Zamora.[88] For this theory there was some support in the fact that, while claiming unlimited rights of patronage, the Spanish kings had cited papal grants in support of its exercise.

Those supporting the national patronage based their contention on the theory of the sovereignty of the people; the king, they held, only enjoyed the exercise in the name of the people. Castillo confused somewhat his defense of the popular right, however, by resting it apparently on the establishment and endowment of churches. These were the conditions set forth in the papal bulls for the enjoyment of the right. Juan Nepumuceno Azuero, a liberal priest of Bogotá, from whom Santander sought an opinion in writing on the theory of the patronage, gave a much stronger defense of the national

---

[86] *Silva, Documentos,* vol. vi, pp. 36-38.

[87] The theory of the church on the patronage is presented well by prominent clerics in protests against the Law of 1824; particularly by Andrés Rosillo, *Venganza de la justicia por el manifestación de la verdad en orden al patronato,* (Caracas, 1824); *Observaciones que el congreso nacional eleva el cabildo metropolitano de la Santa Iglesia de Caracas sobre la ley de 22 de julio de 1824* (Caracas, 1825); Buenaventura Arias, *Exposición sobre patronato eclesiástico dirigida al primer Congreso de Venezuela,* (Caracas, 1832); and Ramón Ignacio Méndez, *Exposición sobre el patronato eclesiástico hecha al supremo Congreso de Venezuela,* (Caracas, 1830). The writings of Méndez on this subject are voluminous.

[88] Zamora, Matías Gómez, *Regio patronato español e indiana,* (Madrid, 1897).

position. He rested it squarely on the grounds that the patronage was an imprescriptible right of sovereignty that the church had usurped.[89] And Juan Antonio Pérez, a liberal priest of Caracas, gave a similar but far more elaborate justification of the patronage as a right inherent in sovereignty in his famous *A vosotros*.[90] It is interesting to note that the clearest and most advanced expositions of the national right came from priests. Other exponents of the national position were not always so careful as these two ecclesiastics to free their contentions from suggestions of papal concessions made to Spain and inherited by the new state or to be secured in new grants; they mentioned concordats while proclaiming the national right to the patronage. Political considerations were responsible in part for this equivocation; they wished to quiet the opposition of the clergy. Also, there was hope of securing national recognition from the Papacy through a concordat; which, in turn, might promote recognition by other powers. Probably, too, there was still some confusion in thinking on the patronage arising from colonial traditions. The clearest defense of the patronage as an imprescriptible right of sovereignty came out in 1850, when friction arose between the Venezuelan government and the Papacy over the confirmation of Pérez as archbishop. It was set forth in the writings of Felipe Larrazábal, A. L. Guzmán, and others. By that time thought had been freed from the colonial precedents.

The proponents of the national patronage found support for their position in the works of the Spanish jurisconsults, especially those produced under the Bourbon régime, during which the defense of the royal absolutism was elaborated. No addition was made to the exercise of the patronage in the Indies under the Bourbon kings, since it was already unlimited. But there was increasing insistence on the theory of the absolute sovereignty of the political power; earlier sovereigns had been content with the exercise of it. The legalists of the eighteenth century did not rest the royal claims to the patronage on the concession theory. Even much earlier Solórzano had been

---

[89] Groot, *op. cit.*, vol. iv, pp. 141-143. He quoted at length from the reply of Azuero.

[90] *Á vosotros cualesquiera que seais, salud, etc.*, (Caracas, 1851). It was reprinted at the time of a serious conflict with the Papacy in 1851.

an advocate of the view that the right was inherent in the monarchy. Ribadeneyra, Villanueva, Llorente, Tamburini, and Campomanes were leading exponents of the regalist view in the later eighteenth century.[91]   These writers found some support for their thesis in the bulls of Benedict XIV of 1753.   In these bulls, the Pope confirmed the patronage in the Indies, declaring that it was acquired by foundation and endowment, by privilege and apostolic concession, and by other legitimate title.   The political theorists mentioned above were well known to Venezuelan and Colombian writers and legislators. Llorente formed the chief support for the argument of Azuero; Groot testified to the widespread influence of Llorente, Villanueva, and Campomanes.[92]   Tamburini was likewise frequently quoted; a special edition of his *Verdadera idea de Santa Sede* was published in Caracas in 1832.   These men possessed especial influence through their contemporaneousness.   De Pradt, the French Gallican bishop of Malinas, a European protagonist of the independence of the Spanish colonies and an ardent advocate of the national control of the church, was also influential through his numerous works on political and politico-ecclesiastical questions and through his friendship with Bolívar and intimate personal interest in the Colombian cause.[93]   But it appears that, with the exception of De Pradt, the influences on the evolution of the civil constitution for the church were predominantly Spanish.   This opinion is implicit in the statements of Groot and explicit in such works as the Cuervos' *Vida de Rufino Cuervo* and Gutiérrez Ponce's *Vida de Vergara*.[94]   The influence coming from Spanish *émigrés* in London, especially from Blanco-White, appears

[91] Ribadeneyra, Antonio, Joachím, *Manuel compendio del regio patronato indiano,* (Madrid, 1753); Tamburini de Brescia, P., *Verdadera idea de la Santa Sede,* (Caracas, 1832); Llorente, Juan Antonio, *Retrato político del papas;* also his *Apología católica del projecto de constitución religiosa escrito por un americano,* (San Sebastian, 1821).

[92] Groot, *op. cit.,* vol. iv, p. 375; p. 383; *passim.*

[93] Of chief interest among his writings on the Spanish colonies is his *Concordato de América con Roma,* (Paris, 1827), a defense of the national patronage.   He carried on a considerable correspondence with Bolívar.   Along with Henry Clay, he was accorded a special vote of thanks in the Colombian Congress of 1821; (*Leyes de Colombia de 1821,* pp. 257-258).   A. L. Guzmán in his *Argos* in 1826 advertised for sale the thirty-two volumes of De Pradt's works.

[94] Cuervo, Angel and Rufino José, *Vida de Rufino Cuervo y notícias de su época,* 2 vols., (Paris, 1892); and Gutiérrez Ponce, Ignacio, *Vida de don Ignacio Gutiérrez y episodios históricos de su tiempo,* 2 vols., (London, 1900).

to have been considerable.[95] While recognizing the Spanish influence, Leturia in his recent study, *La acción diplomática de Bolívar ante Pío VII*, insists upon the fundamental significance of the French civil constitution of the clergy in the evolution of the Colombian Law of the Patronage. Liberal and anti-clerical sentiment no doubt came from both sources; it would be difficult to resolve the relative influence of each. But in the form and content of the constitution of the church, the influence of the Spanish law would appear to be the more prominent. And it might be mentioned in passing that the civilist and regalist legislation under the later Bourbons, especially Charles III, was followed in special laws passed before the general law was enacted. For example, the administration of the tithe in the law of 1821 was based on the Spanish law of 1770, apparently not executed in Venezuela before this time, a law which put the administration almost entirely in the hands of laymen. The Bishop of Mérida complained bitterly of this copying of the "impious ministers of Charles III."[96]

To return to the legislative evolution of the law of the patronage, the government rejected the proposal of the joint *junta* of civil and ecclesiastical officials and introduced its own project in the House of Representatives. Its bill was approved in the lower house on August 4, 1823, but was held up in the Senate by the opposition of the Bishop of Mérida. Certain amendments were offered; it was returned to the House for reconsideration; and the session closed before action was taken on it again.[97] In the session of 1824, it was a chief subject of discussion for two months, the Bishop of Mérida, supported by Ramón Ignacio Méndez and a lay member from Popayán, leading the opposition in the Senate.[98] The *Correo* observed that there was not a party in opposition, but one very ultramontane member with two seconds.[99] Restrepo declared that Lasso de la Vega's extravagant opinions caused embarrassment to the government, not by producing a following in the Congress, but by stir-

---

[95] Blanco-White was well-known in Bogotá through his publication, *El español*, the organ of these Spanish liberals; on his influence, *vide*, Groot, *op cit.*, vol. iv, pp. 31-32; *passim*.

[96] Silva, *Documentos*, vol. vi.

[97] *Congreso de 1823: Actas*, p. 379.

[98] Groot, *op. cit.*, vol. iv, p. 374.

[99] *Ibid.*, pp. 377-378.

ring up agitation out of doors and fomenting the "fanatic party in Bogotá."[100]   In the House of Representatives, the defense of the law was led by Juan José Osio, a priest of Venezuela, whose speech, according to *El patriota* of Bogotá, won great applause both in the Congress and from the galleries, the public attending the session for the first time.[101]   The long and heated discussion of the law became a legend; Lasso de la Vega observed that afterwards it became a common introduction to a question to say that it was not a matter of patronage.[102]   Unfortunately the debates of the Congress have not been published and were not available for use in this study.   But from the comments of contemporaries, it seems the opposition in the Congress was limited to a few very determined members.   Talavera, who later protested to the Venezuelan government against the law, voted for it in this Congress.   The considerable time consumed in the discussion of the law must have been spent in the working out of matters of detail.   The Bishop of Mérida declared the law null because the procedure followed in its passage was not that used in the consideration of treaties.   The church had the right as a sovereign authority to negotiate a treaty with the state, he held; and any unilateral establishment was without legal force.[103]   Still deferring in the formalities to the ecclesiastical authorities, the government asked the metropolitan *cabildos* of Caracas and Bogotá to present opinions on the patronage.   But the legislature did not await these opinions.   Both were published later as protests against the law.[104]

The Law of the Patronage, which was signed by the executive and declared in force on July 28, 1824, is a long document, covering eighteen pages of the Colombian code.[105]   Its importance as the constitution of the church in Venezuela justifies its inclusion in full in the appendix to this study.   The Civil Constitution of the Clergy in France, cited by Leturia as a fundamental influence in Venezuela, is only about one-fourth as long.   The length of the Colombian law suggests the Spanish habit of meticulous care as to written instruc-

[100] Restrepo, *op. cit.*, vol. iii, p. 412.
[101] Quoted in *Iris de Venezuela*, October 24, 1823.
[102] Groot, *op. cit.*, vol. iv, p. 388.
[103] Silva, *Documentos*, vol. vi, pp. 104-105.
[104] See above, note 87.
[105] *Leyes de Colombia, 1823-1824*, pp. 211-228.

tions. It is significant that, although the law makes provision for the celebration of a concordat with the Papacy, it insists that such an agreement shall be made to *sustain* the right of the patronage, not to *obtain* it.

Reference may be had to the text of the law found in the Appendix for interesting details. Only a few general observations are attempted at this point. The thorough-going consolidation of the civil control over the church is apparent even from a cursory reading. An indication of the thoroughness and comprehensiveness of this constitution is to be found in the fact that Venezuela, a state in which the surveillance over the church since 1830 has been unyielding, has yet discovered no need for the amplification of the law.

In the detailed statement of the attributes of the various governmental agencies with reference to the church those of the Congress are the most extensive. To the executive was granted the important functions of conducting relations with the Papacy, of selecting, with the sanction of the Senate, candidates for the non-official prebendaries, of choosing the occupant for each official canonship from three individuals proposed by the ecclesiastical authorities, and of maintaining general surveillance over the church under the laws of the Congress. The instructions to the executive emphasize his responsibility for seizing bulls and briefs not sanctioned by the Congress and for supervising visitations, the administration of ecclesiastical finances, and the external discipline of the church.[106]

But to the Congress was granted the important constructive powers exercised by the Spanish monarchy: the power to decree the erection of new archbishoprics and bishoprics; to establish their limits; to determine the number of prebends that cathedral churches should have, and to appropriate funds for the construction of churches; to sanction the calling of national and provincial councils and approve their rulings; to permit the foundation of monasteries and hospitals and approve their constitutions; to establish the fees that church courts collect; to control the administration of the tithe; to grant permission for the circulation of bulls and briefs; to make all laws necessary for the maintenance of the external dis-

[106] Articles 5 and 6.

cipline of the church and for the conservation and exercise of the patronage; to choose those to be presented to the Pope for bishops and archbishops; and to make laws upon the establishment and the administration of missions.[107]

The superior courts were to enjoy much the same authority in hearing appeals from ecclesiastical rulings that the *audiencia* possessed under the Spanish régime.[108] The High Court was granted jurisdiction in all cases of alleged usurpation of civil prerogatives on the part of archbishops and bishops, of controversies arising over concordats, and of disputes over the delimitation of dioceses. Before it was to come the interesting case against Archbishop Méndez in 1836.

In the procedure set up for filling places, the legislators admitted adherence to the accustomed practice. The entire constitution is, indeed, replete with suggestions of Spanish law and practice. It is less radical than the French law in that it made no provision for a hierarchical reorganization. The French constitution was likewise more radical in the establishment of direct election of pastors without any intervention of the clergy and of direct election of bishops; moreover, it did not require the confirmation of bishops by the Pope.

The Law of the Patronage provided that dioceses and parishes might be reorganized by the government to make their limits conform to the civil jurisdiction. But no attempt was made to execute a sweeping change under this provision such as was made under the French constitution. Friction arose, however, over the attempts to effect even a partial reorganization. This was a point in the controversy with Méndez and will be considered in the following chapter. As to the influence of the French constitution, it seems that it was more considerable through its general spirit and intent than through its form. Spanish law appears to have been the basis for the evolution of details. Nevertheless, the French constitution was well-known and was mentioned frequently, especially by the clergy. The cabildo of Caracas in its protest against the Law of the Patronage pointed to the danger that the results would be similar to those attendant upon the French reforms.

Although the clergy continued to protest against the Law of the

[107] Article 4.
[108] Articles 9 and 10.

Patronage, they acquiesced generally in its execution. The metropolitan chapter of Caracas delayed taking the oath to sustain the Law required by the government, and considerable friction ensued between it and the intendant.[109] The chapter urged that the Law be suspended until a concordat could be secured. But apparently there was little active opposition. In his report as Secretary of the Interior in 1826, Restrepo said the Law was being executed without difficulty, even though some opinions were opposed.[110] Groot attributed acquiescence to a high sense of patriotism, which caused men like Talavera to refrain from anything that might embarrass the government at a critical time; or to mere servility and seeking for place, a fatal source in his opinion, of the progressive subordination of the church. It should be added, too, that there were radical priests who approved the measure in principle. The latter were probably relatively few in number, but some, like Pérez, Osio, and Domingo Bruzual of Venezuela, and Juan Nepumuceno Azuero of Bogotá, were influential.

IV

AN ATTEMPT has been made in the preceding pages to trace the evolution of the place of the church in constitutional and statutory law under Venezuela and Gran Colombia to its final definition in the Law of the Patronage. Attention should be directed now to the development of the anti-clerical sentiment that gave rise to these measures and to certain attacks on the church outside the sphere of legislative action. Anti-clerical sentiment did not wait for the achievement of political stability to seek expression. Mention has been made of the difficulty that Bolívar and Santander had to hold it in check in the early twenties. It reached its height in Bogotá in the years from 1823 to 1826; then a reaction in favor of the church set in. Opposition to the church was never very deep-rooted nor very general in Colombia. But in Venezuela there was a steady progress of anti-clericalism. After her separation from the Colombian union the church suffered further restrictions in the abolition of the tithe, the extinction of all convents for men, the definite grant of liberty of worship, and the institution of certain other reforms.

[109] *Observaciones, passim.*
[110] *Archivo Santander,* vol. xiii, p. 377.

That anti-clericalism was more radical and more persistent in Venezuela than in other divisions of the union was recognized generally by contemporaries of the development. Groot, Restrepo, Páez, Pedro Gual, Roscio, and many others testify to the fact. In the twenties it was evidenced in the greater persistence of her legislators in urging restrictions on the church; in the attacks of the Masons on the institution, a movement which reached its height in Caracas; and in the pronounced resistance to the reactionary decrees of Bolívar in favor of the institution. First of all the Hispanic-American countries Venezuela fought her *Kulturkampf* and won a victory over the church. Although public opinion was not entirely reconciled to the outcome until Guzmán Blanco dragged the church in the dust in his "reforms" of the eighteen-seventies, opposition to the anti-clerical policy, confined largely to the uneducated masses, was silenced. To the strength and persistence of these early attacks on the church the final success is in large measure to be attributed. The depletion and demoralization of the church by the war and its loss of both social and political prestige in these struggles were such that it never recovered the place it had occupied in the colonial period. Certain contributions of that period toward this loss of social power have been mentioned—the fact that the dominance of the church was probably never so complete here over either Spaniard or Indian, the internal decline of the institution in the late colonial period and the consequent loss of power in the eighteenth century, the intense civilist spirit, provoked and strengthened in the *competencias,* and the more general acceptance in this region of European rationalistic philosophy. Nevertheless, the church had remained an important force in society. The caution with which political leaders proceeded with anti-clerical measures indicates this.

And there were certain factors that, it would appear, should have operated to check the further decline of the church, if they were not positive influences in its favor. The attitude of the clergy in the revolution, at least up to 1820, seems to have had little influence in the development of anti-clericalism. The attacks made on the institution on the grounds of its Spanish sympathy arose from the later local uprisings, in which certain priests were charged with participation. But to offset such charges there was the extravagant patriotism of a part of the clergy following the Spanish revolution of 1820. Although class feeling was stirred by the War for Independence, there was no great social revolution in Venezuela that aligned the masses or the classes against the church. Active opposition to the church was, indeed, confined to a minority of the people. It was met apparently by a minority of the clergy. The rest were spectators. From the uneducated lower classes the church received the large measure of such support as it had, a support that was usually passive only. Again, the economic basis for opposing the church did not exist in Venezuela in the sense that it did in Mexico or in Perú or even in Colombia. The revolution had left the institution relatively impoverished; comparatively little could be gained by the confiscation of its properties. There existed, to be sure, certain bases for attack on material or utilitarian grounds: the plan to promote foreign immigration, which the intolerance of the church might impede, and the desire to discourage entrance into the church in the interest of secular occupations.

In spite of these considerations, there was great progress in anticlericalism in the eighteen-twenties. Added to certain special incidents and activities that widened and intensified the hostility to the church, there was a determined effort on the part of certain political leaders to educate the public generally in religious reform. Such an effort began even before independence was thoroughly secured. The following letter written by Restrepo to Santander in 1821 is illustrative of this policy:

I am enclosing the accompanying article which I have taken from *El español constitucional*. It seems to me that it is time to be instructing the people upon ecclesiastical matters. I consider it of the greatest importance that you have inserted in the *Gaceta* these principles of ecclesiastical jurisprudence, which are very enlightened and fitting for a free people. They can be published . . . without its being thought it is done with the consent of the government, in order that the priests and monks, intransigent men with whom we must temporize for some time until we are sufficiently strong, not be alarmed.

I intend to send you another article from the *Español* upon tolerance. I doubt that it is yet time to insert it in our only *Gaceta* because we shall make enemies of the priests. . . . In the same *Español* there is a political history of the Papacy that will serve well for instructing the people upon the weak foundations of this colossus of clay.[111] There are in it some things too bold, on the canonization of saints and other matters upon which we are yet superstitious. I want this little work, which will be a pamphlet of one hundred pages, published, because it will be very useful. In order that it circulate it will be necessary to give it away; and only the government can print it, preferably in a foreign country so that no one know it; for it would discredit itself with the clergy. The article cited, which demolished the power of the popes, is found in the first volume of the *Español constitucional*. You will understand how important this matter is. We must make a hundred reforms in ecclesiastical affairs, which will be useless unless we have created a public opinion in their favor.[112]

For a short time after 1822 the government fostered education in anti-clericalism more openly through official or semi-official publications. In addition to *La gaceta del gobierno* and *El correo*, official organs that favored reforms, *La miscelánea* of the Cuervos, *El conductor* of Vicente Azuero, *El granadino*, *La bandera tricolor*, and many others preached against fanaticism. Under the free press law a flood of radical sheets and pamphlets appeared agitating anti-clerical action.[113] Groot indicated the extent of this propaganda and criticized the government for participating in it.[114] Increasing secularization of education in colleges and universities made through the commission on the direction of studies was another step in the promotion of anti-clericalism. A feature of this program made especially notable through the storm of protest raised against it in Colombia was the introduction of the teaching of Bentham's *Principles of Universal Legislation* through a decree of the government, November 8, 1825.[115] This measure was furiously attacked by certain priests, in particular by a Father Margallo of Bogotá, whom Restrepo designated as the recognized leader of those who had remained a

---

[111] Very likely that of Llorente, *Retrato político de los papas.*

[112] *Archivo Santander*, vol. vi, p. 121.

[113] The extent of these is shown in the lists published in *Bibliografía bogotaña*, 2 vols., (Bogotá, 1925) by Eduardo Posada.

[114] Especially in volumes iv and v; *vide*, also Restrepo, *op. cit.*, vol. iii, p. 368; p. 412; *passim.*

[115] Groot, *op. cit.*, vol. v, p. 61.

century behind the times. This priest attained considerable notoriety through his prosecution for sedition for preaching against the decree, a prosecution led by Vicente Azuero.[116] Anti-clerical and even anti-religious sentiment became prominent, notably among university students and other young men. From such a group the revolt against Bolívar in 1828 received enthusiastic support because of his reactionary decrees, especially his abolition of the teaching of Bentham.[117]

The Masonic organization, undoubtedly anti-clerical in influence, was encouraged by the government.[118] In its inception the movement was indeed led by Santander, Restrepo, Castillo, Azuero, Soto, and others prominent in political circles. The lodges soon provoked the priests to open opposition in the pulpit and the press. The controversies of the Masons and the church became so disturbing that the government considered moving to Ocaña to escape them.[119] And the political leaders, Santander, Castillo, and Restrepo found it necessary to withdraw their active support from the Masons. Bolívar was already writing from the South that the attacks of the Masons on the church were creating extreme agitation among those people.[120] According to the statement of Restrepo, there was general fear in Colombia that the priests would incite the lower classes to civil war. This fear was indeed realized in the uprising in

[116] Groot, *op. cit.*, vol. v, p. 92 *et seq.*

[117] *Gaceta del gobierno*, Caracas, May 17, 1828. There was apparently, however, little active opposition to the Christian religion in the anti-clerical development in this country. Groot declared that in the universities one was considered stupid if not anti-religious. But in spite of all pronouncements against obscurantism, formal regard, and usually something beyond formal regard, for religious traditions was customary. In this fact one finds a distinction, it would appear, between Spanish and French thought and practice. Rationalism is a hard philosophy for the Spaniard.

[118] For a contrary opinion of their influence, *vide* González Guinán, Francisco, *Tradiciones de mi pueblo*, (Caracas, 1927). There is difference of opinion as to the introduction and very early history of the Masonic organization in Venezuela. Some place its introduction in 1797 with the revolution of Gual and España; others in 1808. But it attained great popularity in the revolutionary movement. It suffered some check in the decrees of Bolívar in the late twenties, but it revived again in the thirties and has been strong ever since. Although the Masons in Venezuela are nominally Catholic and protest their support of the Christian religion and the church, their influence has undoubtedly been anti-clerical. For opposing opinions on this question and a brief historical sketch of the organization in Venezuela, *vide*, Valdivieso Montaño, A., *Introducción de la masonería en Venezuela*, (Caracas, 1928) and Navarro, N. E., *La iglesia y la masonería en Venezuela*, (Caracas, 1928).

[119] Guerra, José Joaquín, *La convención de Ocaña*, Biblioteca de la Historia Nacional, vol. vi, (Bogotá, 1908), p. 257.

[120] *Archivo Santander*, vol. xv, p. 258.

Pasto.[121] Even in Bogotá resistance to the teaching of Bentham was prominent; fathers feared the influence his utilitarian philosophy might have on their sons.[122] In Colombia radicalism in religious thought appears to have extended to a very small circle, and reaction soon followed. When Bolívar issued his decree abolishing the teaching of Bentham and substituting religious study for it, his action was in answer to a public demand in Colombia.

But in Venezuela sentiment was different. Statements of Pedro Gual, Restrepo, Groot, Páez, and others testify to the fact that anticlericalism in Venezuela was far more advanced than in Colombia. Páez, warning Bolívar that his reactionary decrees of 1828 favoring the church would be opposed in Caracas, concluded:

> It is useless that I make observations on this; but as there is so much difference between the exercise of the religious power in Bogotá and in Venezuela, I cannot refrain from mentioning it. We have worked much to destroy the horrors of fanaticism and the influence of the priests on the people; in Venezuela they now rarely meddle with public matters in their ministry. . . . I judge that when you tell me the government is to support religion it will be with all the delicacy that the enlightenment of an age which prefers . . . liberty of thought to civil liberty, demands.[123]

The suppression of the teaching of Bentham in national colleges and universities and the substitution of religious studies for it, ordered by Bolívar in answer to popular demand in Colombia, caused more opposition in Venezuela than any of his decrees favoring the church.[124] No force has operated more persistently against clericalism among this people than the desire to break its control over thought and education and thus to remove from the nation any stigma of obscurantism. The success of the campaign of anti-clericalism in causing a loss of prestige in the church is eloquently set forth in the gloomy observations of Archbishop Méndez to Santander in 1830:

---

[121] Restrepo, *op. cit.*, vol. iii, pp. 469-470.

[122] *Ibid.*; also Joaquín Posada Gutiérrez, *Memorias histórico-políticas: Últimas días de la Gran Colombia del Libertador*, 3 vols., (Madrid, 1920), pp. 126 *et seq.*

[123] O'Leary, *Memorias*, vol. ii, pp. 149-150. Briceño Méndez, his secretary, sent a similar warning to Bolívar from Venezuela, *vide*, O'Leary, *Memorias*, vol. viii, p. 275; p. 297.

[124] O'Leary, *Memorias*, vol. viii, p. 275; p. 297.

This pitiable state of the church is what has decreased its ministers; for no one aspires to a position in which he will be the mark of all the malignity of the century, impoverished to the point of being reduced to beggary, and regarded with the utmost scorn. Formerly one parish of this city had more pastors than all of them now. The curacies that I have vacant are infinite. . . . Of the wise and respectable clergy that I knew there barely exists a remnant; a group of barbarians are the pastors here today, except a very few.[125]

To the opposition to the clergy on intellectual grounds were added in the disturbed decade of the eighteen-twenties other causes more immediate and more practical and capable consequently of influencing a larger class against the church. Chief among these was the fear that the church would retard the immigration of foreigners. From the beginning of the emancipation movement the revolutionary and republican governments had sought to promote foreign immigration. The Congress of Angostura had granted great tracts of land in Guayana to James Hamilton and other foreigners for service in the war against Spain with the hope that these grants would encourage the settlement of communities upon them.[126] Immigrants who might be introduced by these grantees were allowed exemption from taxes and military service for six years. The tacit sanction of religious toleration was extended primarily for the purpose of encouraging foreign immigration. When the question of a state church was introduced in Cúcuta, objection was raised that "if we establish intolerant principles, we shall frustrate the invitations we have made to foreigners to come to settle in Colombia."[127]

The objections of the clergy to religious toleration and certain actual or alleged acts of hostility to foreigners strengthened the sentiment against the church. A case of *competencias* between the civil and ecclesiastical courts in 1826 showed the opposing attitudes. Under the law of 1821 which abolished the Inquisition and established the jurisdiction of the ecclesiastical courts, this jurisdiction was restricted to natives and to foreigners whose names might be on the parish register. Saavedra, a priest of Cundinamarca, sought with the

---

[125] *Archivo Santander*, vol. xviii, pp. 206-207.
[126] Monsalve, *Congreso de Angostura, passim.*
[127] Cortazar and Cuervo, *Congreso de Cúcuta*, p. 219.

aid of the *alcaldes* to register all the inhabitants of his parish and to have them give testimony of adherence to Christianity.[128]   A case against him was brought to the Superior Court, but this tribunal, against the argument of the *fiscal* who prosecuted the case, declared it a matter belonging to the ecclesiastical authorities.   But the High Court, to which the *fiscal* carried it, declared it a case for civil juris- diction and fined the members of the Superior Court for not sup- porting the civil prerogatives.   The case was widely advertised as an interference with the rights of foreigners.   Groot declared that Vi- cente Azuero, the president of the High Court, purposely changed the wording of the *cura's* order to read the registration of *foreigners* instead of *strangers* and to demand testimony of adherence to the Catholic church rather than to Christianity, in order to discredit the clergy with the people.   He declared:

> At that time it was believed that all the enlightenment of Colom- bia depended on foreigners; the laws sought to promote immigration, and whatever served as a menace to the coming of foreigners and to communication with them was reputed as the gravest evil, as a crime, as the most serious opposition to enlightenment, to civilization, and to progress and as the work of fanaticism and ignorance only.[129]

From Venezuela came requests for further security of religious liberty to foreigners through law.   For example, the *Cometa* of Car- acas urged in 1825 that a definite grant of freedom of worship be extended and that foreigners be allowed to marry Colombians.[130] In reply, Santander commended the project in principle; but he de- clared that such writings, coming from the Department of Venezuela, were causing alarm in Colombia and that the government must be cautious because of the intolerance of the people.[131]   The municipal *pronunciamentos* from Venezuela in 1826 and 1828 again insisted upon a grant of religious liberty.[132]   The Colombian leader, Mos- quera, declared that the English were responsible for the agitation for liberty of worship in Venezuela.   "Do you remember," he asked

[128] Groot, *op. cit.*, vol. iv, p. 333 *et seq.*
[129] *Ibid.*, vol. iv, p. 337.
[130] *Archivo Santander*, vol. xiii, p. 44.
[131] *Ibid.*, vol. xiii, pp. 47-48.
[132] For example, *vide*, *Documentos para los anales de Venezuela* (Caracas, 1890- 1909), first period vol. ii, pp. 237-238, for the *pronounciamento* of Caracas.

in a letter to Rufino Cuervo in 1830, "with what zeal Hamilton and Campbell sought it in the treaties of 1824?"[133]   The English sought, too, to secure the establishment of cemeteries for non-Catholics.

Pedro Gual was a leading force for anti-clericalism in Venezuela according to the opinion of Don Manuel Segundo Sánchez, who has made a special study of this interesting statesman.[134]   As foreign secretary, minister to the United States, and representative of Gran Colombia in the Congress of Panamá, he was prepared to view the situation at home from the standpoint of its bearing on the status of his country abroad.   He was prominent in the promotion of foreign immigration and fostered several projects to that end himself.   By every means possible he sought to increase foreign friendships.   As minister of Foreign Affairs in 1825 he was active in the encouragement of the English Biblical Society, represented in Colombia by James Thompson; and he became the first president of the local organization.[135]   The introduction of the Bible in the vernacular, a work undertaken by the Society, was impeded by the priests.   In Caracas opposition to the distribution of the Bibles became a chief source of conflict between the clergy and the Masons.[136] Gual deplored not only the actual interference with foreign interests, but the too great absorption in religious disputes and the consequent neglect of material needs.   Writing to Santander from Panamá in 1826, he declared that if the government would get rid of Rosillo, Margallo, Saavedra, and such reactionary priests and not speak of religion for a few years, it would effect a salutary reform.[137]

More serious charges were brought against the clergy than those that have been cited.   They were accused of making outright attacks on foreigners, of impeding the negotiation of treaties with England and the United States, and of encouraging French and Spanish designs against the Republic.   Still further they were suspected to be conducting secret negotiations with Rome hostile to the

[133] Cuervo, Luis Agusto, *Epistolario del Doctor Rufino Cuervo*, 3 vols., (Bogotá, 1918), vol. i, pp. 195-196.
[134] This opinion was stated by Dr. Sánchez in a conference granted the writer.
[135] Groot, *op. cit.*, vol. v, p. 32 *et seq.*
[136] Navarro, *La iglesia y la masonería en Venezuela*, p. 12.
[137] *Archivo Santander*, vol. xiv, p. 115.

Republic. Because of these charges, to which the Republic was peculiarly sensitive at a time when it was seeking recognition abroad, a bitterness was aroused against the clergy that their support of the monarchy in the Revolution had apparently not engendered. The importance of the incidents themselves and the participation of the clergy in them were no doubt greatly exaggerated by the propaganda of the Masons; but their influence in the development of anti-clerical sentiment makes them worthy of attention.

In 1824 some slaves in Petare, a suburb of Caracas, revolted in the interest of the Spanish monarchy. The insurrection was attributed to the preaching of certain priests. Writing to Santander of the incident, Yanes insisted that the security of independence and political stability would depend much on replacing such priests with patriots.[138] The more serious revolution of Cisneros in the same year was also charged to the encouragement of priests. The appearance of Spanish and French squadrons off the coast at the time these disturbances occurred made them the more alarming; those promoting them were suspected of being in collusion with these foreign enemies.[139]

Priests were thought to have obstructed the enactment of treaties, especially the one projected with England.[140] And O'Leary wrote in 1826 that a veritable Saint Bartholomew's Day was feared in Bogotá because of a slight earthquake, which some priests attributed to the presence of foreigners.[141] Letters from Colombian representatives in foreign countries increased the sensitiveness to these disturbances. Tejada, minister to Rome, wrote February 27, 1827, that nothing occurred in Colombia without its being soon known in Europe; that the fight between Méndez and Gómez in the Senate was regarded as the prelude to a division into two great parties on the clerical question, opposition to English Protestants as the beginning of a religious war, and the events in Caracas as a subversion of order.[142]

[138] *Archivo Santander*, vol. vii, p. 136; also the letter of Lino Clemente on the same incident, pp. 130-132.
[139] *Ibid.*, pp. 224-225.
[140] Azuero, Juan Nepumuceno, *El Dr. Merizalde y el Noticiozote*, (Bogotá, 1925), p. 37.
[141] O'Leary, *Memorias*, vol. iii, p. 27.
[142] *Archivo Santander*, vol. xvi, p. 253.

A celebrated pamphlet against the priests appeared in Caracas in 1825, in which their warfare against the Masons was held to be in reality an attack on the independence of Gran Colombia. This polemic was entitled *La cátedra del Espíritu Santo convertida en ataque al gobierno de Colombia* and was signed by the "Patriot Masons."[143] It declared that at the very time Europe was ready to recognize the independence of Gran Colombia, the clergy allied itself with Spanish absolutism to bring civil division in the country and prevent recognition. Responsibility for the revolution of Petare and other civil disorders was laid at their doors. This pamphlet attained wide circulation. A. L. Guzmán stated in his *Argos* that three or four thousand copies of it had been published.[144] Santander wrote to Montilla in June, 1825, that it was to be republished in Bogotá. Caracas already spoke plainly against the disaffected ecclesiastics, he declared.[145]

There stands out in this agitation against the church the famous case of *La serpiente de Moisés*, around which anti-clerical opinion was apparently most completely crystallized.[146] *La serpiente de Moisés*, a protest against religious toleration was published in Bogotá in 1822 and passed without question by the authorities. In 1826, it was reprinted in Caracas. Prosecution was at once brought against it under the famous law of the press of 1821—the first case to be brought under this law. On the day set for the trial of the editor, the prebendary, Miguel Santana, more than a thousand people, it is said, gathered around the Convent of San Francisco, where the case was heard. The jury pronounced the publication seditious, and the *fiscal* prosecuting the case was given a special reward. All Caracas was in tumult over the victory, which was celebrated until late at night.

This incident, widely advertised throughout Venezuela, discred-

---

[143] *La cátedra del Espírito Santo convertida en ataque al gobierno de Colombia bajo el nombre de Mazones*, (Caracas, 1825).

[144] *Argos*, March 30, 1825.

[145] *Archivo Santander*, vol. xiii, p. 39.

[146] Santana, Miguel, *La serpiente de Moisés*, (Caracas, 1826). In the library of the Venezuelan National Academy of History in Caracas there is found an excellent collection of pamphlets on the politico-religious controversies of this and later periods, an invaluable source for the study of the history of the church. *La serpiente de Moisés* and a number of pamphlets provoked by it are included in this collection.

ited the church as obscurantist, as an obstacle to international recognition and foreign immigration so eagerly sought. One writer declared in a disquisition to be presented to the jury: "England and the United States have their eyes on us. This judgment will decide the fate of Colombia."[147]   Francisco Zea's commendation of the annihilation of *La serpiente* was spread from the Atlantic to the Pacific, it was said.[148]   Some Venezuelan historians have indeed attributed the ultimate subjection of the church largely to this incident. Without doubt, the complete defeat of the clergy in it and the loss of prestige it occasioned contributed much toward destroying the power of the institution with an increasing number of the upper classes.

Bolívar returned to Bogotá in 1828 to attempt to restore order to the country rapidly inclining toward civil war and dissolution. A primary feature of his program for correcting the disturbed conditions was the encouragement of the church. With this policy, public sentiment in Colombia, outside a certain circle of political opponents, was apparently in general agreement.[149]   Reference has been made to his decree abolishing the teaching of Bentham in the colleges and universities and the substitution of religious studies for it. He annulled the law of 1821 which had provided for the extinction of convents with less than eight members and ordered their reëstablishment; he restored the chaplaincies and vicars in the army; and he placed the archbishop of Bogotá on his Council of Government.[150] He encouraged the clergy in public pronouncements and private correspondence to use their influence to correct the tendencies toward dissolution and anarchy.[151] His decree against secret societies checked the activity of the Masonic organization, the chief enemy of the

[147] Saldanha, José de la Natividad, *Discurso teológico-político sobre la tolerancia en que se acusa y refuta el escrito titulado, "La serpiente de Moisés,"* (Caracas, 1826). Among other pamphlets in answer were *Reflexiones imparciales acerca del folleto titulado, "La serpiente de Moisés,* (Caracas, 1826); and *Cartas de un alemán a S. E. el vicepresidente,* (Caracas, 1826). The latter spoke of the furor and extreme ultramontanism of the publication and of the commotion it had created in Caracas.

[148] Santana, Miguel, *Día que no se contará entre los de Colombia,* (Caracas, 1826).

[149] Gutiérrez, Joaquín Posada, *Memorias histórico-políticas,* vol. i, p. 126; p. 183; on the contrary opinion held in Venezuela, *vide* vol. ii, p. 74 *et seq.*

[150] Blanco-Azpurúa, *Documentos,* vol. xi, pp. 693-694.

[151] Lecuna, *Cartas del Libertador* vol. viii, pp. 32, 74, 75; Blanco-Azpurúa, *Documentos,* vol. xiii, p. 100; letters to others on the same question, *Cartas,* vol. vii, pp. 370-371; vol. viii, pp. 29-30.

church.[152] Through his policy of social accommodation, the church in Colombia regained in the late eighteen-twenties most of the influence lost in the early stages of the Revolution. It joined the military group as a chief protagonist of the dictatorship of Bolívar. It is difficult to evaluate the weight of these reactionary decrees on ecclesiastical matters as factors promoting the separation of Venezuela from the Colombian Union in 1830. This question will be considered in the next chapter. Attention should now be turned to the external aspects of the relations of church and state to be observed in the negotiations with Rome.

V

THE DIPLOMACY of Gran Colombia in Rome in the years from 1820 to 1835 forms a most interesting chapter in the political as well as in the ecclesiastical history of this state. Her achievements in this field were indeed of continental scope and significance. Her success made easier the approach of other Hispanic-American states to the Papacy. In some instances Colombian representatives acted directly for other states; for example, Tejada spoke for both Bolivia and Mexico.[153] Other distinctive features of the Colombian diplomacy in Rome are its continuity and consistency through this long period and the agreement between the political and ecclesiastical powers in their approach to the Papacy—an agreement made possible by Bolívar's skillful accommodation of political and religious interests, of social facts and politico-social ideals, and by the ardent patriotism of his ecclesiastical ally, the Bishop of Mérida. The letter of Pius VII to the Bishop of Mérida in 1822 was the first direct communication

[152] Ponte, *Bolívar y otros ensayos*, pp. 191-193. For a criticism of the Masonic activities made by Bolívar, *vide*, Lacroix, *Diario de Bucaramanga*, pp. 94-95.

[153] An excellent study of this phase of the politico-ecclesiastical history of Gran Colombia is that of Leturia, *La acción diplomática de Bolívar ante Pío VII, 1820-1823* and his "León XII y Bolivar," *Razón y Fé*, (November 10, 1930, reprint), both made from materials in the Vatican archives. Other studies, made from the Colombian archival resources, are Cadeña, P. I., *Anales diplomáticos de Colombia* (Bogotá, 1878); Zubieta, Pedro A., *Apuntaciones sobre las primeras misiones diplomáticas de Colombia* (Bogotá, 1924); and the short study of Villanueva, "Bolívar et l'église en Amérique" referred to above. Much material on ecclesiastical relations may be found, too, in his general studies on relations with Europe made from the European archival collections, the four volumes in *La monarquía en América* and *Napoleón y la independencia de América*, (Paris, 1911). And Lucas Ayarragaray's *La iglesia en América y la dominación española* (Buenos Aires, 1920) is of value in the study of Colombian relations with Rome.

of the Papacy with Spain's revolting colonies in America; the confirmation of Buenaventura Arias as an auxiliary to the Bishop of Mérida in 1824 was the first recognition of their religious needs; and the confirmation in 1827 of six proprietary bishops for the dioceses of Gran Colombia was the first formal disregard of the Spanish patronage in America. Finally, in 1835, the Papacy granted political recognition first to New Granada, formerly Colombia; an act, however, of less significance than the foregoing, since the independence from Spain was already assured by success in arms and by the recognition of other powers.

The efforts of the revolting colonies to establish ecclesiastical or political relations with the Papacy were inextricably complicated and impeded by the dual character of this power, by the peculiar Spanish royal patronage, and by the entanglements of European politics. As long as there was a possibility of Spain's regaining her power in America, Rome would naturally hesitate to disregard the Spanish patronage. At the same time, to delay too long granting religious aid might mean the loss of the domination of the church in America. The existence of such a contingency was skillfully played upon by the Colombian representatives in Rome and by the bishops in their letters from America. For instance, the Bishop of Mérida wrote Leo XII in 1825 that apparently the only support of Gran Colombia in Europe was England, the value of whose friendship was to be questioned because of the inevitable encouragement of freedom of worship and Protestantism.[154] Cardinal Consalvi defended the compromising policy of the Papacy in America on the grounds that if the Pope had waited for the sanction of Spain before taking steps to aid the church, "our apostolic vicar might have found the country filled with Methodists, Presbyterians, and new Sun worshippers."[155]

In its political aspects, the diplomacy of Gran Colombia before the Vatican was entangled with the fortunes of the revolution in Spain, with the program of the Holy Alliance for discountenancing illegitimacy and republicanism, with French interests in America, and indirectly with the interests and activities of England. The

[154] Silva, *Documentos*, vol. vi, p. 109.
[155] Leturia, *La acción diplomática*, p. 12.

radical revolution of 1820 in Spain gave the Hispanic-American peoples a favorable opportunity to approach Rome; but the reaction of 1823 came before much was accomplished. In 1824, however, even the Holy Alliance sanctioned the Pope's attending to the religious needs of those countries.[156] The French had persuaded the Holy Alliance to this policy by emphasizing the advantage of supporting the church as a means of reviving and maintaining monarchical institutions in America. What France chiefly sought was to secure the same recognition as the defender of Catholic interests in America that she possessed in the Orient in order to offset England's commercial influence. The continued intransigence of the Spanish monarchy toward either ecclesiastical or political contacts of the Papacy with the revolting colonies in the face of its apparent inability to regain dominion in America and the international movement toward a more liberal policy, expressed in recognition by the United States, England, and France, led the new pope, Gregory XVI, the former Cardinal Consalvi and friend of America, to declare upon his accession in 1831 his intention to follow a policy of *de facto* recognition in political relationships.

In the meantime, efforts were being made in America to secure the recognition of the Papacy. Mention has been made of the declarations of the Venezuela Congress of 1811 and of provisions in the Federal Constitution of that year with regard to a concordat with Rome; also to the gesture made by the Congress toward execution of such a policy. Whatever may have been the belief of some leaders with regard to the greater advantages to be derived from a national church, professions of a desire to reach agreement with the center of Catholic unity continued to be made.[157] There was a dual motive in this movement toward Rome; in addition to the religious one, there was the hope of securing political advantage from recognition by the Papacy.

[156] Villanueva, Carlos A., *La monarquía en América: La santa alianza* (Paris, without date), pp. 203-207. Although England did not attack the Catholic church, she was active in trying to secure liberty of worship and the establishment of cemeteries for non-Catholics: *vide,* Villanueva, "Bolivar et l'église en Amérique," p. 181.

[157] There seems to have been some sentiment for reorganizing the church independently of Rome, especially on the part of Santander, Castillo, and some others in 1823 and 1824; also later in 1826; *vide, El ministerio de relaciones exteriores de Colombia en 1826.*

The first contact of the revolting colonies in Spanish America with Rome was through Fajardo, representative sent to Paris by Bolívar upon his flight to New Granada in 1813. While he was in Paris, Fajardo was placed in communication with Pius VII, then resident at Fontainebleau, through the negotiation of Napoleon.[158] Although no practical results came from the contact, it is notable as the first communication the Papacy received from the revolutionary governments and as an expression of the dual objective of those governments in approaching the Papacy. Napoleon failed to follow up this gesture of favoring the colonies, and upon the royalist reaction in 1816, the Pope issued an encyclical exhorting them to submission to the Spanish monarchy.[159]

In 1819 efforts were renewed, or rather taken up for the first time seriously, to establish contacts with the Papacy. Upon the suggestion of Bolívar, the Congress of Angostura encharged Peñalver and Vergara, representatives of Colombia in London, to open communications with the Papacy through the nuncio at Paris and to attempt to treat with him as head of the church, not as temporal sovereign, to secure the confirmation of bishops for the vacant sees and a concordat that would grant the patronage.[160] Although Pius VII and his secretary, Consalvi, received the communication benevolently, its demands were premature and too extensive to be yet granted. . Independence was not assured and had not been recognized by any foreign power. The representation brought to the Papacy, however, the first detailed information about the demoralized condition of the church that had resulted from the Wars for Independence. If aid were not secured, the communication declared, religion would be destroyed within ten years. From this time Pius VII and his secretary recognized that this "peculiar ecclesiastical problem could not easily be confined to the legitimist formula."[161]

The radical revolution of 1820 in Spain furnished the opportune occasion for the revolutionary government to treat with the Papacy.

[158] O'Leary, *Memorias*, vol. ix, p. 403; Leturia, *La acción diplomática*, p. 75 *et seq.*
[159] For a copy of the encyclical, *vide*, Leturia, *La acción diplomática*, Appendix I, pp. 281-282.
[160] *Ibid.*, p. 90 *et seq*; Villanueva, *La santa alianza*, p. 202; Ayarragaray, *La iglesia*, pp. 209-210.
[161] Leturia, *La acción diplomática*, p. 101.

Its first efforts in this direction was not fortunate, however, and the royalist reaction of 1823 came before any definite achievements were realized. In 1820, the government at Angostura gave Francisco Zea, minister to London, a commission to treat with the Pope similar to the one given to Peñalver and Vergara. But Zea's note to the nuncio at Paris was so exaggerated in its demands that it was not even forwarded to Rome.[162] The Congress of Cúcuta provided for a special commission to treat with Rome, hoping thus to correct the mistakes of these earlier efforts. In 1822, Echeverría was named by Santander as minister plenipotentiary to the Papacy, with instructions to attempt to secure recognition of independence, the confirmation of prelates, and the recognition of the patronage. His death prevented his undertaking the mission, and Agustín Gutiérrez Moreno, named in his stead, did not accept the appointment. Finally, Ignacio Sánchez de Tejada was asked in June, 1823, to take the commission created for Echeverría. Tejada remained for many years the representative to the Papacy, first of Gran Colombia, then after 1830 of Colombia and Venezuela. And he conducted negotiations for Mexico and Bolivia also.[163] Until 1835, no other Spanish-American state had a permanent agent and secretariat in Rome. Tejada towered above his American colleagues as a diplomat to the Vatican and became the leader for the defense of the new republics, Ayarragaray declared.[164] For a long time his work was impeded, however, by the tortuous course of Spanish and European politics.

Through the initiative of Bolívar steps had been taken in the meantime toward establishing contact with the Papacy through the Colombian episcopate. The letter of the Bishop of Mérida, October 20, 1821, written upon Bolívar's suggestion, opened a new era in the history of the Colombian church and that of all Spanish America, Leturia declared. Only in Gran Colombia did the episcopate itself undertake to make apology for the revolutionary and republican governments in America. Other states lacked either a government so flexible or bishops so patriotic.[165] In his letter to Pius VII, Lasso de

[162] Leturia, *La acción diplomática*, pp. 104-106.
[163] Ayarragaray, *op. cit.*, p. 297.
[164] *Ibid.*
[165] Leturia, *La acción diplomática*, p. 108.

la Vega undertook to justify the revolution in Colombia and eulogized
the religiosity of her statesmen.   He suggested at the same time the
danger of the final victory of the civil power over the ecclesiastical
through the continuance of uncertainty in the status of the church.[166]
The reply of the Pope of September 7, 1822, was cautious in its neutrality toward the political contest, but gave hope that attention would
be given to the religious needs of Colombia.   He referred to the
wounds given the church in Spain, which would incline him to hear
the call of America.[167]   On February 22, 1822, he had refused to
comply with the request of Spain not to recognize the independence·
of America, declaring his intention to follow a policy of neutrality.[168]
In spite of Spanish objections and protests, the Papacy began to evidence increasing concern for the religious needs of Colombia.   Attempt was made first to meet them without contravention of the
Spanish patronage; later, after 1827, even this right was disregarded.
The communications from the Colombian episcopate had much to do
with making easier this *rapprochement* with the Papacy, Leturia
found from his studies in the Vatican archives.   And their value
was recognized at the time by the Colombian government, not only
as a means of cementing the adherence of the bishops to the government by thus employing them, but also as an agency for advancing
papal negotiations.

The enthusiastic patriotism of the Bishop of Mérida and the desire of the government to capitalize anything to discourage reactionism led, it is true, to exaggeration of the importance of this first letter
of the Pope to a revolutionary government.   The *Iris,* the leading
paper of Venezuela at the time, rejoiced over the fact that the head
of the church did not meddle in political matters, that he was willing
to communicate with a republican bishop, that his action proved that
the interdict, announced by partisan ecclesiastics to induce submission
to despotism, did not have papal sanction.[169]

On March 19, 1823, the Bishop of Mérida wrote at greater
length in defense of the republican order and of its leaders.   The

[166] Silva, *Documentos,* vol. vi, pp. 18-19.
[167] Leturia, *La acción diplomática,* p. 152.
[168] *Ibid.,* p. 185.
[169] *Iris de Venezuela,* May 22, 1823.

new government he described as an aristocracy, no doubt to decrease the fears of republicanism. He wrote in much detail on the needs of the church; and, in union with the government, asked for the provision of bishops, for the secularization of regulars, for the naming of a legate to conclude a concordat, and for the erection of an archbishopric in Quito.[170] With his letter went one from the Bishop of Popayán, who added a request for a nuncio, preferably with the title of Patriarch, so that he might fill temporarily the vacant archbishopric of Bogotá. Santander was particularly desirous of securing the recognition of the Archbishop of Bogotá permanently as a Patriarch with the right to erect new dioceses and confirm bishops named by the government, a concession that would have increased the civil control of the church beyond that exercised by the Spanish monarchy.[171] The Bishop of Popayán was more ardent even than the Bishop of Mérida in his praise of Bolívar, and declared that in the entire history of revolutions he was sure none could be found in which religion had suffered less than it had in Gran Colombia.[172] Letters were also sent from the ecclesiastical cabildos of Bogotá and Cartagena.

To these communications the new pope, Leo XII, replied on November 19, 1823. While he deplored the evils that political perturbation had brought upon the church, he declared that the letters had assured him that the faith had not suffered nor the devotion toward the Holy See "that shone always in that American nation."[173] Lasso de la Vega eagerly insisted upon the significance of the expression "American nation" as equivalent to recognition of Colombian independence. Pius VII, he pointed out, had referred to Chile merely as a "region" when Juan Muzi was sent to that country. And in succeeding letters he insisted that it would be wiser to send such a mission to Colombia because of her paramount political importance.[174]

As a result of the contact established by the episcopate, the Pope

[170] Silva, *Documentos*, vol. vi, pp. 59-69.
[171] Zubieta, *Apuntaciones sobre las primeras misiones diplomáticas de Colombia*, p. 580.
[172] Leturia, "León XII y Bolívar," pp. 10-11.
[173] Silva, *Documentos*, vol. vi, pp. 87-89.
[174] *Ibid.*, vol. vi, pp. 109-112.

consented in 1824 to appoint Buenaventura Arias, named by the
Bishop of Mérida and approved by the government, as an auxiliary
to the former with the title of Bishop of Jericho and apostolic vicar
of Mérida.[175] This was the first practical assistance granted the
church under a revolutionary government in Hispanic-America. Although Tejada and French diplomacy had some part in its achievement, to a very considerable degree it was effected through the
episcopate. But this agency for conducting relations with Rome was
soon to cease to function; with the passage of the Law of Patronage
and with the progress of anti-clericalism, the patriotism even of the
Bishop of Mérida was overshadowed by his fears for the church.[176]
His apology for republicanism became less ardent. The fears of
ultramontane sentiment within the church led the government
finally to suspect all communications with the Papacy not subjected
to its surveillance.[177] Although Lasso de la Vega continued to press
the needs of the church, later achievements in Rome were apparently the results of Tejada's diplomatic skill.

Tejada's first activities in Rome followed a somewhat tortuous
course. The diplomacy of Spain, directed by the intransigent royalist, Vargas Laguna, brought him difficulty in gaining recognition.
He was not given reception at first in his diplomatic character. Although he was given a private hearing by Cardinal Della Somaglia,
Secretary of State, he was asked to retire to Bologna, then later to
Florence, to silence the objections of Spain.[178] And, in 1824, Ferdinand VII prevailed on Leo XII to issue an encyclical to the American colonies to enjoin them to return to the rule of Spain.[179] This
action was so hard to reconcile with the earlier sympathetic attitude
of Leo, both as cardinal and pope, that the authenticity of the encyclical was even questioned in America.[180] This papal order and
the treatment accorded Tejada caused the government at Bogotá to

[175] *Ibid.*, vol. v, p. 224.

[176] Silva, *Documentos,* vol. vi, pp. 112-116; *passim.*

[177] O'Leary, *Memorias,* vol. vii, p. 234; *Archivo Santander,* vol. xiii, p. 17; p. 108.

[178] Zubieta, *op. cit.,* pp. 576-678.

[179] Leturia, "La célébre encyclical de León XII sobre la independencia de Hispano-
America" *Razón y fé,* May, 1925.

[180] *Archivo Santander,* vol. xiii, p. 359 *et seq.*

threaten to retire him entirely and to proceed independently of Rome. Also it provoked cautious surveillance of the clergy.[181]

But in 1826 Tejada was formally received in Rome and in 1827 the Papacy advanced, in spite of the opposition of Spain, to confirm as proprietary bishops those named by the Colombian government. This action constituted the first complete disregard of the Spanish right of patronage. In the bulls of confirmation Leo XII did not, however, recognize the right of presentation to belong to the Colombian government.[182] Among those confirmed was Méndez, named as the Archbishop of Caracas. In 1828, in his efforts to keep peace with Spain, the Pope returned again to a policy of naming only bishops *in partibus;* Talavera was named thus Bishop of Trícala and apostolic vicar of Guayana. In 1829, Lasso de la Vega was promoted to Quito and Arias was confirmed as proprietary bishop of Mérida. But Tejada had not included the presentation of Arias in requesting the promotion of Lasso; and the government, jealous of its patronage, objected to the action of the Papacy in confirming him. Much friction ensued; the government required the chapter to hold an election for the vacancy even though the bull of confirmation had been received.[183] These confirmations completed the achievements of diplomacy in Rome under Gran Colombia. Pius VIII, who succeeded Leo XII in 1829, was more conciliatory toward Ferdinand VII. It was left to Gregory XVI, 1831, to return to the policy of confirming proprietary bishops and to initiate the policy of recognizing

[181] Fears had been aroused earlier by the Muzi mission to Chile, which had been granted authority to act for any part of the Spanish empire in America. It was rumored that Muzi was working in league with Spain and the Holy Alliance and had a bull from the Pope enjoining submission to Spain. Bolívar ordered that care be taken that no such brief be circulated in Gran Colombia, and declared all communications of the prelates with those of Chile and Perú open to suspicion; Blanco-Azpurúa, *Documentos,* vol. xiii, pp. 731-732.

[182] Blanco-Azpurúa, *Documentos,* vol. xi, pp. 163 *et seq.* Those confirmed were Fernando Caicedo y Flórez, Archbishop of Bogotá; Ramón Ignacio Méndez, Archbishop of Caracas; Félix Calixto Miranda, Bishop of Cuenca; José María Estévez, Bishop of Santa Marta; Manuel Santos, Bishop of Quito; and Escobar y Mariano Garnica, Bishop of Antioquía.

[183] *Documentos oficiales que dan noticias exacta de las occurrencias del Iltmo. Sr. Buenaventura Arias . . .* (Caracas, 1830). There was much uneasiness in 1829, too, over a secret correspondence, intercepted by Tejada, between Estévez, Bishop of Santa Marta and the Papacy, conducted through Pomárez, a Spanish resident in Rome. Estévez declared he sent his communications to Pomárez upon the recommendation of Lasso de la Vega. Tejada urged that special vigilance be exercised to stop these communications, hostile to the government and encouraging servile ultramontanism; *vide,* Zubieta, *op. cit.,* pp. 584-586.

the independence of the Hispanic-American states as they achieved political stability.

The success of Bolívar's diplomacy before Rome as compared to that of other Spanish-American statesmen was the result of several forces, among which were the greater political stability of Colombia, his personal prestige abroad, and Tejada's ability as a diplomat. But it may in large part be attributed to the Liberator's accommodation to the Catholic sentiment of Colombia and to his agreement with the church in the approach to the Papacy. In the Colombian episcopate, he had ardent apologists of himself and his republic, one of them a Spanish ecclesiastic. In the definitive years these bishops did much to bring the attention of the Pope to the problem of the American church. In his external ecclesiastical program, as well as in his domestic policy, Bolívar evidenced his conversion to the philosophy of *The Spirit of the Laws*. A free thinker and a deist no doubt in his personal conceptions, as a statesman he appreciated his position as chief of a Catholic people.

CHAPTER III

THE CHURCH UNDER THE CONSERVATIVE OLIGARCHY, 1830-1848

No PERIOD of Venezuelan politico-ecclesiastical history presents such intriguing contradictions as the one considered in this chapter. The fact that the separation of Venezuela from the Colombian Union was the work of a so-called "conservative" oligarchy in league with a military *caudillo* might easily lead one to expect.that the constitutional order established by this alliance would be conservative in ecclesiastical policy. Class interests, it might seem, would unite the upper classes and the army with the church for the maintenance of special privileges and immunities. But, in fact, this régime was distinguished by a pronounced liberalism in politics and radicalism in religious policy. Indeed, the designation of a party as "conservative" in no sense of fact or principle meant that it was conservative. In the boldness of anti-clerical thought probably no period of Venezuelan history has equalled the one under consideration. In it the unique course of the political and social evolution of the church became established. Later advances in anti-clericalism were no more than the crystallization of opinion formed or the enactment into law of policies advocated at this time. There was no advance in theory.

Separated from the Colombian union and freed from the restraints of military necessity, Venezuela for the first time had an opportunity to express in law and practice her distinctive politico-religious philosophy which had resulted from Spanish tradition, colonial evolution, and recent political and social revolution. Certain elements stand out in this thought as it found expression under this régime. First, there was a relentless determination to subordinate all individuals and groups to the supreme power of the state; no place was left for pluralistic notions of sovereignty. The persistence of the Oligarchy in establishing this conception was fatal to the hopes of ambitious clergymen like Archbishop Méndez. Exhibiting much

of the bold spirit the earlier colonial ecclesiastics had evidenced in
their contests with the civil power, he found himself defeated, nevertheless, at the outset.

Along with the determined civilist spirit went an equally strong
sentiment of equalitarianism that sought to abolish all legal distinctions between classes just as it subordinated all to the political power.
In spite of its so-called oligarchical character, no government in Venezuela has been more consistently liberal than this. Its liberalism, in
policy and practice, threatened the position of the church by attacking
its special privileges.

Finally, there was a distinct secularism to the political philosophy
of the period—a desire to remove the religious question entirely from
the domain of political discussion, to make the control of the church
a matter merely of administration, not a fundamental feature of
political policy. Although the philosophy of the Oligarchy did not
disregard entirely the concepts of Montesquieu, it showed a stronger
tendency toward the more radical utilitarianism of Bentham. Its
accommodations with the church evidenced a more practical, material
motive and a less broadly social one than Bolívar had expressed.

The rule of the Oligarchy under the notable instrument, the
Constitution of 1830, is regarded by Venezuelan historians as a sort
of golden era in their history, a period of the reign of law, in contrast
to the earlier and later dictatorships. It must be admitted, however,
and is, that behind the constitutional order stood the military *caudillo*,
Páez. Observance and applications of law were possible only at his
will and through his personal prestige. Nowhere is his respect for law
better expressed than in his attitude in the contest of the government
with the bishops over the taking of the oath to the Constitution of
1830. Long a friend of Méndez, who was his constant companion
in the campaigns on the Apure during the Revolution, he would allow, nevertheless, no exceptions in the Archbishop's favor when the
prestige of the law was at stake. He expressed in his attitude, too, the
whole philosophy of the Conservative régime, its insistence on the
sovereignty of the political power and on the equality of all before
that power. "You must remember," he declared to Méndez, "that

you do not cease being a Venezuelan through being an Archbishop."[1]
The emphasis placed on principles rather than personalities in this contest with the church distinguishes it from the later contest under Guzmán Blanco, who at the risk of the complete demoralization of the ecclesiastical organization chose to insist on obedience to the decree of a dictator.

Although there was some popular support of the church expressed in petitions to Congress for the return of the bishops and in support of ecclesiastical privileges in the military revolts of 1830-1831 and 1835, and probably much unexpressed sympathy, such demonstrations never approached the point of a general uprising in its defense. The prestige of the nation, represented in the government, was greater than the prestige of the church. The church itself, moreover, was not united in defense of the privileges of the institution. There were prominent protagonists of the government in its ranks—men like Pérez, long the opponent of the government at Bogotá, Domingo Bruzual and Juan José Osio, extreme radicals on ecclesiastical reform, and others. Even those in sympathy with the resistance of the bishops were timid in the expression of it. There was much opportunism in the policy of the church, or possibly of unwilling submission to what was recognized as a preponderant force. Active resistance at this time and in later conflicts was confined to a very few. There was, however, throughout this period and especially in the thirties much of what might be termed "passive resistance" by the church in the disregard of the government's administrative orders.

The plan of this chapter is to consider the clerical question in the separation of Venezuela from the Colombian Union and in the political reorganization; conflicts with the church under the Oligarchy; relations with the Papacy; progress in anti-clerical legislation; the material and personal status of the church in this period; and the church as a political question in the party battles of the eighteen-hundred-forties.

I

IN THE PRECEDING chapter it was indicated that Bolívar consolidated opinion in Colombia for his dictatorship with the aid of the

---

[1] Páez, José Antonio, *Autobiografía*, 2 vols. (Caracas, 1888) vol. ii, p. 156.

clergy and the army. He is regarded, indeed, as the founder of the clerical party in that republic.[2] With the assistance of these groups he hoped to hold Venezuela loyal to the Union and to his leadership. In September, 1830, he wrote his secretary, Briceño Méndez, from Cartagena that letters from Caracas declared that the clergy were enthusiastic for him and that each pastor was a general in his *pueblo*.[3] There are frequent references in his correspondence and that of others to this clerical support of his dictatorship. Neither the clergy nor the army in Venezuela, however, was a unit in his favor. Páez, the foremost *caudillo* of Venezuela, chose to ally himself with the secessionist group of Caracas to effect a separation from the Colombian union. Although there was undoubtedly strong sentiment for Bolívar among the clergy, that group did not undertake to oppose the separation of Venezuela from the Union nor the leadership of Páez. The priests joined with other influential persons of Caracas to request Bolívar to intervene to effect a pacific dissolution of the union.[4] Méndez wrote Santander on January 20, 1830, that he had had nothing to do with the separation and hoped only for tranquillity.[5] He sent his benedictions to the Constituent Congress of Venezuela upon its convention.[6] Talavera, who was suspected of disaffection because of his prominence in Bogotá at the time, declared in answer to investigation by Venezuelan officials that even if his people had not decided for secession, he would have urged it in the interest of peace.[7] Pérez and other liberal priests openly advocated separation; Pérez, indeed, had led the opposition in Caracas to the Bogotá government from the beginning of the Union. Priests figured in the various municipal bodies that issued *pronunciamientos* for separation from Colombia.[8] Although the general sentiment of the church was apparently in favor of Bolívar and a conservative régime, it did not undertake to oppose openly the developments in Venezuela.

Among the factors, economic, political, social, and personal, to which the secession of Venezuela from the Colombian Union has

[2] *Archivo Santander*, vol. xvi, p. 19.
[3] Lecuna, *Cartas del Libertador*.
[4] Restrepo, *op. cit.*, vol. v, p. 268.
[5] *Archivo Santander*, vol. xviii, pp. 203-207.
[6] *Anales de Venezuela*, 1st per., 1829-1830, vol. vi, p. 263.
[7] *Ibid.*, vol. ii, pp. 301-308.
[8] *Ibid.*, vol. iii, *passim*.

been attributed, it is not possible to evaluate exactly the weight of the clerical question.   Most of the municipal *pronunciamientos* were silent on the matter of religious reforms, a silence attributable in part, no doubt, to the desire to gain the support of the lower classes. The declaration of Caracas insisted on a grant of religious liberty; those of Barinas, Araure, and other towns declared opposition to Bolívar's decrees against the teaching of Bentham; but chief attention was directed to economic reform.[9]   The press of Caracas contrasted the liberalism of Venezuela with the military and religious reactionism of Colombia.[10]   Without doubt the reaction in Colombia on ecclesiastical questions was one of several factors that promoted opposition to the Union and to Bolívar.   On the other hand, there were sections of Venezuela that favored the separation with the hope of securing protection for the church.   Arias declared that the delegates from Mérida to the Constituent Congress were instructed to vote for the establishment of the Catholic Church as exclusive, that this, indeed, was a primary reason why Mérida favored separation.[11] But the hostility to class distinctions was indicated in the fact that one of its representatives, Juan de Díos Picón, demanded persistently the abolition of all political and ecclesiastical *fueros* on the strength of instructions from his constituents.

The Constitution of 1830 contained no article on religion.   It was proposed in the Constituent Congress that the Catholic Church be declared the state religion, but that freedom of worship be allowed to foreigners.   Neither proposal was adopted.[12]   There was much insistence from the press of Caracas that religious freedom be granted to aliens as a means of encouraging immigration.   The following interesting extract from the recommendation of the *Semanario político* to the Congress will indicate the tenor of these pronouncements:

[9] *Anales de Venezuela*, 1st per. vol. ii, pp. 237-238; vol. iii, 182-185.

[10] *Ibid.*, vol. ii, p. 252; *passim.*

[11] *Documentos oficiales . . . de las ocurrencias del Iltmo. Sr. Arias.*

[12] *Anales de Venezuela*, 1st period, vol. vii, p. 254.   The clergy declared at this time that failure to recognize the Catholic church as that of the state constituted a virtual grant of freedom of worship.   Arias protested against this as contrary to the wishes to the people of Mérida in their instructions to their delegates and insisted on their right of reclamation.   The clergy were correct in their assumption, but the government was not long satisfied with this implicit recognition of religious toleration. An explicit grant was soon made in the law of 1834, mentioned below.   Article 218 of the constitution had granted to foreigners equal rights with Venezuelans; and Article 188 granted to these civil liberty, interpreted to include freedom of religion.

1. Without liberty of worship to foreigners, we shall have no immigration.
2. If there is no foreign immigration, there will be no population.
3. Without population we can not have liberty, wealth, and general happiness.
4. Without these benefits, we shall be less than we are today! Nothing!!![13]

With an enthusiasm equal to that of the famous Argentine publicist, Alberdi, the Oligarchy continued to urge that "to civilize was to populate." Foreigners, it was declared, were needed to bring European enlightenment as well as wealth to Venezuela. The examples of the United States and England flourishing under religious freedom were constantly in mind. William Burke's famous declarations of 1811 on the material advantages of religious toleration were never forgotten. Other incidents of the period will indicate this further.

On October 13, the Congress received a representation from Archbishop Méndez, urging that the Law of the Patronage be suspended. On the following day it declared the law in force temporarily, leaving for future congresses the final settlement of the question.[14] There was much discussion in the Constituent Congress of the abolition of all personal *fueros*. Article 188 of the Constitution declared that civil liberty, personal security, security of property, and equality before the law should be enjoyed by all Venezuelans. Article 215 went further to declare that taxes should be distributed proportionately and without any exceptions of personal *fueros*. These provisions did not satisfy some. Juan de Díos Picón of Mérida led a vigorous discussion for the definite abolition by law of all eccle-

---

[13] *Anales de Venezuela*, vol. v, p. 350.
[14] *Ibid.*, 1st per. vol. vii, p. 8; Méndez, Ramón Ignacio, *Exposición sobre el patronato eclesiástico hecha al supremo congreso de Venezuela*, (Caracas, 1830); idem, *Exposición del Arzobispo de Caracas al soberano congreso de Venezuela*, (Caracas, 1830). On September 30, Méndez had submitted some observations on the project of a constitution: that only the Catholic church should be tolerated; that prelates should be accused only before the Pope, not before the senate or any national tribunal; that provincial assemblies encharged with the administration of schools should not have control over seminaries; that freedom of printing should not extend to writings against dogma or religion; that in these matters reliance should not be placed upon silence nor on an allocution to the constitution recommending religion; *Observaciones que al Arzobispo de Caracas hace al soberano congreso de Venezuela sobre el projecto de constitución*, (Caracas, 1830).

siastical and military *fueros*, on the grounds that they were contrary to the republican system and the rights of citizens and were merely a part of Bolívar's despotic system. He expressed well the sentiment of legal equalitarianism characteristic of the Oligarchy:

The privileged *fuero* attacks liberty, because it inspires a certain pride and superiority that makes some believe they are superior to others; that it is their due that all should submit to their will. . . . From this is born the spirit hostile to liberty, the fatal division that keeps us separated, that weakens and enervates the social ties so necessary for conserving good harmony in a republic.[15]

This question was brought up a number of times in the Congress in connection with other articles. Díaz of Caracas declared that he had voted several times against having special tribunals, military or ecclesiastical, except for cases purely military or clerical. But the Constituent Congress, absorbed in the political questions of the separation from Colombia and the attitude that should be taken to Bolívar, preferred, it seems, to leave these ecclesiastical questions to be settled in later congresses.[16] It did abolish military *fueros*.

These general provisions, however, were regarded as a *desafuero* of the clergy. In the military revolts of 1830 and 1831 and in the later uprising of 1835, one of the primary features of the program of the Reformists was the reëstablishment of military and ecclesiastic *fueros*. Although the following of this group never became general, it approached more nearly a clerical party than any that Venezuela has had. In the east—in Cumaná, Barcelona, and Margarita—the disaffection was apparently strongest, under the leadership of José Tadeo and José Gregorio Monagas in 1831 and of these two and General Mariño in 1835. During his exile, Talavera issued a pastoral supporting the revolution of the Monagas brothers and union with Colombia on the grounds that the constitution of Venezuela had attacked the foundations of religion in its

---

[15] Azpurúa, Ramón, *Anales de Venezuela; Documentos para la historia de Venezuela desde el año de 1830*, (Caracas, 1877), p. 549 *et seq.*

[16] An interesting petition was received by the Constituent Congress from Pablo Chacón, without date or place, asking that it sanction the matrimony of priests, urging in defense of his proposition that matrimony being a civil contract and priests subjects, this was a question within its jurisdiction, *Anales*, vol. vi, p. 436.

desafuero of the clergy.[17] The *pronunciamientos* of the towns emphasize the same objection.[18] The clergy were, no doubt, generally in sympathy with this movement and in some cases openly supported it. There were, on the other hand, priests who led the forces of the government against them. Máximo Pérez, a priest of Cumaná, received special commendation from General Gómez for his able support.[19] Another interesting case is that of Andrés Torrellas, the famous royalist chief of Coro, who fought so fiercely for the cause of Spain. In 1830, he was the foremost leader in the west for the government at Caracas.[20] It will be seen in the discussion below that in the Congress as on the field some of the most pronounced protagonists of the government were found among the priests. They were never united in defense of their institutional privileges.

II

ON SEPTEMBER 23, the Constituent Congress issued a decree that on the day following the publication of the constitution all citizens should assemble at their respective cathedrals or parochial churches, that a mass should be said, the oath to support the constitution taken, and a *Te Deum* sung. The seventh of November was fixed as the day for taking the oath and Ramón Ayala, Governor of Caracas, sent notice to Méndez on October 30. On November 3, Méndez wrote Ayala, objecting that the order had not come from the national government and protesting that, by ordering the oath taken in the cathedral with religious ceremonies, the government was interfering in the liturgy of the church.[21] This peculiar regard for solemnizing civil acts with religious forms on the part of a government, not only anti-clerical, but in many respects radical in religious thought, might be observed in passing. It is one of the intriguing

---

[17] *Documentos de Secretaría del Interior y Justicia*, (1831), vol. xxv, exp. 32, folios, 384-387. These documents are found in the Archivo Nacional of Caracas.
[18] For example, that of Aragua, *ibid.*, vol. xxiv, exp. 13, folio 300. Folios 292 to 388 are concerned with this revolution in Barcelona.
[19] *Anales de Venezuela*, 2nd per., 1831-1840, vol. i, p. 483.
[20] Gil Fortoul, *op. cit.*, vol. ii, p. 164.
[21] These documents and the correspondence of Méndez with the government are published under the following title: *Documentos oficales que dan justo concepto acerca de la expulsión del Iltmo. Sr. Dr. Ramón Ignacio Méndez, dignísimo arzobispo de Caracas y sobre otras circumstancias interesantes que ocurrieron en ella*, (Caracas, 1830).

contradictions in Venezuelan religious evolution that one finds frequently recurring. In connection with this incident the formula of the oath to the Constitution of 1811 might be recalled and Guzmán Blanco's insistence on *Te Deums* mentioned. Ayala insisted that the procedure of the oath was taken from Spanish practice. Méndez replied that the constitution of the church as well as that of the state should be different under the Republic.[22] He admitted that he had sent the order to the ecclesiastical *cabildo* and given license to the vicar to celebrate the acts prescribed, observing that in the interior many priests were, no doubt, complying with the order without this license. They should not be censured too severely, he declared, since they were acting under compulsion. But he insisted that he could not take the oath in the cathedral; he would take it only in the Government House, where he might make protests and reservations.

On November 7, Méndez issued a statement of his objections to the constitution. The Catholic worship should be recognized as the exclusive state religion. The power of the Congress to establish territorial delimitations should be limited to civil divisions. The freedom of speech in Congress should not extend to discussions of dogma and the discipline of the church, matters belonging solely to ecclesiastical control. The power granted the Congress to promote public education should not extend to the control of seminaries. The provision for the judicial organization should be amended to make recognition of the ecclesiastical jurisdiction. Similar explanation and exceptions he would make to grants of power to the provincial legislatures. Finally, he insisted the provision that one might do anything not prohibited by law should be interpreted to include divine and ecclesiastical law as well as civil. And he protested that the execution of Article 215, which provided that taxes be levied without distinction as to class privileges, must be preceded by negotiation with the Papacy.[23] Méndez offered to take the oath with the understanding that the Catholic church remain the exclusive church

---

[22] Spanish precedents in ecclesiastical law and practice were constantly cited.

[23] *Juramento de la constitución del estado que el Arzobispo de Caracas presta en manos del Sr. Gobernador de la Provincia en su despacho hoy 7 de Noviembre de 1830,* (Caracas, 1830).

of Venezuela; that the government conclude a concordat with the Papacy with reference to Article 215; and that the liberty, independence and discipline of the church be maintained. The other points he would be willing to trust for clarification to later congresses.

The objections of Méndez to the order of the government were presented to the Council. On November 13, that body replied through A. L. Guzmán, Secretary of the Interior, that the constitution as the fundamental law of the nation was so sacred that anyone who failed to recognize its authority was not able to be a public functionary; that an archbishop who refused to take the oath was dangerous to the public tranquillity; that if he did not take the oath he would be suspended from his office and exiled at once.[24] On November 17, the decree of exile was issued, since Méndez persisted in his objection. There ensued then difficulty and much correspondence between him and Ayala over the naming of a vicar. Ayala insisted that he must name one before the decree of suspension was issued or the appointment would not be valid; Méndez delayed, and when he finally named José Suárez Aguado on November 20, he delegated to him only such faculties as he judged convenient, reserving those he thought necessary "to maintain the unity of his people with their pastor."[25] In a communication to Páez on November 19, Méndez offered to take the oath with a general reservation that it not be interpreted in a way to destroy the immunities of the church. Páez replied in a letter notable both for its touching expression of friendship for Méndez and for its unyielding defense of the national prerogatives. One of his greatest consolations, he declared, had been to have Méndez for a companion; he had anticipated the greatest harmony of church and state under his administration. "Demand of me," he said, "as many personal concessions as you wish, and I will grant them. . . . If my fervent supplication can at any time

[24] *Documentos oficiales . . . de la expulsión*, pp. 33-39.

[25] *Ibid.* Páez showed the same personal concern in the cases of these bishops as in that of Méndez. To Arias he offered the hospitality of his home in Valencia for a conference with the hope of effecting a reconciliation. Arias considered accepting the suggestion but an old priest, Juan Antonio Monagas advised against it. (Picón Febrés, Gabriel, *Datos para la historia de la diócesis de Mérida*, Caracas, 1916, pp. 287-288).

have any weight, I wish that it may be effective on this occasion."[26]
The Council of Government, too, expressed regret that harsh terms
had to be used against a venerable patriot. But it was a case of an
intransigent ecclesiastic opposed to an equally uncompromising political power, claiming authority as representative of the national will.
The decree of exile was executed on November 21, and the Archbishop passed to Curaçao to join his nephew, Briceño Méndez, and
other Bolivarians. Upon their refusal to take the oath to the constitution, decrees of exile were issued also against Talavera and
Arias, Bishops of Trícala and Jericho. In a letter to Páez on
November 12, Arias had protested against the silence of the constitution on religion, a silence sure to be fatal to the rights of the
church; and he deplored the sad exhibitions of intolerance on the
part of the political authorities.[27] Guerrero, the governor of Mérida,
reported difficulties with Arias similar to the friction between Ayala
and Méndez over the matter of appointing a vicar. Arias had
named Ciriaco Piñeiro, whom Guerrero declared subversive, ultramontane, and as disaffected as the bishop. In spite of the objection
of the governor, Arias refused to make another nomination on the
grounds that there was no other person suitable to fill the office.[28]
Decrees of exile were issued also against the priests, José de la Cruz
Olivares and Esteban Arias, for refusal to take the oath.[29] Some
other priests sought to take the same course, but desisted when they
saw the intention of the government.[30]

Talavera and Arias joined Méndez and his nephew in Curaçao.
The *Gaceta de la Sociedad Republicana* in June 22, 1831, observed
that the island was a political council, a military barrack, and an
ecclesiastical synod, all for Bolívar. The coincidence of the intransigence of the bishops with the uprisings for Bolívar made their
conduct less pardonable in the minds of Venezuelans, for it gave it
the appearance at least of having a political motive. This conviction

[26] González Guinán, *Historia contemporánea*, vol. ii, p. 200. He quoted the letter
of Páez.
[27] *Documentos oficiales . . . de las ocurrencias del Iltmo Sr. Dr. Buenaventura
Arias*, pp. 20-26.
[28] *Documentos de Secretaría del Interior y Justicia* (1831), vol. xviii, exp. 1, folios
1-36.
[29] *Ibid.*, vol. xviii, exp. 22, folios 397-408.
[30] González Guinán, *Historia contemporanea*, vol. ii, p. 202.

was strengthened by the favor Méndez was known to have shown the dictatorship of Bolívar.[31] Nothing, Páez declared later, proved so clearly the unanimity of the opinion of Venezuelans for the separation as the tranquillity with which the exile of the bishops was carried into effect.[32] Although there were some petitions received afterwards for the return of the prelates, opinion at the time seemed decidedly for the action of the government in the contest with them. The *Gaceta de la Sociedad Republicana* had declared at the beginning of the trouble with Méndez that the government should not retain him in office:

It should be known that a man with a mitre and a man with a plow will suffer equal penalties when infringing the law. Away with privileges! It is not men but principles that rule in Venezuela; and our government, with the example of the Spanish Cortés, ought to resolve upon a vigorous measure that will save the national dignity and the equality of the law.[33]

A few days later it congratulated the government on the double victory, first over Bolívar, now over the ecclesiastical pretensions, declaring that the philosophy of the century had revealed to society that it was absurd that some citizens should be independent of the sovereign authority. "In the state there is only one supreme power. It is in virtue of the luminous principles written by nature in the code of reason that the supreme government of Venezuela has acted."[34]

Other expressions of opinion are in agreement with this defense of the sovereignty of the state and equality before the law, both fundamental tenets of the Constitution of 1830 and the government of the Oligarchy. A paper of the time emphasized the difference between the term, *expulsión*, expulsion, used by the clerics and the term *extrañamiento*, exile, used by the government. The former made the act appear as an unconstitutional exercise of violence, the latter as a legal act equivalent to denaturalization. The periodical protested that the bishops "sought to be Venezuelans, not under the Venezuelan law, but under a law apart"; that the Congress had the

[31] Páez, *Autobiografía*, vol. ii, p. 120.
[32] *Ibid.*, p. 124.
[33] Issue of November 13, 1830.
[34] *Gaceta de la Sociedad Republicana*, November 25, 1830.

right to say to them, "Here one cannot be a Venezuelan, unless he submit himself completely to the nation."[35]

In January 1831, Méndez wrote Páez from Curaçao, requesting the President to use his influence with the Congress to secure his return to his archbishopric.[36]   In a protest against the expulsion of the bishops, the clergy of Caracas urged the government to issue passports for their return; they deplored the political intolerance that sought to create a servile church similar to that of France under the civil constitution of the clergy.[37]   In a second representation they insisted that it was not improper for the sovereign power to treat with a bishop as head of the church and that the "general will" of the people was demanding a return of their pastors.[38]

In February, 1832, the question of permitting the return of the bishops was taken up in Congress.   Alegría, a priest in the House of Representatives, proposed that they be allowed to take the oath with a clause added that it would not be understood to contradict the vow made upon consecration.   He was supported in this by Ávila, Unda, and Pulido, prominent priests of the lower House.[39]   Such a condition was vigorously opposed, however, by members of the Oligarchy, Quintero, Santos Michelena, Rendón, and others.[40]   On February 27, 1832, a petition signed by one hundred thirty-five people was received from Barquisimeto, asking for the return of the bishops and the celebration of a concordat.   This petition reopened the question; Rendón led in the opposition to any exception in favor of the clergy and held that a concordat could be made only with the Papacy as sovereign to sovereign and not with the bishops.[41]   There was no

---

[35] Vallenilla Lanz, *Críticas*, pp. 408-409.

[36] *Al excmo. Señor José Antonio Páez, Presidente del Estado de Venezuela,* (Curaçao, January 2, 1831).

[37] *Noticia razonada de lo ocurrido en la expulsión del M. R. Arzobispo de Caracas, Dr. Ramón Ignacio Méndez,* (Caracas, 1831).   The folowing appeared also in his defense: *Verdadera idea del poder de la iglesia según las escrituras, la razón, la historia y la política, repuesta por abora al Fanal, Gaceta constitucional, Tamburini, al elector Pallero, al papel, A vosotros cualesquiera que seais, salud, y otros folletos que han corrido de algunos meses á esta parte*—unos eclesiásticos al Iltmo. Sr. Dr. Ramón Ignacio Méndez, (Caracas, 1831).

[38] *Segunda representación que el clero de Caracas hace al soberano congreso de Venezuela sobre la vuelta de su benemérito prelado el Iltmo. Sr. Dr. Ramón Ignacio Méndez y la justicia que demanda la concordia entre el estado y la iglesia,* (Caracas, 1832).

[39] *El Conciso,* February 18 and 22, 1832.

[40] *Ibid.*

[41] *Ibid.,* February 29, 1832.

point on which the Oligarchy was more sensitive than this; there could be no sort of an agreement with the clergy that recognized it as having a status above that of ordinary citizenship. *El Conciso* reported a noisy session in the House on the fourteenth of March over the question of the bishops.[42] On March 16, the Senate took action with little discussion. It was resolved that the bishops should take the oath according to Article 220 of the constitution and "satisfy a dogma which is irrevocable."[43] In the Senate, the clerics voted for the measure. On April 17, the government issued a decree for their return and on April 21, Méndez and Talavera took the oath required and were restored to their sees. Arias had died in exile.[44] Although the nation had supported the exile of the bishops, it would seem from the discussions in the Congress and from the press as well as from the representations of the clergy that there was popular support for their return.[45] The religiosity of the people was still strong, and the church was yet able to provoke some expressions of it.

III

AT THIS POINT it may be well to go ahead to the consideration of the renewed difficulties of the government with Archbishop Méndez, which led to his second exile in 1836. Immediately upon his return in 1832, he issued a pastoral against certain errors propagated in his

[42] *El Conciso,* March 15, 1832. The English, it declared, would have thought the discussion treated of saving the country from an imminent danger. When told that it was only a matter of three bishops, they would have thought the Venezuelans, children or fools. The paper deplored the spending of ten sessions and ten thousand pesos on the question.

[43] *Ibid.,* March 17, 1832. Article 220 read :"No officer shall be able to enter upon the exercise of his functions without taking the oath to sustain and defend the constitution and to perform faithfully and exactly the duties of the office."

[44] In 1831, Arias had left Curaçao for Pamplona in Colombia, which was still a part of his bishopric. From this place he expected to direct the administration of it. Colombia, however, forbade transit through her territory, and Arias died in Río Hacha. (*Memoria del Interior y Justicia,* 1833, pp. 12-13). This incident hastened the settlement of the matter of the territorial limits of the dioceses. Upon the request of Colombia, made in a decree of January 28, 1832, Gregory XVI added the parishes of Pamplona, San José de Cúcuta, Limoncito, and San Faustino de los Ríos to the Archbishopric of Bogotá, setting forth the delimitations in an apostolic letter of May 6, 1834. The Congress of Venezuela on May 14, 1836, gave *pase* to the letters of the Pope with regard to the first three, since they were within the civil jurisdiction of New Granada, suspending that as to the last until the limits between the two with reference to it were fixed. (*Recopilación de leyes y decretos de Venezuela,* 52 vols., Caracas, 1874-1931) vol. i, pp. 292-293.

[45] For example, *vide, Los venezolanos,* May 26, 1832, as to the rejoicing over the return, indicative of the religiosity of the people.

diocese. Although of a general character, it was obviously directed against the radicalism of the Oligarchy. He pronounced a regular diatribe against the "impious" century called the "age of enlightenment"; condemned the notion of the state controlling the church in external affairs as a Jansenist principle, beginning with Marsiglio of Padua; and denounced the distribution of Bibles in the vernacular as a work of proselytism on the part of certain Biblical societies.[46]

On the latter point, the Oligarchy was especially sensitive because of its desire to promote close friendship with England. In February, 1833, a more serious charge was brought against Méndez on the grounds of his impeding the attainment of this objective. In a long letter to Santos Michelena, the Minister of Foreign Affairs, the British consul, Robert Kerr Porter, complained that the preaching of the Archbishop on his pastoral visit was prejudicial to the security of foreigners, that he had been delivering "injunctions tending most strongly to subvert the good feeling in which strangers have been held hitherto by the natives of these districts," that he had called on native Venezuelans to hold no communication with heretics and foreigners. If such ideas took root, he held, it would soon be dangerous for foreigners to enter on business. Such intolerance, he protested, "must in a short period materially injure the prosperity and well-being of the state"; it would paralyze the efforts of the government to promote immigration and at the same time "check the liberal social and political sentiments that have already made so considerable advance." The conduct of the Bishop, he considered, had already trespassed seriously on the treaty with Great Britain, which granted to subjects of that country "the most perfect and entire security of conscience without their suffering molestation . . . on account of their religious beliefs." Other foreigners, he asserted, had expressed disturbance, and as the only foreign representative resident in the country, he spoke for all.[47]

The Secretary of the Interior, to whom the complaint was communicated, instituted an investigation of the conduct of the arch-

[46] *Reflexiones que el Arzobispo de Caracas y Venezuela, Dr. Ramón Ignacio Méndez, dirige á sus diocesanos sobre varios errores que se propagan en la diócesis*, (Caracas, 1832).

[47] *Documentos de Secretaría del Interior y Justicia*, (1833) vol. i, exp. 31, folios, 429-431.

bishop, the reports of which fill many folios of the *Documentos* of the Department.[48] He urged the governor of the province to see that the Law of the Patronage was observed with regard to pastoral visits.[49] He was alarmed, he declared, for the peace and prosperity of the country. Through the local justices of the peace he made an investigation of the preachings of the Archbishop. Most of these, however, reported that they had not attended the sermons and had had to rely on the statements of individuals who had attended. These failed to bring charges against the Archbishop, a fact that suggests his continued influence with the people. The incident shows, however, the disposition of the administration.[50]

With the abolition of the tithe in 1833 and the passage in 1834 of a law granting freedom of worship, measures discussed below, the protests of Méndez became more direct. In a circular to his diocesans in 1834, he denounced bitterly these measures and the exercise of the patronage by the civil power, which was declared in force by the Congress of 1833. In imitation of the United States and France, Venezuela was trying to institute reforms wholly foreign to her traditions and spirit, he protested. He advised against all association with foreigners and heretics.[51] In the same year, he declared resistance to the decree of the governor of Caracas, who ordered the erection of a new parish, San Juan, pronouncing the act null as contrary to canon law.[52] Finally in 1836, he refused categorically to give canonical institution to Rafael Escalona, for dean, and José Ambrosio Llamoras, for archdeacon, of the cathedral of Caracas,

[48] *Documentos de Secretaría del Interior y Justicia*, (1833) vol. i, exp. 31, folios 432-575.

[49] *Vide*, Appendix, Law of the Patronage, Article 5, section 9; Article 7, section 6; Article 8, section 7.

[50] There were other instances in this period of trouble over interferences with foreigners, especially Jews; *vide*, for example, *El Conciso*, February 21, 1832, with reference to the attacks on Jews in Coro; also in *Documentos de Secretaría del Interior y Justicia*, (1831), vol. xxxviii, exp. 285, fol. 5-112.

[51] *Reflexiones que el Arzobispo de Caracas y Venezuela, Dr. Ramón Ignacio Méndez, dirige á sus diocesanos sobre varios errores que se propagan en la diócesis* (Caracas, 1834).

[52] *Contestación que el Arzobispo de Caracas da al govierno de la provincia sobre la erección de una nueva parroquia en la iglesia de Capuchinos*. (Caracas, 1834). The erection of new parishes belonged to the civil power under the Law of the Patronage, Article 7, Section 4, and Article 8, Section 10. Méndez did not recognize the validity of this law. He had protested, moreover, against Article 5 of the Constitution of 1830 on the grounds that it did not restrict the control of the government over territorial delimitations to civil jurisdictions only.

upon their presentation by the President of the Republic. In an explanation of this action to his diocesans, he declared that, upon the abolition of the tithe and the payment of these officers by the government, the places had ceased to be benefices, the incumbents becoming mere civil employees, who did not require canonical institution.[53] In the same representation he insisted that the payment of the tithe was still obligatory in conscience, in spite of the law decreeing its abolition. The government, on receiving notice of this pastoral, forbade its circulation and ordered seized copies that had already been distributed.[54]

Charges were brought by the government before the Supreme Court against the Archbishop under Article 6, Section 16, of the Law of the Patronage and heard by this body in accordance with Article 9 of the same law. Méndez contested the jurisdiction of the court in the case, holding that he was subject only to the Papacy. The Court answered that such jurisdiction applied only to grave criminal charges, that in cases of the disregard of the national patronage judgment belonged to the civil courts as under the Laws of the Indies; that the judicial department could only follow the laws and rules laid down by the sovereign legislature in the Law of the Patronage. It declared the Archbishop deprived of his jurisdiction and subject to exile if he did not obey the law in forty-eight hours.[55] The decree was executed November 30, 1836. There seems to have been little discussion of a return following this exile. A group of the clergy of Caracas petitioned for such.[56] And Monseñor Baluffi, papal internuncio to Colombia, sought to secure the Archbishop's return and a concordat; but the government of Venezuela refused to treat with him.[57] Méndez died in Colombia in 1839.[58]

[53] Méndez, Ramón Ignacio, El Arzobispo de Caracas á sus diocesanos, (Caracas, (1836), and Continuación del empreso titulado "El Arzobispo de Caracas á sus diocesanos," (Caracas, 1836).

[54] Memoria del Interior y Justicia (1837), pp. 16 et seq.

[55] Gaceta de Venezuela, no. 305, quoted in La opinión nacional, October 5 and 6, 1870.

[56] Representación que el clero de Caracas preparo para darle al soberano congreso de Venezuela con mótivo de la expulsión de su digno prelado el Iltmo. Sr. Dr. Ramón Ignacio Méndez ocurrido el 30 de Noviembre de 1836. (Caracas, 1837).

[57] Memoria del Interior y Justicia, (1838) pp. 10-13.

[58] He spent three years in Curaçao. Upon the insistence of the Archbishop of Bogotá that he come to live with him, Méndez left in 1839 for Bogotá, but died on the journey in Tunja.

Certain national historians of Venezuela, imbued with the decided anti-clericalism that has characterized the intelligentsia of that country, have presented Archbishop Méndez in a light wholly unfavorable. Gil Fortoul, for example, emphasizes his impetuosity, his irascibility, and his lack of evangelical virtues, giving as support for his interpretation certain incidents in the life of Méndez, in which he displayed undoubtedly something of the character of the *llanero*.[59] He quotes, moreover, in support of his interpretation, the opinion of an English officer, that Méndez was mediocre, ignorant, uneducated, and dissolute.[60]   Such an interpretation fails to find support in the life of the Archbishop or in the opinions of contemporaries who had an opportunity to know him.   Méndez was a creole of high social status and a doctor of both laws in the University of Caracas.[61]   As rector of that university, Vargas esteemed him a great credit to the institution.[62]   Bolívar praised both his patriotism and his theological learning.[63]   His discussions on the patronage attracted attention in the literary circle of the Cuervos and Mosquera of Bogotá, in which knowledge of theology and canon law was of high rank.[64]   The list of his writings indicates the extent of his intellectual labor.[65]   And his work evidences a familiarity not only with theology, church history, and canon law, but with much of the political and social philosophy of his age and others.   The frequency with which he appealed to Rousseau and Montesquieu has been mentioned; he showed acquaintance, too, with Machiavelli, Pufendorf, Vattel, Siéyès, Constant, William Cobbett, and others.   As to his character, Páez com-

[59] *Historia constitucional*, vol. ii, p. 41 *et seq.* In 1826, Méndez came to blows with Diego Fernando Gómez in a dispute that arose in the discussion of the law as to the age for taking religious orders. It led to the expulsion of Méndez from the Senate (*vide*, Groot, *op. cit.*, vol. iii, pp. 373-378). An altercation with A. L. Guzmán, when that one was Secretary of the Interior in 1831, is also given as proof of the violent character of the Archbishop.

[60] This is given in the first edition of his history, vol. i, page 36, note. It is omitted from the second edition.

[61] González Guinán, *Historia contemporánea*, vol. iii, p. 117.

[62] Navarro, *Anales eclesiásticos*, pp. 188-189, note.

[63] Lacroix, *Diario de Bucaramanga*, p. 214.

[64] Cuervo, *Epistolario del Doctor Rufino Cuervo*, vol. i, p. 185.

[65] In addition to those that have been cited, there are many others listed in the bibliography of this study. Méndez had begun before the dissolution of Gran Colombia to protest to Bolívar against the Law of the Patronage. His writings on that subject, against William Burke's teaching, on the tithe, and on ecclesiastical immunities are able as well as voluminous.

mended his moral integrity and austerity, although admitting his defects of disposition.[66]   And it should be said that even his warmest apologists recognize that his violence of temper and too great aggressiveness often injured the cause for which he labored.[67]

The exile of Méndez, it might be said, ended an era in the Venezuelan church.   His administration represented, in a sense, a recrudescence of the colonial character of the episcopate in its determined battle for the privileges of the church.   He might be considered the last of those colonial ecclesiastical statesmen who battled with the civil power for precedence and with society for moral predominance.   He was very much of a Mauro de Tovar.   He knew he fought a losing battle against the prestige of the political power, which spoke in the name of the new nation, and against the attractiveness of the philosophy of the age of enlightenment; and his last years were embittered by the fact.[68]   He saw the inevitable decline in the character of the clergy through the loss of prestige of the office and its subordination to and dependence on the civil authorities.   After him there were some notable Venezuelan ecclesiastics, chiefly his contemporaries, Talavera, Unda, Peña, and Fortique, and later Boset, Guevara, Silva, and some others.   But these shone, on the whole, through intellectual and pastoral virtues rather than in statesmanship.

Mention has been made of the fact that the Papacy suggested the conclusion of a concordat with Venezuela through the internuncio, Baluffi, sent to Colombia in 1836.   At this point further consideration might be given of relations with the Papacy during this period.   Upon the dissolution of Gran Colombia, Tejada was asked to continue to represent Venezuela in Rome.   In reply to the note of Baluffi, the government, however, answered that it preferred to treat directly through a special minister.   Baluffi had made the return of the archbishop, a matter which the government did not choose to consider, a necessary preliminary to further negotiation.[69] General O'Leary was sent to Rome, but nothing resulted from the

[66] Páez, *Autobiografía*, vol. ii, p. 120.
[67] Navarro, *Anales eclesiásticos*, p. 203.
[68] His bitterness appears not only in his public writings, but is well expressed in his correspondence with Santander; *vide*, *Archivo Santander*, vols. xviii and xix, *passim*.
[69] *Memoria del Interior y Justicia*, (1837), pp. 10-13.

mission.[70]   He was soon in London with Fortique.[71]   With reference to the Baluffi note, *El Liberal*, the paper of José María de
Rojas, a prominent member of the Oligarchy, observed that it was
after all not a matter of great importance to enter into negotiations
with Rome, a court that dealt in celestial interests. It feared, moreover, that the Pope was attempting to reëstablish the Jesuits and
thought the mission to America should be kept under strict surveillance.[72]   No further efforts were made during this period to treat
with the Papacy. In spite of the fact that the Law of the Patronage
provided that the government should conclude a concordat, it must
be observed that Venezuela's gestures in that direction have never
been sufficiently vigorous to convince one that she desires such.[73]

Although no agreement was accorded with regard to the exercise of the patronage, Pope Gregory XVI confirmed José Vicente
Unda as Bishop of Mérida upon his presentation by the government
in 1836.[74]   In the bulls of confirmation no recognition was made,
however, of the fact of presentation. And certain conditions placed
on the bishop the government regarded as contrary to its prerogatives; some duties "whose fulfillment never will be permitted," it
declared. On November 19, 1836, the Congress issued a decree,
placing such restrictions on the *pase* to be given to bulls as might be
needed to protect the prerogatives of the nation.[75]   Upon the resignation of Talavera as Bishop of Trícala in 1837, the government
at once asked Congress to declare the see vacant and to name a pro-

---

[70] *Anales de Venezuela*, 2nd period, vol. ii, pp. 337-338.

[71] Fortique, who had been in Europe some time, expressed regret in a letter to
Santander in 1834, that the attacks on the church had been such that it would probably
be difficult to establish relations with the Papacy. (*Archivo Santander*, vol. xx, pp.
340-341).

[72] *El Liberal*, May 16, 1837.

[73] Apparently considerable sentiment existed in the thirties for a national church.
The celebrated pamphlet, *A vosotros*, published in 1832, was a very pronounced attack
on the Papacy. The suggested *Project of Ecclesiastical Reform* discussed below proposed changes in complete disregard of the Papacy and of canon law. Both of these
works were productions of priests. A translation from the French of a two-volume
attack on the Papacy, *Ensayo histórico sobre el poder temporal de los papas*, was
published in Caracas in 1834. The translator, J. D. L., stated in the introduction to
his work, that he had been urged by friends to undertake a work "very useful for the
present epoch when we establish . . . the cements of our political society."

[74] *Documentos de Secretaría del Interior y Justicia*, (1832) vol. i, exp. 12, fol.
290; a copy of the bull is found here with the documents of 1832.

[75] *Memoria del Interior y Justicia*, (1836), pp. 15-16.

prietary bishop to avoid conflicts that might arise from the naming of an apostolic vicar.[76]   And on May 13, 1841, the following decree with regard to the oath required of prelates was issued:

The Congress, considering: (1) that the Supreme Power of the Republic would suffer in its integrity and in the efficacy of its action if it should be permitted that it be embarrassed by a foreign power; (2) that there have abounded in the history of other nations, and have not been lacking in that of Venezuela, unfortunate examples of resistance to the supreme power of the state on the part of the ecclesiastical authority; (3) that such can be attributed primarily to the compromise into which the prelates enter with respect to the obedience that they swear to the Roman Pontiff and that they owe to the laws and the government of the Republic, decree: Article 1: That the *pase* that the government gives to the bulls of the Pontiff to any Venezuelan prelate shall contain the statement that such a *pase* is conceded only in so far as the rights and prerogatives of the nation are preserved; Article 2: That, before delivering the bulls of institution, the prelate shall take the following oath, "I, such a one, archbishop or bishop of such and such a diocese, swear that I will never consider directly nor indirectly annulled or diminished in any respect the oath of obedience to the constitution, to the laws, and to the government of the Republic which I gave before my presentation to the Pope, by that of obedience to the Apostolic See which I gave at the time of my consecration, nor by any later act under any motive.[77]

In keeping with its secular spirit, the government sought a decree from Gregory XVI in 1836 for the reduction of the number of feast days to the limits conceded Colombia in 1831 and 1834, citing in support of the request the devastations of the war, the need of work for reconstruction, the fact that the small number of priests made impossible the hearing of mass in widely separated churches, and the social disorders that attended the frequent holidays.   In 1837, the Pope recognized the request to the extent of granting some reductions, but not so much as the government had asked.[78]

---

[76] *Memoria del Interior,* (1840) pp. 17-18; the Pope had earlier delegated to Talavera the power to name a *provicario apostolico* to whom he might communicate his faculties.

[77] *Recopilación de leyes y decretos de Venezuela,* vol. ii, p. 76.

[78] *Ibid.,* vol. i, p. 293; vol. ii, p. 551, decree of Congress, March 16, 1840, giving *pase* to the bull.

IV

THE ATTITUDE of the conservative government to the church was expressed not only in its resistance to the pretensions of the bishops and its close inspection of relations with the Papacy, but also in restrictive legislation and in the persistent surveillance over the church in the administration of these laws and the Law of the Patronage. With reference to the latter, the Constituent Congress of 1830 had, it will be recalled, declared it only temporarily in force, leaving a final ruling to the regular Congress.   No action was taken until March 21, 1833, when the Congress issued a decree that it be recognized as a formal law of the republic.[79]   The action was provoked by the expositions of the Archbishop of Caracas and the Bishops of Jericho and Trícala, who urged the suspension of the law, and by the fact that the executive had had doubts regarding its execution without further legislation by Congress.   Interestingly, Andrés Torrellas was the President of the Senate to declare it in force.   The uncompromising insistence of the government on its observance was such as to make it seem, indeed, as an official in Guayana observed, "the vital institution of the country."[80]

On April 6, 1833, a law declaring the abolition of the the tithe was passed.[81]   This question had been considered since 1831.   In that year Santos Michelena, Secretary of the Treasury, had urged its absolute suppression on the grounds that it was an impost unequal, unjust, and detrimental to the public welfare, bearing as it did on a class least productive and subject to a system of collection that was vicious.[82]   When this question was introduced into the Congress, some who favored the abolition advised delay, because they feared the attitude of the people.   Others declared that popular opinion supported the measure.   This would appear to have been true, since priests who opposed the bill admitted it, declaring that public opinion

[79] *Recopilación de leyes y decretos*, vol. i, p. 145.   The representation of Méndez was referred to above; the others are: Arias, Buenaventura, *Exposición sobre patronato eclesiástico dirigida al primer congreso constitucional de Venezuela*, (Caracas, 1831) and Talavera, Mariano, *Representación sobre patronato eclesiástico dirigida al congreso de Venezuela*, (Caracas, 1832).
[80] *Documentos de Secretaría del Interior y Justicia* (1830) vol. vi, exp. 165.
[81] *Recopilación de leyes*, vol. i, p. 148.
[82] *Memoria de la Hacienda*, (1831), pp. 20-22.

on the question had been formed by an anti-clerical press.[83]   The arguments of Michelena were emphasized in the Congress.   It was insisted in addition that in the Republic no one should have the power of demanding public contributions except the government.   Although there was some opposition both in the Congress and out to the state's paying the clergy upon the suppression of the tenth, such seems to have been slight, then as later.   There has never been strong sentiment in Venezuela for separation of church and state.   A pamphlet of this period presented arguments for continuing the pay of the clergy that seem to have had general acceptance; it asserted that the pastors would have no support without it and that to retire the pay would be to abandon the Law of the Patronage, "which is needed to moderate the preponderance of the church, to repress attempts made daily against the rights of the nation, and to control the discipline, which for lack of equilibrium of any other worship, is able to influence public negotiations."[84]   Twenty-five of the twenty-nine members in the House of Representatives voted for the measure granting salaries.[85]   This law, passed April 25, 1833, fixed the appropriation at 48,000 pesos for the diocese of Caracas, 24,000 for that of Merida, and ordered that the clergy in Guayana should be paid individually from the public treasury, as under the Spanish practice then in force.[86] The law provided that the clergy should continue to enjoy primacies and other parochial subventions.   Annates and semi-annual and monthly exactions from the clergy were abolished.

There were protests from the clergy that the amounts appropriated were inadequate and the system of distribution outlined in the law inequitable.   Méndez declared that they were not equal to the return from the tenth for the period from 1822 to 1827, which the government had taken as a basis for its estimates, and that they were far below those for the colonial period.[87]   Figures given in the Introduction to this study will indicate the correctness of the latter assertion.   The income for the diocese of Caracas at the end of the

---

[83] *El Conciso*, February 21, 22, 23, 24, and 26, 1832.   In the House the priests, Ávila, Unda, Pulido, and Alegría, opposed the measure; the liberal priest, Osio, defended it.

[84] Published in *El Liberal*, February 14, 1837.

[85] *El Conciso*, February 24, 1832.

[86] *Recopilación de leyes*, vol. i, p. 152.

[87] *Arzobispo á sus diocesanos*, (1836).

eighteenth century was 316,215 pesos. But, according to figures compiled by the church, the amount collected for the six years from 1822 to 1827 was 339,824 pesos, or an average of something more than 56,000 pesos.[88] According to the *Memoria* of the Treasury Department in 1831, the returns from the tithe of 1830, payable to the church, were 98,110 pesos.[89] The appropriation to the church in 1836, under the law of 1833, was 82,270.[90] Although the amounts were less than those derived from the tenth, they were not considerably so. And regarded as civil officials, the clergy were about as well paid as others under the Conservative régime, which practiced rigid economy in order to pay the foreign debt. Only the president received a salary larger in amount than that of the archbishop, whose salary of five thousand pesos was, nevertheless, meagre compared to the seventy thousand often received by that dignitary under the colonial régime. On the whole, the meagerness of the income of the church was a result of the general impoverishment of the country by the Wars for Independence. Nevertheless, the church has suffered economic loss from the abolition of the tithe, particularly in certain periods. Governments have failed to pay even the salaries allotted. But there appears to have been no complaint in the latter respect under the Conservative régime. Under a law of 1841, the apportionments for the church were increased.[91] By 1845 the appropriation was 110,147 pesos.[92] The moral effects of the law abolishing the tithe were, it would seem, more serious than the economic, in that it placed the clergy in dependence on the civil authorities and hence tended to make it mercenary. This result Méndez feared particularly.

There were complaints, too, against the system of distribution outlined in the law; according to it one hundred fifty pesos were to be paid each parish priest; two thousand to each of the universities of Caracas and Mérida; and the remainder was to be divided as under the Spanish law. The income of vacant offices was to revert to the

[88] *El dean y cabildo de Caracas sobre las asignaciones eclesiásticos y su cuenta,* (Caracas, 1833).
[89] *Memoria de la Hacienda,* (1831), pp. 20-22.
[90] *Memoria del Interior y Justicia,* (1837), p. 15.
[91] *Recopilación de leyes,* vol. ii, pp. 78-80.
[92] *Memoria del Interior y Justicia,* (1845).

public treasury. The *cabildo* of Caracas protested that the salary of pastors in cities should be more than that of occupants of rural parishes and that the income of vacant offices should remain with the church; and it pointed out difficulties in the distribution, which was left to the *cabildo* under the law.[93]   These complaints led the government to take over the control of the distribution in a decree of 1835, and it has continued to exercise this power.[94]

On February 18, 1834, the Congress passed a law granting the right of freedom of worship. Justification for it was found in Article 218 of the Constitution, which extended to foreigners an invitation to live in Venezuela.[95]   The *Nacional* declared that the clergy and the Camaras had lost a lot of time in the discussion of a question not worth so much attention, since there were not enough foreigners in Venezuela to support churches.[96]   In the same year, however, the first non-Catholic chapel was erected in Caracas by members of the Anglican Church, the work being promoted by the British consul, Sir Robert Kerr Porter.[97]   But the grant of freedom of worship has affected little the monopoly of the Catholic Church so far as nominal adherence is concerned.   There are few non-Catholics in Venezuela today.

Under the decree of Bolívar of July 10, 1828, providing for the rëstablishment of convents, the foundations of the Dominicans of Mérida and of the Franciscans of Maracaibo had been ordered restored.   The Constituent Congress of Venezuela had taken no action with regard to this decree or the earlier laws of 1821 and 1826 under which the extinction of these convents had been ordered. There was much friction over the uncertain status of these establishments, especially under Guzmán's administration as Secretary of the Interior in 1831; the *Documentos* of the Department are filled with reports of investigations on the condition of the convents and demands for their delivery to the state.[98]   In 1837, the Congress passed a

[93] *El dean y cabildo de Caracas sobre los asignaciones eclesiásticos, passim.*
[94] *Recopilación de leyes,* vol. i, pp. 232-233.
[95] *Ibid.,* vol. i, p. 166.
[96] Issue of March 1, 1834.
[97] Gil Fortoul, *op. cit.,* vol. ii, p. 39.
[98] *Documentos de Secretaría del Interior y Justicia* (1831), vol. xxi, exp. 96, 114, passim.

law declaring the laws of Colombia in force.[99]   This accomplished
the extinction of all convents for men.   A pension of three hundred
pesos was granted to any friar who was unable to serve a curacy; in
1841 all who had not already received pensions under the law were
granted them.[100]   The buildings and incomes of the convents passed
to the service of public education.   According to reports of the Department of the Interior some of these were in a sad condition, having been completely despoiled by the war.[101]   Although there was
general agreement, apparently, in the opposition to convents, some
of the Conservatives opposed the measure extinguishing them as contrary to the principle of the inviolability of property guaranteed by
the Constitution.[102]   Thus, radical anti-clericalism was not able to
conquer their scrupulous regard for property rights and constitutional
guarantees.

The Conservative administration and public opinion in the thirties
sought to check the influences of the clergy in education.   Venezuelan legislators in Colombian congresses had shown this attitude
in their opposition to convents both for men and for women and in
their support of liberal laws for public education.   In 1833, a decree
was issued prohibiting priests from holding places in national *colegios*,
or secondary schools, either as rectors, vice-rectors, or teachers.[103]
In 1836, José María de Rojas in his *Liberal*, a leading periodical of
the time, issued a pronouncement against the teaching of the clergy in
the university; their tuition, he protested, was "poisoning the foun-
tains of learning" and from it "the institutions of the country received
daily attack."[104]   José Bracho, as Secretary of Interior in 1837,
favored the separation of the seminary from the University; the
union, he declared, made the entire university ecclesiastical in character, when it should be national and scientific.[105]   It should be noted
that the clerical interests favored the separation on the grounds that

[99] *Recopilación de leyes*, vol. i, p. 364.

[100] *Ibid.*, vol. ii, pp. 450.

[101] *Documentos*, (1830) vol. xx, exp. 80, folios 175-198; vol. xxi, (1831), exp.
120, folios, 194-199.

[102] *Anales de Venezuela*, 2nd per., vol. ii, p. 391.

[103] Castillo, Pedro del, *Teatro de la legislación colombiana y venezolana vigente
que contiene en forma de diccionario*, (Valencia, 1852), vol. i, pp. 273-274.

[104] Quoted in Zuloaga, Nicomedes, *Bibliografía y otros asuntos*, (Caracas, 1925):
9-10.

[105] *Memoria del Interior*, (1837), p. 64.

the teaching of Bentham in the university was ruining the spirit of the seminary. When the separation was made in 1856, it was largely through the efforts of the clergy.[106] The Conservative government found it necessary in 1841, however, to allow priests to teach in national *colegios*. Páez issued a resolution in that year, repealing the decree of 1833; he pointed out in justification of this action the fact that in the provinces there were frequent vacancies attributable to the lack of educated persons outside the ranks of the clergy and that the small salaries attached to those positions did not attract those who were capable of filling them.[107]

A law passed both Houses of the Congress in April, 1834, for the abolition of all ecclesiastical *fueros*, but it was vetoed by the President, Páez.[108] In the same year a Project of Reform of Ecclesiastical Policy was presented as the report of a special committee of the senate composed of Domingo Bruzual, Martín Tovar, and Gabriel Picón. Bruzual, the chairman of the committee, who drafted the report, was a priest. In the introduction to the report the committee stated that some still hesitated to make reforms necessary to the happiness of the country and urged that all the restraints of the Spanish traditions and dependence on Rome be broken. It recommended that complete freedom and equality be granted to all religions with full rights of public worship; that all distinction between the clergy and other citizens be abolished; that all foreign manuscripts and printed matter be prohibited from being read in religious meeting, unless approved by the government; that ministers of all religions be prohibited from teaching in public schools, universities, and colleges; that the government refuse to recognize seminaries established under the rules of the Council of Trent and subject all to strict national control; that the clergy be subjected to the jurisdiction of civil courts, the ecclesiastical tribunals being allowed to retain authority in spiritual matters only; that all priests be appointed by the government; that no minister be allowed to wear dress peculiar to his office except when performing its functions;

---

[106] *El Patriota*, January 12, 1845.
[107] Castillo, *Teatro*, vol. ii, pp. 273-274.
[108] *Documentos de Secretaría del Interior y Justicia*, (1834), vol. ii, *exp.* 74, *fol.* 187-202; *Anales de Venezuela*, 2nd. per., vol. ii, p. 391.

that all regular orders be extinguished, both of men and of women; that a foreign minister who married a Venezuelan be *ipso facto* a Venezuelan and that the government grant him ten *fanegados* of land; that it grant twenty *fanegados* to all Venezuelan priests who married; that impediments to matrimony be restricted and that the government establish dispensations for violation of these except certain ones; that civil matrimony and civil registry be established.[109]

The proposal was not enacted into law except as to certain features on which there was later legislation; but the extent of its recommendations suggests the progress of anti-clerical thought. It was answered in an able writing by some Catholics of Carabobo, who stated that their objections had all been presented before, but that they wished to bring them together in a single work on this leading question of the day. The Congress was enjoined to remember that it did not represent merely its own members but a Catholic people; that it should not follow Llorente and the example of the United States. They criticized especially the attack on the ecclesiastical *fueros,* the abolition of which, it was declared, would be fatal to the prestige of the clergy; deplored the erroneous notions as to matrimony; and protested against the restriction on the reading of foreign documents, which was pronounced beyond the most ample scope of the Law of the Patronage.[110] This and other writings in the periodicals and in pamphlets indicate that religious sentiment in the population was still strong and often found expression.

Although there was no outright resistance on the part of the clergy to the Law of the Patronage and other legislation on ecclesiastical matters, aside from the action of the bishops, which has been discussed, there was much friction between civil and ecclesiastical authorities as to the administration of the laws. These conflicts were comparable to the ancient *competencias.* There was, besides, much passive resistance on the part of the clergy in their delay in complying, or failure to comply, with government demands for reports. Mat-

---

[109] *Reforma de la política eclesiástica,* (Caracas, 1834). Article 12 of the organic law of the provinces provided that the governor report on births, deaths, etc., according to the system outlined in the civil code. Since no civil code was enacted in this period, the law remained without effect. (*Memoria del Interior y Justicia,* 1841, p. 13.)

[110] *Breve impugnación del folleto intitulado "Reforma de la política eclesiástica ó sentimientos de la provincia de Carabobo,"* (Caracas, 1834).

ters of external discipline in processions, of formal relations with the civil authorities on ceremonial occasions, of the delivery of the convents, of the filling of curacies with provisional appointees, of division of parishes, and of interference with the rights of foreigners under the law of 1834 were sources of disputes. The reports of these fill many folios of the *Documentos* of the Department of the Interior and Justice. No subject produced so much correspondence; on none was the government more persistent in efforts to secure the execution of its orders.

A few illustrations will suggest the nature of these controversies. In 1830, Archbishop Méndez undertook to order a religious procession in Caracas without the sanction or instructions of the governor. When the police attempted to stop the procession, Méndez contested the right of the civil authorities to any voice in the matter. In reply, the governor cited royal orders of 1770, 1777, and 1780, and Article 248 of the police regulations of Venezuela, which declared that it belonged to the civil authorities to preside at all processions and religious acts apart from the churches.[111] In 1833, the governor of Cúmana reported trouble with the provisor of the bishopric of Guayana, who had refused to invest the governor with the keys to the ciborium in the solemnities on Holy Thursday. For this refusal, which the governor pronounced in violation of the Law of the Patronage and the *sinodales* of Caracas, he blamed Talavera. Urbaneja, Secretary of the Interior, ordered that no relaxation be made in the insistence on the supremacy of the civil authorities and in the prevention of such disrespect displayed in public to the government.[112]

Article 34 of the Law of the Patronage was the source of much conflict with the clergy, particularly with Méndez. According to this article, the prelates had the right to fill curacies provisionally. This expedient, it would seem, was used to excess to prevent the government's having a voice in the matter. Foreign priests were often put in. On this basis the government claimed the right under Article 39 of the Law to have all appointees submitted to it in order

[111] *Documentos de Secretaría del Interior,* (1830), vol. i, exp. 30, folios 401-473. The reference to cédulas of the Bourbon monarchy, which emphasized the control of the civil authorities, might be noted. There were many instances of such.

[112] *Documentos de Secretaría del Interior,* (1833) vol. iii, exp. 70, folios 1-57.

that it might be assured that curacies were provided with natives or naturalized citizens. In a note to Guzmán in 1833, Méndez protested against this rule, claiming that Article 39 did not apply to *interinos*, and asked that his communication be submitted to the President, Páez. In reply Guzmán asserted that Article 39 applied to *interinos* as well as to proprietary appointments and that it did not belong to the bishop nor to the president to decide in the matter. "The interpretation of the law belongs to the legislator," he declared, "and disobedience is a crime."[113] As a result of this controversy, a resolution was passed on October 17, 1833, requiring that *interinos* be presented to the governor of the province for his approval. On November 23 of the same year, a second resolution on the matter ratified the note of Guzmán in respect to his assertion that the president had no right to set aside a law through interpretation, a statement that Méndez had contested.[114] There continued to be complaints concerning failure to fulfill the law with respect to *interinos*, but no ecclesiastic showed the intransigence of Méndez in the matter.[115]

Civil officials protested against absences of pastors from their parishes. In a resolution of June 27, 1843, the government decreed that they should notify civil officials of absence, that ecclesiastics were civil employees with civil functions to perform and must act subject to civil authority.[116] It went further on July 6, 1849, to require that they get a special license for leaving their parishes.[117] Reports of governors indicated much delay in securing information required from ecclesiastics.[118] This could well have been the result in many cases, however, of slowness of communication and the difficulty of compiling the data requested rather than of the intentional dilatoriness or negligence of the ecclesiastic.

[113] *Documentos de Secretaría del Interior*, (1833), vol. xxxiv, exp. 30, folios 389-390.

[114] Castillo, *Teatro*, vol. i, pp. 434-435.

[115] There was question over the use of stamped paper against which the clergy had frequently protested. In an executive order of April 23, 1845, it was stated that *interino* appointments need not be made on such, but continued the requirement of its use for proprietary ones (Castillo, *op. cit.*, vol. i, p. 433).

[116] Castillo, *op. cit.*, vol. i, pp. 436-437.

[117] *Ibid.*, vol. i, pp. 437-438.

[118] *Documentos de Secretaría del Interior*, (1832), vol. iii, exp. 168, folios, 6-16; *Memoria del Interior*, (1834), p. 43. An executive order of November 21, 1833, declared ecclesiastics subject to certain penalties if they failed to furnish promptly information required. (*Gaceta de Venezuela*, no. 152).

V

SOME FACTS on the status of the church in the period will indicate these difficulties in administration and contribute something toward an explanation of the progressive loss of influence of the institution in Venezuela. Reports from the several provinces in 1831 described the deplorable state in which the War for Independence had left the ecclesiastical organization. The Governor of Barinas stated that for forty-eight parishes there were only ten pastors, three of these being very old. Many of the people in the provinces were Indians; and these, he declared, could only be governed by a strong hand; in spite of the existence of "beneficent laws based on the most luminous principles of the rights of man" they required "a sort of theocracy."[119] There were only eight priests in the Province of Apure, according to the report of the governor; and two of these were very old. There were no sacristans, no provisors, no friars, no hospitals, no chapels, no *cofradías*. The Indians were wandering without missionaries to control them.[120] The communications from Maracaibo and Barcelóna were similar.[121] In a letter to Páez in September, 1831, Méndez deplored the sad state of the archdiocese of Caracas; one hundred seven parishes were without pastors; thirty were served by substitutes. There were probably not more than twenty aspirants to the ecclesiastical career, "miserable young men without learning."[122] In taking possession as *vicario apostólico* of the bishopric of Guayana in 1829, Talavera encountered, he declared, "a desert in the spiritual order." All the missionaries were gone, and the college of the Franciscans in Barcelona contained only two very aged friars. The few priests in the bishopric served four or six parishes: there were no pastors or missionaries in Río Negro. The lack of centralization in administration was even more pronounced than under the colonial régime. The governor of the bishopric had moved the seat of his residence to Cumaná, and Guayana remained in complete isolation. When he arrived as apostolic vicar, he found that the observance of the *sinodales* of Caracas

---

[119] *Documentos*, (1831), vol. xxiii, exp. 152, folios, 213-217.
[120] *Gaceta de Venezuela*, September 7, 1831.
[121] *Ibid.*, December 14, 1831; February 8, 1832.
[122] *Documentos de Secretaría de Interior*, (1832), vol. iii, exp. 77, folio 236-237.

had never been extended to Guayana. To remedy this defect of administration, he sought to furnish copies to all the priests. There was no press nearer than Caracas, and to avoid the delay of three or four months that would have been required for securing the printed copies, he had them made by hand. In 1833, he made a visit to the Island of Margarita, belonging to the bishopric, a district which no bishop had visited, however, for fifty-six years. Here he found the church lacked everything.[123] In the vast extent of the bishopric of Guayana there were in 1832 only thirty-six priests; of these, ten were regulars from Spain, six priests from other dioceses, five septuagenarians, and five habitual invalids. The two canons were so poorly paid that each office had been filled four times since he arrived because of the resignation of incumbents.[124] With regard to the higher clergy, Urbaneja reported, in his *Memoria* as Secretary of the Interior in 1834, only seven prebendaries in the cathedral of Caracas, three in Mérida, and one in Guayana.[125] According to Depons there were seventy in Caracas alone at the time of his visit in 1801.

There was no considerable improvement in the status of the church during this period. Méndez had predicted that this would be true; the times were evil for the church. The Catholicism of a great number, he declared, was reduced to two acts, baptism in life and absolution upon death. The church had lost its prestige in society. There was, in addition, no sufficient pecuniary attractions to the career to draw men into the church. In the three dioceses there were only three hundred twenty-nine priests and eighty-four friars in 1843; even the secular clergy were less in number than at the end of the colonial period.[126] In 1847, after the government for reasons discussed below had made some efforts to increase the clergy, there were only four hundred forty priests for the four hundred eighty-one curacies. One-third of these were too old to serve, or were ill, or had other ecclesiastical offices; hence, there were two hundred eight curacies without pastors. There was an average of one pastor for

---

[123] Talavera, *Apuntes de historia de Venezuela*, pp. 106-108.
[124] Talavera, *Representación sobre patronato eclesiástico*, p. 24.
[125] *Memorial del Interior*, (1834), p. 42.
[126] *Ibid.*, (1843), p. 21.

every 2,893 people; in Europe at the time, it was asserted, there was one for every ninety-eight.[127]

To supply the vacant curacies and to serve the missions, which the Conservative government undertook at this time to restore, the plan of bringing priests from foreign countries was adopted. The Secretary of the Interior in 1832 had called special attention to the needs of restoring the missions, but had no solution to offer, since the regular clergy, "in our day against the dominant ideas, the habits, the doctrines, and even the public interest," had formerly been the base. He reported that the lands granted to James Hamilton, Colonel Needham, and others had been reassumed by the government. In Upata, the central mission, the houses were in ruins. The government should learn the actual condition in order that decay not continue; but information he declared was hard to secure.[128] The Province of Guayana made some efforts toward the reduction of the Indians under the promotion of the Governor, Tomás Herés, but the work was retarded by lack of funds. The national government made small appropriations for the purchase of agricultural tools, 1,744 pesos in 1840. In the work of reduction the governor used civilians and sometimes Indians for lack of priests. Some served without pay; others received a small remuneration.[129]

A law passed in 1841 gave the president the power to promote the reduction of the Indians by such a system as he might establish, to bring missionaries from foreign lands, and to determine their duties.[130] In virtue of this law, there issued on October 15, 1842, a decree outlining the organization of the missions of Guayana. The administration was put in charge of a director-general serving under the Department of the Interior. The territory, divided into four districts, was placed under the immediate supervision of vice-directors and chiefs of circuits. Under these civil officials the missionaries served; they might be suspended from their offices by the vice-director. They were subject, moreover, to the ordinary clergy in the administration of their ecclesiastical functions.[131] The system was

[127] *Memoria del Interior*, (1847), p. 22.
[128] *Ibid.*, (1832), p. 36.
[129] *Ibid.*, (1837), pp. 11-12; (1840), p. 4.
[130] *Leyes y decretos*, vol. ii, pp. 29-30.
[131] *Ibid.*, vol. ii, pp. 30-37.

very different from the virtual *imperium in imperio* that the ancient missions of Caroní had constituted. Emphasis was placed on the obligation of the missionary to teach the Indian to work and submit to the government. There was less insistence on the need of conversion. One may readily conclude that this was not an important consideration with most members of the government, except as it might serve civil needs. The evangelical spirit of the Catholic kings was lacking. Reduction was to serve secular and utilitarian ends.

On October 22, 1842, a decree was issued outlining a similar system of reduction for the district of Maracaibo.[132] A contract was made in the same year with the priest, Alegría, to bring missionaries and artisans; it extended also to the introduction of pastors for vacant parishes. The government was to pay the passage of the immigrants and one hundred pesos to those who served as missionaries.[133] Under this contract Alegría brought fifty-nine men, twenty-nine missionaries and thirty priests, in 1843. Of the twenty-nine, twelve went to the upper Orinoco and central Guayana; six to Río Negro, two to Cumaná, three to Maracaibo, and six to Apure.[134]

The operation of the system was not fortunate; moreover, its initiation as well as its execution became the source of a political attack on the government. In 1844, the Secretary of the Interior, José Manuel Manrique, reported trouble with the civilians in the districts, due to the fact that they did not wish to submit to the mission authorities. Of the few missionaries who had come, some had died, some were ill, and others were not willing to undertake work so difficult.[135] According to the *informe* of a visitor appointed by the government in 1845, only two missionaries remained in the Upata district and on the lower Orinoco, the center of the mission system. One of these, Bernardo de Mamesa, was commended for his good work. The system, however, was held to be defective. It had led to exploitation of the Indian by the directors and by the traders, whom the directors favored. Little had been accomplished toward the reduction to civil life.[136] In virtue of this report, the

[132] *Leyes y decretos,* vol. ii, pp. 37-42.
[133] *Memoria del Interior,* (1842), p. 20.
[134] *Ibid.,* (1843), p. 13.
[135] *Memoria del Interior,* (1844), p. 15.
[136] *Ibid.,* (1846), p. 37 *et seq.*

government issued a decree on November 6, 1845, changing some features of the administration and giving the missionaries more prominence in it.   A missionary-general was named to serve under the director-general.[137]   The changes in the system, however, did not improve its operation.   Although there was some good work done, especially in Río Negro, the enterprise as a whole was a failure. One cause of this was recognized to have been the inadequacy of funds for the proper promotion of the work; another, as has been suggested, certain defects in the civil administration, criticized as mercenary in spirit rather than civilizing, as seeking the profit of a few and as isolating the Indian—the same criticism, it is interesting and instructive to note, that had been brought aganst the Capuchins, but now directed against the civil administration.[138]

But the ineffectiveness of the effort may be attributed in part to the missionaries themselves, to their conflict with civil officials, and to their failure to adjust themselves to the hardships of life on the Orinoco; and, in addition, to political opposition by the new Liberal Party that exaggerated the shortcomings of the missionaries and the government and tended to nullify any good results the undertaking might have obtained.   In 1848 the government reported the failure of the effort at reduction.   The priests had abandoned the region and fled, resisting naturalization required in the contract with Alegría; they had disobeyed the prelate of Guayana and the government officials; and only five were left of the entire number.[139]

The greater part of those who had come to Venezuela were of the secular clergy and remained in the towns; these were denounced by the Liberal press as fanatic and obscurantist Carlist clerics, with whom the Godos sought to reëstablish the reactionary régime of the Spanish.   El venezolano, the organ of the chief of the Liberal Party, Antonio Leocadio Guzmán, announced the arrival of sixty-two priests in November, 1842; more were said to be on the way, and it was supposed that the 83,000 of Ferdinand VII would arrive finally, if General Soublette proved as devout as his predecessor.[140]

[137] Leyes y decretos, vol. ii, pp. 42-44.
[138] Memoria del Interior, (1846), p. 44.
[139] Ibid., (1848), p. 34.
[140] El venezolano, November 15, 1842.

Those who entered, it was stated, were stopping in Caracas to "reduce the natives of the Cathedral, Altagracía, Santa Rosalie," etc., and were promoting in the pulpit "the old system that men have not advanced for thirty years."[141] Criticism from *El agricultor*, *El patriota*, *El liberal*, and other papers of the party were similar.[142] An attempt was made to arouse nationalist sentiment against this policy of the Conservative Party. Although it was admitted that priests were needed, the Liberal press advocated the promotion of seminaries, so that native priests might be trained, men loyal to the institutions of the country, especially to the "holy doctrine of equality," and so that the money might be kept at home.[143]

In emphasizing, thus, the doctrine of equality, appeal was made, also, to democratic as well as to nationalist sentiment against the Conservative Party. It was pronounced the party of the Clergy, the Administration, and the Bank. This alliance elected General Soublette in 1842, Rojas asserted.[144] In addition to attacks directed against its introduction of foreign priests for the promotion of what was pronounced its reactionary policies, it was criticized for filling the ecclesiastical *cabildos* and the ranks of the higher clergy when pastors were lacking.[145] The pulpit and the confession, Guzmán declared, had been made into political machines.[146] The pastors were supporting the minority against the majority and must be delivered to the judgment of public opinion. The preaching of a certain *cura* of San Pedro against a teacher belonging to the Liberal Party attained widespread notoriety through the press.[147] Some of these priests were brought to trial in 1848 for disaffection to the Liberal government, which followed upon the assumption of power by Monagas on January 24 of that year. The trial of these provoked discussion again of the abolition of the ecclesiastical *fueros*.[148] In this case attack was made on the feature of the Law of Patronage

---

[141] *El venezolano*, November 1, 1842.

[142] For example, *El agricultor*, November 21, 1844; *El liberal*, July 23, 1842.

[143] *El venezolano*, September 5, 1843.

[144] Rojas, J. M. de, *Bosquejo histórico de Venezuela*, (Paris, 1888), p. 83. Along with other prominent Liberals, Rojas had formerly been a leader in the Oligarchy.

[145] *El agricultor*, November 21, 1844.

[146] *Editoriales de "El venezolano,"* 4 vols. (Caracas, 1883), vol. iv., p. 408.

[147] *El patriota*, November 1, 1845.

[148] With reference to these trials, *vide*, *Dilate de la Corte Suprema*, (Valencia, 1849); *Defensa practicada el día 19 de los corrientes ante S. E. la Corte Superior del primero distrito de centro por Antonio Suárez en favor de la disciplina eclesiástica*, (Caracas, 1853).

that subjected priests to higher courts for disaffection to the government. In a representation signed by "some parishioners" it was objected: "Is it equality for a farmer to be tried in one court and a pastor in a higher?" The protest continued: "Who deserves more dignity, that is, more honor, a *cura* or Capuchin, unproductive consumers, or an honest head of a family who by his toil contributes to the rich income of the state?"[149] It is probable that considerable popular criticism of the clergy had been provoked by the propaganda of the Liberal Party, which identified the clergy with the Conservatives, who were called the party of monopolists; it is impossible, however, to evaluate the strength of this sentiment or its contribution to the continuous loss of influence of the clergy over the masses.[150]

Although the Conservative Oligarchy was accused of being the party of the clergy, there is, in fact, no evidence of reaction from the philosophic radicalism of the thirties. As the party standing for the maintenance of order and the inviolability of property rights, it attracted the support of the church at a time when the Liberal Party was demanding the abolition of the *censos*, the chief source of income of the clergy.[151] If there appeared to be reaction in the Conservative group in favor of the clergy, it was for practical and utilitarian ends. Priests were allowed in *colegios*, because other teachers could not be secured. The restoration of the missions was attempted with ecclesiastical aid, but the end was civil and secular. If in the social realm it showed some tendency toward accommodation with the church at a time when the propaganda of the Liberals was threatening social revolution, it was with a purpose strictly

---

[149] *El republicano*, May 16, 1848.

[150] Venezuelan historians differ in their conception of the bases of these political groups. Vallenilla Lanz and Gil Fortoul agree in attributing the division to a class struggle, although they differ in their explanation of its origin. Vallenilla Lanz sees the political conflict of the eighteen-hundred-forties, which developed later into the Federal war, as the continuance of the class struggle of 1810 for political and social democracy. Gil Fortoul gives greater emphasis in his explanation of it to the economic unrest of the eighteen-hundred-forties. His interpretation inclines to a conception of the struggle as based on socialistic principles. Pedro Arcaya, on the other hand, holds that there was no integrating factor, such as class interest, that produced these groups; in his conception the only cohesive force was the prestige of the *caudillo*. Professor Pierson, in his *Lectures on Venezuelan History*, states an opinion in general agreement with that of Gil Fortoul: that unrest due to economic causes was a primary factor in giving rise to the political conflict. He does not find support, however, for the thesis of the latter that the political philosophy underlying the struggle was that of socialism.

[151] This question is discussed in the following chapter.

utilitarian.[152]   And its injunctions to the clergy to aid in the maintenance of order have more the tone of commands to civil employees
than of appeals to venerated pastors.   There was no tendency to
relax the insistence on the rigid enforcement of the Law of the
Patronage.   Nor was there any tendency to condone the excesses of
the priests connected with the mission experiment.   Conservative ministers were as severe on their shortcomings as their opponents.[153]

Although there were priests who supported actively the Conservative Oligarchy against the Liberal Party, the clergy were not
united in such a program.   The election returns of 1846 show
priests in both groups.[154]   In 1861, Guzmán himself was praising
the clergy for not mixing themselves prominently in political contests, but for being nevertheless enlisted on the whole in the Liberal
ranks.[155]

The Conservative Oligarchy had not only accomplished important advances in anti-clerical legislation: the abolition of ecclesiastical immunities with regard to taxation and other public contribution; the abolition of the tithe; the definite grant of freedom
of worship; and the abolition of all convents for men; but it had
defined the attitude of the nation toward the civil constitution of the
clergy.   No amplifications have been made to its interpretation of the
Law of the Patronage in the interest of civil supremacy.   It had,
moreover, established the policy toward the Papacy to be followed
later with little change, a policy of evading the question of a concordat and yet not advancing to a complete break with Rome and
the establishment of a national church.   The Oligarchy had suggested many radical reforms in ecclesiastical policy that for one reason or another, the negative of Páez or the fear of public disturbance,
were not enacted into law—steps taken later by Guzmán Blanco in
a spirit very different from the legalist and civilist sentiment of the
Oligarchy.[156]

[152] *Memoria del Interior*, (1847), pp. 22-23.
[153] *Ibid.*, (1844), (1845), (1846).
[154] Guzmán, *Editoriales*, vol. iv, p. 202.
[155] Guzmán, A. L., *Datos históricos sur-americanos*, 4 vols.   (Brussels, 1878-1882),
vol. ii, pp. 42-46; p. 265.
[156] Domingo Olavarría in his *Estudios histórico-políticos* (Valencia, 1894) gave a
good statement of the contributions of the two parties to the evolution of the church
question.

CHAPTER IV

THE CHURCH UNDER THE MONAGAS RÉGIME AND IN THE CIVIL WAR, 1848-1870

IN THIS PERIOD of civil conflict and confusion, of reaction and revolution, there is found no such a consistent program of policy and action on the church question as in the period of the Conservative Oligarchy. There were radical and, on occasion, reactionary currents in policy. Little change is observable, however, in practice. Definitions established by the Oligarchy were maintained in all fundamental relations with the church. The tendency in the period was on the whole toward more radical reforms; the abolitions of all *fueros*, the establishment of civil marriage and registry, the secularization of cemeteries—steps suggested by the Oligarchy but not made effective·in law. The revival and progress of the Masonic organization promoted the agitation of these questions; also the liberalism provoked in the period of the Federal war and by the government of Falcón.

Along with this tendency toward radical reform, there went a recrudescence of a spirit of active resistance in the church. These developments ended in the war between the institution and Guzmán Blanco, who established the anti-clerical reforms by dictatorial decrees and exiled clerics who opposed his orders. In the period under consideration, however, the archbishop, Guevara y Lira, sought to maintain harmony with all the governments and to magnify the pastoral functions of his office in the interest of peace. His high character and his beneficence in a period of serious distress arising from continuous civil war probably revived to a certain degree the social prestige of the office. He was able to secure considerable aid for the reconstruction of the church. His promotion of ecclesiastical education and of the discipline and morale of the clergy produced a group of able and devoted followers, who supported him in his opposition to Guzmán Blanco. In the period under consideration some of these ardent churchmen passed beyond his control to enter into bitter conflict with the Masons and even with the public authorities. The agitation of the reduction of the *censos*, a fixed burden on land from which the clergy and the church secured most of their income, threatened division in the institution and brought criticism to Guevara, who supported compromise. But when the question became, in 1870, a matter of the abolition of the *censos*, the church united to oppose the measure. In the contest with Guzmán Blanco there was probably more unity of sentiment in the body than had existed at any time under the Republic; but, even so, not many members were willing to enter into active opposition to the government.

In the fluctuation of party alignments in the period, it is not possible to follow the attitude of the clergy. They had, it has been stated, probably been as a rule in opposition to the Liberals in 1846. This fact, or belief, led to radical gestures and some action against the clergy in the Liberal government that followed upon the assumption of personal rule by José Tadeo Monagas on January 24, 1848. As Secretary of the Interior in 1849, Guzmán led in the pronouncements against the clergy. In 1861, however, he declared they were largely Liberals. The pronounced intellectual radicalism of the Conservatives aroused probably more fear from the clergy than the propaganda of their opponents. Antonio José Sucre, the fire-brand of the clerical group in 1870, declared that he had up to that time been in the Liberal files. But in spite of the fact that he was the choice of the Liberal government, Guevara, head of the church, had shown great favor to the Páez-Rojas dictatorship for reasons which will be indicated below. In the political changes of the period the church question was never foremost. In 1850 and again in the years from 1862 to 1864 incidents concerning relations with the Papacy brought it, however, into considerable prominence.

José Tadeo Monagas, who came to the Presidency in 1847 as the candidate of the Conservative Oligarchy, named upon the recommendation of Páez, had been, it will be recalled, a leader of the revolutions of the thirties for the reëstablishment of military and ecclesiastical *fueros*. Upon his assumption of personal rule following the overthrow of the Congress, January 24, 1848, one might have expected that he would put such a program into execution. That he did not even attempt it might be taken as an indication of the crystallization of opinion in favor of the reforms of the Oligarchy. One of the early acts of his personal government was a decree of August 31, 1848, against the entrance into Venezuela of any individuals of either sex belonging to the Jesuit organization. Any members of this order who might be in the country were to leave at once.[1] On November 24, 1848, a representation came from the provincial assembly of Caracas to the Secretary of the Interior, which sought the expulsion of five women established under the name of Sisters of the Oratorio of San Felipe, alleging their membership in the Jesuit Order.[2] This *informe* was received by Guzmán, recently appointed to the secretaryship of the Interior.[3] It led to a second executive resolution communicated by Guzmán to the governor of the province. All foreign ecclesiastics both regular and secular were ordered to leave the country at once.[4] In issuing this decree, Guzmán took occasion to emphasize the bad conduct and intransigence of foreign clerics and to insist that, since convents were not allowed in Venezuela, regulars could not live there according to the constitutions of their own orders.

In the Congress of 1846 the project for the abolition of ecclesiastical *fueros* that Páez had vetoed in 1834 was revived. Trial in special tribunals, it was declared, was contrary to the equality of legal rights guaranteed in the Constitution of 1830; the abolition of these *fueros* was urged, moreover, on the grounds that it would free the clergy from the power of the bishop. The establishment of civil

---

[1] *Leyes y decretos*, vol. ii, pp. 244-245. This he issued in virtue of an earlier act of Congress, of March 15, 1845, that gave the executive the authority to order out of the country, or to refuse entrance to, foreigners who might be considered prejudicial to the interest of the state. (*Leyes y decretos*, vol. ii, p. 244).

[2] *Ordenanzas, resoluciones, y acuerdos de la H. Diputación Provincial de Caracas vigentes el día 10 de Deciembre de 1853*, (Caracas, 1854), p. 119.

[3] Guzmán had been found guilty on a charge of conspiracy in a famous trial in 1846 and was subject to the penalty of death; the sentence was commuted by Monagas to permanent exile on the condition that it would be executed if he should return to the country. In 1849, however, he returned and was given the office as Secretary of the Interior.

[4] Castillo, *Teatro*, vol. ii, p. 83. *Vide*, also, Villegas Pulido, G. T., *Los extranjeros en Venezuela*, 2nd edition (Caracas, 1919), pp. 20-21.

matrimony was also discussed. On neither question was action taken, but the introduction provoked protests from the clergy.[5]

Guzmán's *Memoria* of 1849 may be taken as a sort of liberal *pronunciamiento* on the clerical question. The church, he declared, was enslaved in points where it should be independent and in others, essential to the peace and harmony of society, it was out of balance with the public powers. It should be supreme in beliefs, but subject to control in all its relations to society. The patronage and tuition of the state was supreme, imprescriptible, and inalienable. Ecclesiastical *fueros* were declared a contradiction to the institutions of the country. Pastors, he considered, should be elected by the people. This process alone would free the clergy from political slavery and put it in the hands of the people whose consciences it directed. He issued another long pronouncement against foreign priests and advocated the establishment of seminaries as a means of increasing the clergy. Civil matrimony he declared essential to the promotion of immigration. Civil registry should also be made effective.[6]

The nationalistic gestures of the Liberals found an opportunity for expression in a controversy with the Papacy over the confirmation of the archbishop-elect, Pérez, in 1849 and 1850. Fernández Peña, named archbishop on the exile of Méndez, died in 1849, his death being hastened, it is said, by unhappy relations with Guzmán as Secretary of the Interior. The latter had demanded the removal of Peña's provisor, Domingo Quintero, for partisan and personal reasons: he was the brother of Angel Quintero, a conservative leader and bitter enemy of Guzmán. Objection was raised, too, on partisans grounds to the one named by Peña as the successor of Quintero. A bitter interview followed, and Peña died soon afterwards.[7] Upon the death of the archbishop, the notable liberal priest, Pérez, was elected by the Congress and on January 19, 1849, presented by the President to the Pope. Pius IX refused confirmation, stating in

[5] Among protests from the clergy are the following: *Observaciones sobre el projecto de desafuero eclesiástico archivado en la legislatura de 1834 y revivido en el senado en 1848* (Mérida, 1848) and Piñeiro, C., *Objecciones del desafuero y soluciones del fuero eclesiástico*, (Caracas, 1851). From Mérida there came decided opposition to anti-clerical proposals. Piñeiro was the leader in this opposition.

[6] *Memoria del Interior*, (1849), p. 13 *et seq.*

[7] González Guinán, *Historia contemporánea*, vol. v, p. 10, note.

explanation of his rejection that the ill-health and advanced age of Pérez rendered him unfit for the arduous task of administering a diocese where visits were made only by long and toilsome journeys. The government through Lecuna, Minister of Foreign Affairs, insisted on the confirmation, basing its insistence on precedents. No presentation of the Republic had been refused up to this time; nothing, it declared, was more contrary to Venezuelan desires than a change in the relations with the Papacy. But Pius IX remained firm in his refusal. He was urged to maintain this position, the government was convinced, by the secret information of its enemies in Venezuela. This assertion, made in a letter to the Pope, remained unanswered. Lorenzana, Colombian representative in Rome, was the agent of the Venezuelan government in the negotiations.[8] He declared in a letter to persons in Caracas that the Secretary of the Papacy had stated thus the position of Pius IX: that it belonged solely to the Pope to pass on the fitness of candidates, that he had never recognized the right of patronage in the Venezuelan government, that the principles professed by Pérez and not his age or health were the basis of the rejection.[9] Pérez was the author, it will be recalled, of the radical attack on the Papacy, *A vosotros*, published in 1832. Moreover, after the European revolutions of 1848, Pius IX had entered upon a program of uncompromising defense of the Church against the inroads made by nineteenth century nationalism and liberalism. His Venezuelan policy is merely an interesting expression of his general ecclesiastical program. No action was taken by the government to relieve the *impasse*, which continued until the death of Pérez in 1852. Guevara, elected upon the recommendation of Monagas, was confirmed at once.

The incident provoked much discussion and writing in periodicals and pamphlets. Members of the clergy and other orthodox Catholics saw unity with Rome endangered and took advantage of

---

[8] *Memoria del Interior,* (1851) pp. 15-16; (1852), p. 37. The Pope had not sanctioned, moreover, the erection of two new bishoprics, Barquisimeto and Calabozo, ordered by the government in 1847.

[9] Larrazábal, Felipe, *Colección de artículos sobre la cuestión arzobispo de Caracas y Venezuela publicados en "El patriota,"* reprinted, (Caracas, 1852). These give a detailed discussion of the incident with much of the correspondence.

the occasion to urge a concordat.[10] Anti-clerical writers, one of the chief of whom was Larrazábal, insisted that the government should place Pérez in office with or without the bulls of confirmation. The old argument that Venezuela inherited the right of patronage from Spain he insisted should be discarded; the right was inherent in sovereignty; it was inalienable and imprescriptible. "If Venezuela possesses the right of patronage as a sovereign regalia," he declared, "the chambers now about to assemble will respect the supreme act of the election of Pérez, and he will unquestionably be Archbishop of Caracas."[11] *El republicano* declared that, if confirmation were delayed longer, the President should order the Venezuelan bishops to consecrate Pérez for the office.[12] Another writer, who stated that he was a Catholic, seventy-three years old, insisted that the Republic should declare categorically to the Pope that it did not recommend Pérez, but presented him; that he should be placed in office at once "to show that the government had head and members capable of ruling the church in perfect accord with the Republic."[13] Although there was much talk of separation from Rome, no change was made in the anomalous position of the state with reference to the Papacy. No concordat was concluded with the Pope; yet the government did not declare independence nor establish a national church.

It may be well at this point to pass on to consider further relations with the Papacy during this period. Under the dictatorship of Páez, on May 6, 1862, Guevara, then in Rome on a religious mission, was given authority by the government to open negotiations with the Papacy for the establishment of a concordat. He was instructed to take proper care that any agreement formed did not

---

[10] Among the many pamphlets that appeared, the following might be mentioned: Yépez, José Marcario, *Origen de las dos potestades, civil y eclesiástica: La independencia de la una respecta de la otra y sus consecuencias,* (Barquisimeto, 1852); *Respuesta al papel titulado "Las bulas,"* (signed C. P.) Mérida, 1851; *Un católico á "El patriota" en la cuestión Arzobispo de Caracas,* (Caracas, 1851). Yépez, the author of the first, was one of the most vigorous protagonists of the rights of the church in this period; C. P., the author of the second, was, no doubt, Civiaco Piñeiro, of Mérida, equally outspoken in the defense of the institution.

[11] Larrazábal, *Colección de artículos,* p. 31.

[12] *El republicano,* August 28, 1850.

[13] *Las bulas ó sea lo que se debe hacer en el cuestión acerca del arzobispo electo,* (Caracas, 1851). Pérez's *A vosotros* was reprinted at this time. In answer to it there was published, *A la reimpresión del "A vosotros"* (Caracas, 1851), which declared it a recapitulation of common errors.

contravene the Law of the Patronage. In September, 1862, he brought back a concordat, which he had signed in Rome with Cardinal Antonelli, Secretary of State to Pius IX. This agreement contained the following provisions:

Article 1. The Catholic, apostolic, Roman religion shall continue being the religion of the Republic of Venezuela and the government shall recognize the duty of defending it with all the rights and prerogatives that belong to it by virtue of the ordination of God and the authority of the sacred canons.[14]

Article 2. The education of youth in universities, colleges, and other schools, public and private, as well as in other establishments of instruction shall be entirely conformable to the Catholic religion. Bishops and the ordinary clergy shall have the direction of the doctrine in faculties of theology, canon law, and other ecclesiastical institutions with complete freedom. They shall also be able to determine whether there is anything contrary to the Catholic religion and purity of customs in other studies.

Article 3. The existing seminaries shall be conserved, and, conformable to the rules of the Council of Trent, the bishops shall be free in the erection, discipline, and administration of said seminaries. The rectors and professors of these institutions shall be named by the bishops and removed when they esteem it necessary.

Article 4. Bishops shall examine and censor books of all kinds relative to faith, ecclesiastical discipline, and public morals; and the government shall lend the assistance of its authority and shall coöperate to sustain the dispositions of the bishops with reference to the canons.

Article 5. The bishops as well as the clergy and the people shall communicate freely with the Roman Pontiff, since, by divine right, he is head and center of the universal church.

Article 6. By means of its minister plenipotentiary the government of Venezuela shall seek and obtain from the Papacy a concession that, considering the extraordinary circumstances, the ecclesiastical appropriations be substituted for the tenth. In consequence of this concession, the government shall be obliged to pay from the

[14] This is not a complete translation of the document.

public treasury as a national debt the assignments that are expressed in the note adjoined to this concordat. The clergy shall continue to enjoy the right of receiving the primacies and the stole according to the custom of each diocese and the rates prescribed by the *sinodales* or that shall be established in the future by the ecclesiastical authority.

Article 7. As a consequence of the obligations assumed by the government, the Supreme Pontiff concedes to the President of the Republic of Venezuela the right of patronage and the privilege of proposing the bishops according to the terms established by the present convention.

Article 8. The President shall propose those with qualities required by the sacred canons, and the Pope shall confirm them, according to rules prescribed by the church; they shall not enter on their duties, however, until the bulls are received.

Article 9. All the dispositions that have been in force with regard to the *espolios* of the archbishop and bishop shall remain in force; and as a result, the said *espolios* shall belong to the respective cathedral churches.

Article 10. The President shall name those for all the offices of dignitaries, except the official ones, and also the remaining prebendaries and present them to the ecclesiastical prelates, so that if they be worthy, these may give them canonical institution. But the first dignitary of the metropolitan shall be reserved always to the free disposition of the Papacy and in the other cathedrals one of the Canons of Merced.

Article 11. The official canons shall be provided according to the rules of the canon law, and the bishops shall present three from whom the president shall choose one.

Article 12. As soon as the state of the public treasury permits, the prebends in the metropolitan church shall be reëstablished.

Article 13. As soon as possible, a seminary shall be established in Guayana.

Article 14. In case of a vacancy in the episcopate, the chapter shall elect freely according to the canons the one who shall govern the diocese, and such an election shall not be revoked.

Article 15. All parishes shall be provided in concourse accord-

ing to the rules of the Council of Trent. Lists shall be formed by
the ordinary clergy, and the president or provincial executive shall
choose one.

Article 16.   The ordinary clergy shall choose their coadjutors.

Article 17.   The Papacy shall erect new dioceses in agreement
with the government.   In each there shall be a chapter and a seminary.   The endowment of each shall be according to the norm of
those existing.

Article 18.   Parishes shall be erected by the ordinary clergy in
each diocese according to the canons and in agreement with the
government.

Article 19.   All causes of faith and of duties and rights belonging to the ministry, questions of matrimony, and any other of an
ecclesiastical nature shall belong to the jurisdiction of the ecclesiastical
authority.

Article 20.   The ecclesiastical *fuero* shall be conserved in the
Republic in the civil causes of the clergy.   As to the criminal causes,
the same shall be conserved, the Papacy consenting that it remain
within the limits to which it is now reduced by law.

Article 21.   The bishops shall be free to correct the clergy who
do not live conformable to the rules of the church.

Article 22.   The church shall retain the right that it now has to
acquire and possess properties and sacred foundations under any
proper title, which right shall be inviolable and therefore not to be
suppressed without the intervention of the Papacy.

Article 23.   In consideration of the circumstances of the times,
the Pope consents that ecclesiastical goods be subject to common im-
posts, churches, seminaries, and other institutions of worship being
excepted.

Article 24.   To ease consciences the Pope shall remove all obligations as to the tenth under the law of 1833; also, as to other ecclesiastical goods received or the *censos* redeemed under the laws of the
Republic; but it shall be kept in mind that these abusive alienations
shall never be repeated.

Article 25.   Convents of nuns shall be conserved, and prelates
shall be able with entire freedom to erect others.   As to those of

monks, the prelates shall be able to establish them according to the canons, placing itself in agreement with the government.

Article 26. The government shall continue trying to promote the conversion and instruction of the Indians.

Article 27. The ecclesiastics shall be able to take the oath in this form: "I swear and promise God by the Holy Evangel to obey and be faithful to the government established by the Constitution of the Republic of Venezuela; and I promise, also, not to be concerned personally nor by means of counsel in any project that may be contrary to the national independence and the public tranquillity."

Article 28. It shall be permitted that in the ancient collect the name of the President of the Republic shall be mentioned after those of the Pope and the bishops.

Article 29. Everything not mentioned in the concordat shall be regulated according to the discipline of the church approved by the Papacy.

Article 30. All laws, ordinances, and decrees of the Republic of Venezuela that are contrary to this convention shall be abrogated by it, and it shall be considered in force always and be regarded as the law of the Republic. If any difficulty should arise over the points contained in this treaty, the Pope and the President of the Republic shall resolve them by common agreement.

Article 31. The ratification of the present concordat shall be exchanged in Rome within a year, or sooner if it should be possible.[15]

This convention, submitted by Páez to the Council of State, was approved by that body on February 28, 1863, with a single objection raised: it would strike out the adjective "abusive" applied in Article 24 to the alienation of church property. Páez signed it on March 6.[16]   Soon afterwards, on June 6, 1863, the dictatorship of Páez ended in a treaty with Falcón, an agreement effected through the efforts of Guevara. In accordance with the Law of the Patronage

---

[15] Guevara y Lira, Silvestre, *Observaciones sobre el concordato de Venezuela celebrado en Roma en julio de 1862 y ratificado por su Santidad, May 25, 1863,* (Caracas, 1864). This gives the text of the concordat. It is found also in González Guinán, *Historia contemporánea,* vol. viii, pp. 93-99.

[16] *Memoria del relaciones exteriores,* (1863), pp. 87-88. It is hard to understand this conduct of Páez except as a policy adopted possibly to strengthen his dictatorship by securing the support of the church. Soon afterwards he praised in his *Autobiografía* the action of the Venezuelan government against the church.

the new government sent the concordat, approved by the Páez dictatorship, to the Congress as the only authority for amending that law. The Congress submitted it for investigation to a commission composed of María Salón, J. D. Landaeta, and Maximino Castillo. This committee returned an unfavorable report. Objections were raised on the grounds that the convention was not in harmony with the Law of the Patronage; the powers of Congress under the Law of 1824 were ignored; the naming of dignitaries was given to the President alone; and the granting of licenses to bulls and briefs was omitted altogether; the erection of dioceses was granted to the Pope; religious societies of women were placed beyond the control of the government; the ecclesiastical authority was granted the right of inspection of teaching and of books. Special objection was raised to the conservation of ecclesiastical *fueros,* which were pronounced improper in a democracy. Conflicts between the concordat and the spirit and letter the Constitution of 1864 were also pointed out; it was opposed to the rights of religious liberty and freedom of the press granted in that instrument. Finally, it was pointed out, the concordat annulled all laws, ordinances, and decrees of the Republic not in harmony with it; this provision contravened the fundamental principle of the sovereignty of the state. The commission proposed that the executive open anew negotiations with the Papacy in order to place the concordat in harmony with the laws of the country and with the spirit and letter of the constitution that had just been sanctioned.[17]

This report was adopted by the Congress. In June, 1864, Lucio Pulido was named minister to Rome to negotiate a new concordat. Nothing came, however, of the mission.[18] This ended the efforts, or gestures, of the Republic toward according an agreement with the Papacy with regard to the recognition of the patronage. It is interesting to note that, although Venezuela had enacted three constitutions within a period of seven years, all governments, with the single exception of the dictatorial administration of Páez, had refused categorically to admit any change in the civil constitution of

[17] González Guinán, *Historia contemporánea,* vol. viii, p. 293 gives in brief the report of the commission.
[18] *Memoria del relaciones exteriores,* (1865), p. 90; (1867), p. 76.

the clergy. In a century of the life of the Republic there have been twenty political constitutions, but only one constitution of the church. As Navarro points out, Venezuelan historians have regarded the failure to effect an agreement with Rome as a national victory without admitting that ecclesiastical affairs have thereby remained backward and discipline decrepit and in many respects anachronous.[19]

II

THERE WAS little legislation of a fundamental character on the church in the two decades under consideration. Provisions on religion in the Constitutions of 1857, 1858, and 1864 should, however, be mentioned; also, certain laws affecting directly or indirectly the interests of the institution should be considered. The Constitution of 1857, dictated by Monagas, was reactionary on the question of religion. Article 1 of this instrument stated: "The state shall protect the Catholic, apostolic, Roman religion and the government shall sustain always this worship and its ministers according to the law." This resulted, however, in no change in practice. Monagas would not have dared, Gil Fortoul observed, to establish an exclusive religion of state, as he had sought to do in his insurrection of 1831.[20] The Constitution of 1858 suppressed this article. The fundamental law of 1864 granted freedom of worship, but declared that the Catholic religion alone could be exercised outside the churches. In the constituent assembly that framed the Constitution of 1858, the abolition of political privileges of the clergy was advocated. This proposal was introduced also in the constituent assembly of 1864.[21] It might be noted here that Venezuela has never dispossessed the clergy of the political rights as Mexico has done. Since 1830 churchmen have been prominent in political office; Talavera, José Félix Blanco, and Guevara had been members of the Council of State. This participation of the clergy in politics is another of those curious contradictions in Venezuelan anti-clericalism; it in-

---

[19] Navarro, *Anales eclesiásticos*, p. 215 note. Gil Fortoul gave, in his *Historia constitucional*, vol. ii (1st edition) p. 492 *et seq.*, a criticism of this proposed concordat and congratulated the nation on its failure.

[20] Gil Fortoul, *op. cit.*, 1st edition, vol. ii, p. 318.

[21] *El federalista*, September 21, 1864.

dicates, no doubt, the assurance of the government of its predominance of power. The clergy are politically innocuous.

In a decree of April 22, 1856, the separation of the Seminary of Santa Rosa from the University of Caracas was ordered. It was provided that the prelate should draw up a constitution in agreement with the institutions of the country and submit it to the Congress in the next session. Guevara never submitted the Constitution, an omission overlooked possibly in the confusion of the period.[22] The seminary continued under the direction of the archbishop until it was suppressed by Guzmán Blanco in 1872. Guevara was tireless in his efforts to promote ecclesiastical education. Upon his request, Felipe Larrazábal wrote a *History of Clerical Seminaries* in encouragement of the work. Talavera used for the same purpose the columns of his scholarly religious periodical, *Crónica eclesiática*, which had been recently established. Guevara experienced great difficulty, however, in securing funds. By the law in which its separation from the University was ordered, the seminary was to enjoy the incomes from certain chaplaincies.[23] Guevara declared in force the disposition of Mauro de Tovar for the imposition of a three per cent tax on the income of all benefices. The narrowness of these, however, restricted the returns from this source.[24] In spite of these difficulties, nevertheless, he was able by his zeal to achieve much toward the improvement of clerical education.

Ecclesiastical appropriations were increased by law in 1853.[25] There were, in addition, many special grants made for the construction and repair of churches. Such were frequent, too, in the next decade. Since little had been done for this purpose under the Republic, the buildings were in great need of repair. Earthquakes, too, destroyed many churches; a serious one in Cumaná in 1854 brought special grants to that section for the building of churches. In the almost constant disturbance and civil war of the period, governments failed, however, to meet these obligations. In his opposition in 1855 to the reduction of the *censos*, Yépez complained that the eccle-

---

[22] *Leyes y decretos*, vol. iii, p. 86.
[23] *Ibid.*
[24] Larrazábal, Felipe, *Historia de los seminarios clericales* (Caracas, 1856), pp. xvii-xxi.
[25] *Leyes y decretos*, vol. iii, pp. 77-78.

siastical appropriations had not been paid for eight years, or, in other words, since the Liberal government came into power.[26] In a protest against an executive decree of July 14, 1865, which reduced by one-half the ecclesiastical appropriations, the bishop and the chapter of the diocese of Mérida declared they were reduced to misery, that the appropriations had not been paid for years.[27] There are many similar statements of the precarious condition of ecclesiastical incomes in these years. Such complaints had not been heard against the Conservative Oligarchy.

Curacies, moreover, were still unfilled. In 1855, only one hundred fifty-four of the four hundred seventy-five parishes were occupied by regular pastors.[28] During the war parishes were suppressed on account of lack of resources. Although the restoration of the missions continued to be discussed for a time, nothing was accomplished. Andrés Level, sent by the government in 1850 as visitor to Upata, issued a notable report on the status of the reduction. Of sixteen of the ancient missions of Caroní only the sites remained. There were ten parishes that contained some Indians; four of these had no churches and the buildings in others were hardly fit for use. Eleven parishes contained only inhabitants of Spanish descent. The Indians had been touched but slightly.[29] Michelena y Rojas, sent in 1855, issued likewise an able report on the conditions.[30] There were, however, neither funds nor missionaries with which to promote the work. In 1858, the executive was again given the authority to bring foreign priests, but there are no records of the introduction of any.[31] Reports mentioned only the futile efforts of the two or three that remained. The promotion was finally discontinued altogether, to be revived again only at the end of the century.

The erection of two new bishoprics, Barquisimeto and Calabozo, had been decreed in 1847.[32] This, it was thought, would promote the increase of the clergy and improve the administration and the

---

[26] Navarro, *Anales*, pp. 211-212, note.
[27] *Memoria del Interior* (1866), *Documentos*, pp. 12-13.
[28] *Ibid.*, (1855), *Documentos*, p. 45.
[29] Level, Andrés, *Informe sobre el estado actual de los distritos de reducción de indígenas en el Orinoco*, (Caracas, 1850).
[30] Michelena y Rojas, Francisco, *Exploración oficial*, (Brussels, 1867).
[31] *Leyes y decretos*, vol. iii, p. 574.
[32] *Ibid.*, vol. ii, pp. 377-378.

discipline by reducing the distance from the episcopal center. The creation of neither of these became effective, however, until 1867, when a bishop was named for the former. Difficulties over the selection of an episcopal center and over the confirmation of a bishop delayed further the erection of the latter.[33] The lack of unity in administration was exaggerated by the disturbed conditions of the times. The Secretary of the Interior in reporting the appointment of bishops for the new sees took occasion to comment on the excesses of the clergy in deserting their duties to take part in the revolution.[34] The government in 1859 had asked the archbishop to dictate measures to prevent the participation of priests in the war.[35] Objection was raised that this was contrary to the Law of the Patronage, that it belonged to the government, not to the archbishop, to restrain rebellious clerics.[36] Apparently the control of neither was effective. In 1863, the government again urged the archbishop to discipline the clergy in the interest of their pastoral functions, stating that pastors were frequently found deserting their parishes to serve others or to serve none.[37] Although there was still rigid insistence on the Law of the Patronage, its execution in these years in the control of the clergy was not so effective.

There was trouble with some of the higher clergy as well as with the lower. In 1864, complaint was brought by the governor of Mérida against the Bishop, Boset, for a year's unexplained absence from his see.[38] In answering the complaint the chapter declared that governments changed so often that the bishop might be in his see without the knowledge of the government. And, it protested, "Is the bishopric a dependency of the president of the state that the bishop must notify him when he wishes to be absent?" It objected to the use of the term, *usted*, in addressing the bishop. Even cultured France, it asserted, gave the title Monseñor; but in Mérida the mitre was addressed only in the form the constitution required for all civil

---

[33] *Memoria del Interior*, (1861), pp. 23-24; (1869), pp. civ-v. *Memoria de las relaciones exteriores*, (1869), p. 115.

[34] *Memoria del Interior*, (1861), pp. 23-24.

[35] *El heraldo*, September 21, 1859.

[36] *Ibid.*, September 24, 1845.

[37] *Memoria del Interior*, (1863), pp. 55-57.

[38] He had gone to Rome, it seems.

employes. The chapter declared that the action of the governor was destroying all respect for the clergy in Mérida; that it would probably be necessary to move the seat of the bishopric, and, hence, the province would lose the material and moral advantages derived from it. The government, it declared, sought to exile from that soil the profound respect that ministers had always inspired. The chapter went on to criticize the work of the Constituent Congress then in session. "To avoid useless contests in the future," it stated in closing, "the chapter concludes by declaring that from this time it will accept no law or disposition contrary to the canons of the church whatever be the authority from which it emanates."[39] In 1870, further trouble arose with the ecclesiastical government of Mérida over the publication of an interdict. The government ordered the raising of the interdict on the grounds that it threatened to produce disturbance and that the authority for the declaration came from a bull of 1867 to which the government had not given license. The chapter contended that the civil government had no right to intervene. It protested, further, against the refusal of the civil authorities to attend the solemnities on the anniversary of the earthquake of 1812.[40]

These incidents indicate the recrudescence of a spirit of resistance resembling that of an earlier period and contribute to an explanation of the intransigence of 1870. The comments of the chapter of the bishopric of Mérida as to the ignorance of the various governments that came into power with regard to the state of the diocese suggests, too, a reason for the ineffectiveness in the execution of the Law of the Patronage. Even in normal times it was difficult of administration in the more distant dioceses of Mérida and Guayana. In 1857, complaint was made that in the latter the collection of fees under the old rates of the bishopric of Porto Rico was still allowed.[41] Fortique had found on entering upon his duties as bishop here in 1846 that there was no uniform practice observed by pastors in the administration of their parishes, in spite of various efforts made earlier to extend the *sinodales* of Caracas to the diocese. To correct

---

[39] *El federalista*, September 21 and 27, 1864; October 4, 1864.
[40] *Documentos de Secretaría del Interior* (1870), No. 75.
[41] *Memoria del Interior*, (1857), p. 3.

the lack of unity within his own diocese, he issued in 1847 a detailed statement of instructions, a very able document celebrated in Venezuelan ecclesiastical history.[42]   As to Mérida, the secretary of the Interior declared in 1869 that even before the war little was known of it because of the slowness of communication and that since the outbreak of civil strife the government had no knowledge of "that remote diocese."[43]

The question of the reduction of the *censos,* or of its redemption by certificates of public indebtedness, was a further source of unrest and resistance among the clergy.   Most of their income came from this form of fixed contribution from landed property; moreover, the income of the church itself was largely from this source.   The seminary depended almost solely on it, since the income of the chaplaincies belonging to it came from the *censos.*   The contribution was, however, a great burden upon agriculture; some reduction had been made in it on that ground under the government of Gran Colombia in 1824.   In the economic crisis of the early eighteen-hundred-forties it had become a leading factor in the Liberal opposition to the government of the Oligarchy.[44]

The Congress of 1855 considered the question of the reduction of the *censos;* it was opposed in the Senate by Guevara and Boset.[45] But when it was proposed that it be extinguished entirely by certificates of public indebtedness, these bishops, after a conference with a group of the clergy, favored the reduction from five to three per cent.   Although there was criticism of their action by a part of the clergy, notably José Marcario Yépez of Mérida, they defended it on the grounds that a reduction was preferable to the complete redemption by compensation in government notes.[46]   No action was taken on the question at the time.

Following the Federal war, however, the question of the reduction or redemption of the *censos* was reintroduced.   In his report of 1866 the Secretary of the Interior admitted that reduction involved

[42] Fortique, Mariano, *Instrucción pastoral,* (Caracas, 1847).

[43] *Memoria del Interior,* (1869), p. cv.

[44] *Vide,* for example Guzmán, *Editoriales, passim.*

[45] *Diario de debates,* May 2, 1855.

[46] *Crónica eclesiástica,* April 4, May 2, June 13, and August 22, 1855.

grave interests that were worthy of consideration; that the clergy and other holders of the *censos* should be considered as well as the agriculturists and an attempt made to reconcile the interests of the two groups.[47] By a law of 1866, supported by a special representation of the bishops, the *censos* was reduced to three per cent on all capital, whether civil or ecclesiastical; that due for the period of the war, from March 1, 1858, to June 30, 1863, was cancelled altogether.[48] The matter was not considered settled, however, and the unrest among the clergy over it continued. Although some were willing to compromise, all would unite to prevent complete extinction. González Guinán stated that he knew only one priest who favored the decree of Guzmán Blanco issued in 1870 for the abolition of the *censos*.[49]

Conflict between the clergy and the Masons was renewed in this period. Although the organization had been revived and was flourishing by 1840, no trouble appears to have been provoked with the church under the Conservative Oligarchy and the Monagas government. In this period of partial accommodation between the church and the government, the clergy seemed to have adopted a tolerant attitude toward the Masons.[50] Some were, no doubt, members of the lodges. By 1860, however, a different attitude was evidenced; it was a further indication of the growing spirit of resistance in the body of the clergy. The Masons accused the church of circulating bulls against the order without the license of the government.[51] However that may be, it seems that opposition was encouraged by closer contacts with the papal government of Pius IX. The visits of Guevara and Boset to Rome have been mentioned, and the rebellious spirit of certain groups of the clergy against further infringement on canon law indicated.

A notable controversy with the Masons arose over the refusal of a certain priest, Andrés Domínguez, to give confession and eccle-

[47] *Memoria del Interior*, 1866, pp. 39-43.
[48] *Leyes y decretos*, vol. iv, p. 483.
[49] González Guinán, *Historia contemporánea*, vol. ix, p. 440.
[50] Navarro, *La iglesia y la masonería en Venezuela*, p. 19.
[51] Ascanio Rodríguez, J. B. *Apuntes y documentos para la historia del registro civil en Venezuela*, (Caracas, 1925), pp. 4-14.

siastical burial to a Mason, José Ruíz.[52] A commission of the Grand
Lodge of Caracas appealed to the archbishop. Although the latter
deplored the incident and promised that such would be discouraged,
he did not censure the conduct of the priest.[53] He wished, however,
to prevent controversy. The protagonist of the church in the matter
was the archdeacon of the metropolitan church, Antonio José Sucre,
who defended the action of Domínguez in a series of fiery articles in
the press.[54] This incident, with others that might be mentioned,
brought more widespread discussion of civil marriage and civil registry. The Masons of the country united in a petition to the Congress in 1867 for civil matrimony. This Congress, the Masons
declared, was, however, under clerical influence, and nothing was
done.[55] Páez stated in his *Autobiografía* that it interpreted badly
the object of the representation; he hoped that the next legislature
would act favorably upon the petition.[56] The attack of the Masons
on the church was to reach its climax in the following period in the
apotheosis of Guzmán Blanco by the order and its support of his anti-
clerical decrees.

In the unrest of the period Guevara had been praised by all political groups. He had shown zeal and energy in his office. Felipe
Larrazábal proclaimed him the model pastor. Cecilio Acosta was
equally extravagant in praise of him. In a period of social distress
from war, plague, and earthquake, he had been untiring in acts of
beneficence. He had been prominent, too, in political life as senator
under the Monagas régime and as a member of the Council of State
under the dictatorship of Páez. He had attempted to accommodate
conflicting interests. On the clerical question he had shown a willing-
ness to compromise—he hoped to win by conceding something. The
growing spirit of rebellion against civil restrictions among the clergy
is indicated by its criticism of his concessions. But Guevara was not
a mere opportunist. When the battle became drawn between the

[52] *El federalista*, April 29, 1864.
[53] Ascanio Rodríguez, *Apuntes*, 4-14.
[54] *La iglesia y la masonería: Casos de consciencia suscitados por el arcediano de esta Santa Iglesia Metropolitana* (Caracas, 1865).
[55] Ascancio Rodríguez, *op. cit.*, pp. v-xv.
[56] Paéz, *Autobiografía*, vol. ii, p. 124.

church and Guzmán Blanco, he became inflexible in his defense of the rights of the church. And resistance on the part of the clergy became open rebellion in the case of some of its members. In the renewal of conflict and evidences of intransigence in the ranks of the clergy, the period from 1848 to 1870 prepared the way for the ruthless attacks of the Dictator on the institution.

CHAPTER V

GUZMÁN BLANCO AND THE CHURCH

I

THE CONTRAST between the constitutional government of the Conservative Oligarchy and the personal rule of Guzmán Blanco is displayed nowhere more distinctly than in the attitude of each toward the church. The Oligarchy opposed the institution as a force presuming to assert independence of the nation; an institution whose immunities were destructive to civil equalitarianism and whose obscurantism was hostile to the enlightenment of the age. Its leaders sought to reduce the church to submission to the national will and to destroy its intellectual dominance. Its policy was radical and uncompromising, but it was consistent, based on principles, and it followed a course prescribed by law. If personal bitterness was not absent from the contest—and it was not absent under the administration of Guzmán as Secretary of the Interior—such an attitude did not remove the conflict from the high plane of constitutional and legal procedure.

Under Guzmán Blanco the situation was very different. It could hardly be said that his intellectual reaction to religion and the church was radical. Certainly his expressions of a personal attitude are not consistently so. Indeed, as a young man, he was noticed in the society of Caracas for his orations on religious subjects, and he continued to display on occasion a decided religiosity.[1] His conception of his "providental mission" as head of the Venezuelan state and his desire to magnify, even to deify, himself as *caudillo* of his people could only issue, it would seem, from a mind with much of mysticism in its content. He was, in addition, leader of a party that had advocated

---

[1] Orations given in the "Sociedad de María" are found in *Glorias del ilustre americano, regenerador, y pacificador de Venezuela, General Guzmán Blanco*, (Caracas, 1875). For contradictory statements made later on religion and the church, *vide.*, Olavarría, *Estudios históricos*, pp. 469-470.

greater freedom for the church intellectually and religiously, even though radical in its attacks on its privileges.

But upon his assumption of dictatorial power Guzmán Blanco found his will opposed by the intransigence of a prelate, and success in that intransigence would have reduced his own personal prestige. Persuasive methods having failed, he set out to break the resistance of Guevara and his supporters by any means at hand. Archbishop Méndez had been exiled for violation of a law and only after a trial according to legal forms. Guevara was expelled for an act against which there was no law; he was given no hearing under judicial process. Priests were exiled or thrown into prison for expressing sympathy with him. Guzmán Blanco went on to destroy then the work that Guevara had built up with such untiring efforts; some of it, too, under the express encouragement of the Liberal Party. His first attack was directed against the seminaries in which the Archbishop had taken a peculiar pride; no part of his reconstruction of the church had been so close to his heart, and Guzmán Blanco knew it. Their destruction was a personal affront to Guevara. There followed then the extinction of the convents for nuns—institutions in which Guevara had taken a special interest—and the expulsion of the members from the one in Caracas in the midst of unedifying scenes. The abolition of all ecclesiastical *fueros,* the extinction of primacies, restriction upon the rights of the clergy to inherit property, the establishment of civil marriage and civil registry, the removal of the prohibitions on the marriage of the clergy, were steps in the continuance of the war on the church.

But it was not so much the reforms instituted as the method and spirit in which they were brought about that distinguished the anticlericalism of Guzmán Blanco. The reforms, to be sure, had been advocated by the Oligarchy; demands for civil marriage and civil registry had recently been made prominent in the conflict between the church and the Masons. And in instituting these measures the dictator appealed to the principles of national sovereignty and the supremacy of the law—traditions established by the Oligarchy and still possessing high prestige—and to the liberalism and fraternalism of the Masonic program. He paid tribute, also, to the growing liberalism of thought in Europe on religious and clerical questions. But behind his acts and giving chief motive to them, one may well believe, was personal resentment at finding his will obstructed by a churchman and his own prestige lowered thereby: they issued from injured egotism. Added to his own outraged emotion as a motive for the attack was the personal grudge of his minister, Urbaneja, toward Guevara for the refusal of the latter to grant him a marriage dispensation. Decrees against the church and against individual clergymen were executed, moreover, with an absence of dignity and decorum, to put it mildly, that reduced the clergy to contempt in the minds of the people; indeed, to an ignominy from which it has never been able to regain any prestige. The most unlovely features of the anti-clerical war in Venezuela, aside from certain brutal acts of the uncultured Castro and possibly some proscriptions of Gómez can be attributed to the Guzmáns, father and son, and they issued in each case from personal or partisan motives. A. L. Guzmán's war on Méndez and his controversy with Peña over the Quinteros have been cited.

For the bitterness of the conflict with Guzmán Blanco, the clergy cannot, however, be entirely freed from responsibility. They laid themselves open to attack through their partisanship and intransigence; they sought to excite a religious war against the Liberal *caudillo* and his supporters. This was true, at least, of a part of the body. One of the first acts of Guzmán Blanco, after he was proclaimed provisional president following his victory of April 27, 1870, was the declaration on May 7, 1870, of a decree ordering the redemption of the *censos* by certificates of public indebtedness. This decree consolidated the clergy for the opposition, identified by the Guzmanistas as the Conservative or *godo* group; it was, in fact, a combination of former Liberals, Conservatives, and followers of Monagas. The war then assumed a ferocious character, González Guinán asserted, the opposition taking advantage of the religious fanaticism aroused.[2] For example, Guzmán Blanco wrote from Valencia, September 19, 1870, to the ministry at Caracas that Delgado should be removed and a liberal priest appointed; that this priest had almost succeeded in covering the Oligarchical cause in

---

[2] González Guinán, *Historia contemporánea*, vol. ix, p. 440.

Carabobo with religious sanctions; that the church in Valencia was the headquarters of the reactionary Oligarchy of the west.[3] Similar complaint was made of the church in Cojedes and other places.[4] Both the extent of the activity of the clergy and their effectiveness in consolidating support to the opposition were, no doubt, exaggerated, but their action was sufficient to identify the institution with the group. The *Opinión nacional,* organ of the Liberal Party, declared in June, 1870, that writings were circulating in the name of the clergy of Caracas with the aim of fomenting revolution against the government.[5] Domingo Quintero, governor of the archbishopric in the absence of Guevara, who was then in Rome, replied that he knew nothing of this.[6] None of these complaints, moreover, touched the archbishop. Returning from Rome in July, he met Guzmán Blanco in La Guaira, and cordial courtesies were exchanged between them. Indeed, it was believed that Guevara would be able to reconcile any difficulties that had arisen or might arise.[7]

In the metropolitan church, however, there was an ecclesiastic destined to play a leading part in the events that followed the exile of the archbishop and in later armed revolts against the Guzmán Blanco government. This was Antonio José Sucre, who, it will be recalled, led in the attacks on the Masons in 1864. Sucre is not one of the least interesting personalities in this war of personalities. His rôle in the present controversy merits some brief review of his earlier career. Nephew of the great Revolutionary leader, Antonio Sucre, the grand marshal of Ayacucho, he was a student in Caracas at the time of the famous incident of January 24, 1848, the dissolution of the Congress by José Tadeo Monagas. He had urged Palacio, the President of the House, to remain at his place.[8] As a consequence of his participation in this event, he fled to Colombia. Here for a time he followed the military career, then entered the church and was ordained by Archbishop Herrán. At the time of his return to Caracas in 1862, he was a prebendary in the Cathedral of Bogotá.

[3] *Documentos para la historia de Venezuela, Memorandum del General Guzmán Blanco,* (Caracas, 1876), p. 76.
[4] *Ibid.,* p. 107.
[5] *La opinión nacional,* June 30, 1870.
[6] *Ibid.*
[7] *Ibid.,* July 27, 1870.
[8] González Guinán, *Historia contemporánea,* vol. iv, p. 469.

His association with the church in Colombia, where the integrity of the institution had not been weakened, probably accounts in a large part for the vigor of his defense of ecclesiastical privileges in Venezuela. Upon the recommendation of Páez he was made archdeacon of the cabildo of the metropolitan church of Caracas in 1863. Guevara gave him a place in the seminary, where he became known as a gifted teacher, a fact that explains, no doubt, his great influence over the archbishop, who regarded the promotion of ecclesiastical education as his chief work. Sucre became, indeed, a force throughout the church in Caracas; a man of exemplary life and scholarly attainments, he was recognized as the foremost champion of the rights of the institution. He was always, however, a disturbing influence. A severe critic of Guevara's accommodating attitude on questions of clerical interest, in 1867 he came into open dispute with the archbishop over a pastoral of the latter against usury and brought upon himself the censure of the *cabildo*.[9] His attacks on the Masons became so upsetting that the government, according to the statement of L. D. Landaeta, gave him two thousand *pesos* to make a trip to Rome in order to get rid of him.[10] He was back in Caracas, however, in 1870 and opposing in the press the government decree on the *censos*.[11] In the political revolts of this year, he seems, on the other hand, to have had no part, and was still on friendly terms with the Liberal Party.

The decisive victory over General Matías Salazar on September 21, r870, gave Guzmán Blanco hope of a definitive consolidation of his control and the advent of peace. He instructed José Ignacio Pulido, head of the government at Caracas during his absence in the war, to order a *Te Deum* said in gratitude for this favor of the deity and as a further means of consolidating peace. This order was communicated to Guevara on September 27 through Diego B. Urbaneja,

[9] *Opiniones sobre el préstamo á interés y justificación de ellas*, (Caracas, 1867). For facts relating to his career, *vide* Navarro, *Anales*, pp. 259-260, note. After the suppression of the revolution against Guzmán Blanco, Sucre went South through Ecuador to Chile. In Santiago he belonged for some years to a religious community; he left it as a result of an impulsive rudeness to the superior, who had declared that the Venezuelans were cowards to submit to the oppression of Guzmán Blanco.

[10] *La opinión nacional*, April 14, 1873.

[11] *Ibid.*, July 1, 1870.

Secretary of the Interior.[12] In reply Guevara took occasion to pro-
nounce judgment on the conduct of the war; he went further to
suggest that the celebration of a *Te Deum* should be deferred until a
"frank and perfect amnesty" had been declared and political prisoners
released. "These are the motives," he concluded, "that induce me
to postpone the celebration of the religious . . . solemnities that the
government demands until it shall accord . . . the measure of magnanimity and political wisdom I have been permitted to indicate."[13]

From Urbaneja there came an immediate reply, pronouncing
exile on the archbishop to be executed within twenty-four hours. No
reconsideration was granted. The government, he asserted, did not
find it strange that Guevara should have desired amnesty, but it found
it surpassingly so that he should have made it a condition for the
fulfillment of an order of the civil authorities.[14] The archbishop
accepted this fate, protesting "against the violation that the national
government makes of our person, of our rights, divine and human,
ecclesiastical and civil."[15]

The political circle in Caracas were justly surprised: they had no
reason to anticipate such opposition from the archbishop. He had
accommodated his administration to the frequent political changes
that had occurred since he entered office. He had celebrated with
Te Deums the entrance into power of Páez and Falcón with the
hope of hastening thereby the establishment of peace and order. To
the dictatorship of Páez he had shown special favor, declaring in its
defense that "beyond the supreme chief there is chaos."[16] In spite
of this, the Liberals had considered Guevara an adherent to their
party; he owed his place to their election. Larrazábal, an enthusiastic admirer of the archbishop, expressed astonishment and grief
over his objection to the order of the government and its consequences; he could believe only that Guevara meant to defer its fulfillment.[17] The Guzmáns were equally astounded and regretful.

---

[12] *Documentos de Secretaría del Interior*, (1870), no. 45.
[13] *La opinión nacional*, September 28, 1870.
[14] *Ibid.*, September 28, 1870.
[15] *Ibid.*, September 28, 1870.
[16] *Documentos de Secretaría del Interior*, (1870), No. 75; Urbaneja, D. B., *El
Arzobispo S. Guevara y Lira*, (Caracas, 1872).
[17] *La opinión nacional*, October 7, 1870.

Guzmán Blanco was not hunting occasion for a war with the church; his power was yet too insecure. Indeed, he looked to the archbishop for support. On October 2, he wrote Guevara whose departure was delayed by illness:

Account has not yet been given me of what took place. Since I am so good a friend of you, since my government desired to depend upon your aid, and since you were giving it so discreetly, what has been able to cause that collision between the head of the Venezuelan Church and the government of the Republic. . . ? I believe I said to you, and I am sure I told Doctor Sucre, that as soon as the government had conquered the serious resistance of those that wished war, it would modify the rigor with which our duties oblige us to treat them until the attainment of peace. . . . I wish to know what you think in order to see if there be not some means by which we may again be as we were before that unfortunate and inexplicable conflict.[18]

In the same sentiment A. L. Guzmán wrote the Archbishop on October 19. If he had been in Caracas, he declared, such an unhappy complication would never have arisen.[19]

The news of the order of exile caused consternation among the people of Caracas, since the archbishop was very popular. A commission of prominent men, Modesto Urbaneja, Luis Vallenilla, and Nicanor Bolet Pedaza, offered their services to attempt to effect a reconciliation of the difficulties.[20] The government agreed not to recognize the notes passed between the Ministry of the Interior and Guevara. These efforts were ineffective; the archbishop refused to modify his answer to the order for the *Te Deum*.[21]

Responsibility for the failure to reconcile the conflict may be attributed in large measure to Sucre and to Urbaneja. Guevara was inclined to recede from his position, but Sucre insisted that to do so would be to sacrifice the honor and dignity of his office.[22] He hastened, moreover, to publish the official note that contained the archbishop's reply to the decree of exile.[23] What influence Sucre or

[18] *Documentos, Memoria del Interior*, (1873), pp. 69-77.
[19] *Ibid.*
[20] *La opinión nacional*, September 28, 1870.
[21] *Documentos, Memoria del Interior*, (1873), pp. 55-56.
[22] González Guinán, *Historia contemporánea*, vol. xiv, p. 447.
[23] Navarro, *Anales*, p. 252.

other ecclesiastics brought to bear on his reply to the order for the *Te Deum* is problematical. The government declared that the archbishop was allowing himself to be used as the tool of the Conservative opposition.[24] It was easy to put that interpretation on his conduct. Probably Guevara was not convinced of the ability of the Guzmanistas to secure peace; or perhaps he desired an amnesty merely as a preliminary to sanctioning the government with a religious celebration. The government protested that such had never been insisted upon before; but the severities of this war had been great, and hundreds were confined as political prisoners. Whatever may have been the motives for his first reply, he seemed willing to concede until the insistence of Sucre decided him. The fact that Urbaneja had in charge the administration of the order for the *Te Deum* helps to account, also, for the difficulties that developed. He was in disfavor with the church. Having failed to secure a dispensation to marry his step-daughter, he had married her abroad without one. Later, as governor of the Federal District, he had occasion to attend officially the celebration on Holy Thursday and to receive the key to the sepulcher. Guevara notified him in advance to send a deputy, since he could not present the key to one under such censure. Urbaneja disregarded the suggestion and suffered public humiliation as a consequence. He never forgave Guevara.[25] Instead of attempting to obtain a modification of Guevara's reply to the order, he issued a decree that gave no place for reconsideration.

The execution of the decree of exile was attended with public indignities which the character of Guevara and his status in Caracas made even less defensible than if they had been applied to an aggressive cleric like Sucre. It is probable that nothing went so far toward destroying the respect and even prestige that the clergy had been able to maintain, to some degree at least, in spite of anti-clerical legislation and education, than the excesses committed in this event and others that followed. Urbaneja was the principal promoter of these atrocities.[26] The Guzmanistas, having failed to secure an accommodation with Guevara, attempted apparently to make political capital out of

[24] *Documentos de Secretaría del Interior* (1870), no. 75.

[25] Navarro, *Anales*, p. 245.

[26] *Ibid.*, p. 254.

the event by arousing the lower classes of the city. Cristóbal González de Soto described the scene of departure as one of violence and disorder. The women of the city, who gathered about the Palace of the Archbishop to say farewell, were rudely dispersed by soldiers; some were wounded; all were insulted.[27] The entire body of the clergy of the city with the chapter issued a public memorial of support to their pastor upon his expulsion.[28] Guevara passed on to Barcelona where illness stopped him. At this place he received the letters of the Guzmáns mentioned above. An order from Urbaneja came about the same time to the president of that province, instructing him to see that the decree of exile was executed as soon as the archbishop was able to travel.[29] On January 6, 1871, Guevara emmarked for Trinidad. Up to this point the whole matter had been in the hands of this provisional Secretary of the Interior. Guzmán Blanco was now to assume the direction of further negotiations.

In his first public statement after his exile, a pastoral issued from Trinidad two years later, Guevara declared that he answered the letters of the Guzmáns, leaving open a way for reconsideration. After a silence of three months, Guzmán Blanco wrote to him in Trinidad, offering to allow him to return on the condition that he issue from that place a pastoral counselling peace. Guevara declined, declaring that an injunction issued under such conditions would have no effect, because it would appear to have been secured by force; moreover, he did not desire "to buy return to the country by an act of subjection." Restored to his diocese, he would be willing to support the government in a pastoral.[30] Nothing came of this effort, or gesture, of Guzmán Blanco for reconciliation. His long silence and his failure to continue communication after this reply would seem to indicate that his desire to adjust the controversy had cooled.

A series of incendiary letters written by Sucre to Guzmán Blanco and printed and circulated surreptitiously made more difficult a cordial adjustment with the church, if such, indeed, had ever been possible.

[27] González de Soto, Cristóbal, *Noticia histórica de la republica de Venezuela*, (Barcelona, 1873), pp. 361-363.
[28] Navarro, *Anales*, p. 253.
[29] *Documentos de Secretaría del Interior*, (1870), no. 9.
[30] *Documentos, Memoria del Interior* (1873), pp. 69-77.

These letters were begun in Caracas on October 6, 1870, and continued in Trinidad and Ciudad Bolívar until November 1, 1871. The first number appeared in the semi-official publication, *La opinión nacional* in which Sucre's articles against the redemption of the *censos* had recently been published. That such freedom of the press was to be no longer allowed was at once apparent. Guzmán Blanco issued an order for the suspension of the publication.[31] These writings in defense of Guevara and in criticism of the government, Navarro insisted, went beyond all the limits of moderation and injured the cause of the archbishop and the church.[32] In a memorial to Cardinal Antonelli, Secretary of State to the Papacy, on February 17, 1873, the government attributed the continuance of the revolution to the activity of the clergy, especially to that of Sucre, and to its encouragement by Guevara.[33] In the last of these letters, Sucre declared indeed that he wrote, if not under the direction, at least under the inspection of his prelate.[34] And Sucre left Guevara to go to Ciudad Bolívar to bless the banners of the revolutionists there. In his pastoral of 1872, Guevara asserted that he had refused the asylum offered him in the Oriente, which was still in control of the opposition, and appeared to disclaim any connection with the activities there. Olavarría contended that the Archbishop was in no way responsible for the activity of Sucre; that, in fact, he opposed it.[35] It seems probable that this is true so far as direct encouragement is concerned. But the resistance of the Archbishop gave occasion for the conversion of the war into a sort of crusade in defense of the rights of the church.

On July 11, 1871, upon the petition of the clergy of Caracas, Guzmán Blanco issued a decree suspending the exile; a commission was sent to notify Guevara.[36] The archbishop refused to accept the concession. The clergy, he declared, had been forced by threats to

[31] The editor appealed against the order, declaring that he had printed the article suspecting nothing improper in it, and the paper continued to appear; *Documentos de Secretaría del Interior*, (1870), communications of October 10, 1870, unnumbered.

[32] Navarro, *Anales*, p. 257.

[33] *Documentos, Memoria del Interior*, (1873), pp. 31 *et. seq.*

[34] Quoted in Navarro, *Anales*, p. 258.

[35] Olavarría, *Estudios históricos*, p. 466.

[36] *Documentos de Secretaría del Interior*, July 10, 1871; *Leyes y decretos*, vol. v, p. 233; pp. 236-237.

make the petition and to state that they were convinced of the good dispositions of the government; moreover, the decree contained no word of vindication for him or guarantee of his rights and dignity for the future. The government had threatened his provisor, violated his correspondence, and sacrificed prelates for no other reason than their loyalty to him.[37]

A year later Guevara decided, however, to act on the decree suspending his exile. He arrived at La Guaira on August 31, 1872. The following communication from Guzmán Blanco was delivered to him on the boat:

The justice of the cause that I represent makes it proper to expect that the authorized word of Señor Guevara condemn the calumnies that bad priests have spread under pretext of his defense, if not actually in the name of his Eminence; likewise, the future peace of the Republic demands that Señor Guevara explain also in a public manner what are his aims with regard to the Liberal cause, already triumphant, and the national government that it has constituted.[38]

Guevara answered that he wished to land so that he might rest and deliberate on a reply. This request was refused, and he returned to Trinidad.[39]

Devoted admirers of Guevara among the clergy deplored his uncompromising attitude on this occasion. Castro, Silva, and Navarro have pronounced his conduct unreasonable.[40] He could hardly have expected to be allowed to land unquestioned. He had ready to publish upon his arrival a pastoral in which he stated that he wished to return to heal the wounds of the church and with no other object than to help to consolidate peace. He should at least have presented this to the government, González Guinán has concluded.[41] If he had done so and the government should have imposed further conditions, it would have freed him from responsibility for the deplorable state into which the ecclesiastical organization had fallen.

[37] *Documentos, Memoria del Interior,* (1873) pp. 69-77; Olavarría, *op. cit.,* p. 466.
[38] Documents in Navarro, *Anales,* p. 267.
[39] González Guinán, *Historia contemporánea,* vol. x, p. 116-117.
[40] Navarro, *Anales,* pp. 267-268.
[41] Gonzalez Guinán, *Historia contemporánea,* vol. x, p. 120. He gave the text of the pastoral, pp. 116-120. That Guevara did not present it to the government caused some to suspect that he changed it before it was published later in the form that González Guinán has quoted.

The archbishop stated later in defense of his action that the note of Guzmán Blanco contained grave charges against him and his colleagues and demanded time and deliberation for an answer. It is probable that Guevara foresaw that it would be impossible to come to terms with Guzmán Blanco; perhaps his attempt to return was merely a gesture to show his concern for his diocese.

Whatever may have been the motives that actuated his conduct, the results are clear. War was now declared by Guzmán Blanco on Guevara and the church. The extinction of the convents of nuns, the closing of the seminaries, the abolition of primacies, the establishment of civil marriages and registry, and the secularization of cemeteries followed. On January 31, 1873, a second degree of exile was issued against Guevara, on the ground that he had made himself the center of revolution against the government, that he had suspended the clergy who resisted his seditious plans, and that he had refused the generous condescension of the government in suspending the decree of exile, preferring to reside abroad and direct the rebellion. The decree declared that he should remain in exile, that the government should go directly to the Papacy as the head of the church, that all acts of Guevara should be declared null, and that all who obeyed them or introduced and circulated his orders should be exiled.[42] On the same date the penalty of exile was pronounced against all who violated the Law of Patronage and the laws of civil marriage and registry.[43] On March 18, 1873, Guzmán Blanco suspended the exile of all who had been exiled except Guevara; and on May 8, 1873, he instructed the Congress to make the presidential decree for his exile a law.

It now became a *idée fixe* of Guzmán Blanco to secure by any means possible the vacancy of the archbishopric. In his attempts to do so he made himself *de facto* head of the church as well as of the state, presuming to exercise spiritual functions as well as temporal; he threatened to establish a national church independent of Rome; and acting under his dictation, the Congress was on the point of declaring independence of the Papacy, when a solution that averted

[42] *Leyes y decretos*, vol. v, pp. 232-233.
[43] *Ibid.*, vol. v, pp. 237-238.

that extreme step was reached. The dictator seized the opportunity, for he had no desire to break with Rome; all he wished was to remove Guevara. It was not the ecclesiastical question, but the personal one that absorbed him. His *amour propre* was injured so long as Guevara was in office.

The ecclesiastical organization was indeed in urgent need of attention; it had reached a state of complete paralyzation. Some of the clergy had voluntarily followed Guevara into exile; others had been exiled by Guzmán Blanco for supporting the archbishop or obeying his orders. As to the occasion for these expulsions, the archbishop declared in his pastoral from Trinidad that one was expelled for accepting his appointment as vicar, some for accepting other offices or for coming to Trinidad for his ordination, others for opposing the *Te Deum* or for not attending it when it was celebrated.[44]

On the other hand, Guevara suspended from the exercise of ecclesiastical functions all those who submitted to the orders of the Dictator. On October 14, 1872, he suspended thus Domingo Quintero, dean of the metropolitan church, José Manuel Mendoza, and José Antonio Ponte, for accepting the chairs of ecclesiastical science established by Guzmán Blanco in the University upon the extinction of the seminaries. On November 11 of the same year, he issued a new decree of suspension against Domingo Quintero for the celebration of a *Te Deum* upon the order of the Dictator.[45] Twelve other ecclesiastics of the city were included in the same order. These orders were circulated in Caracas by a few devout women, the only means left the archbishop for the transmission of his dispositions. With the suspensions of November 11, he issued a decree stating that since he had no vicars left he would use the unusual method of issuing his orders direct.[46]

Guzmán Blanco attempted to secure the removal of Guevara by getting the suffragan bishops to accuse him before the Papacy of deserting his diocese, of leaving his church headless by dissolving the chapter, and of converting himself into a "*caudillo* of conquered

[44] *Documentos, Memoria del Interior*, (1873), pp. 69-77.
[45] Navarro, *Anales*, pp. 270-271, note.
[46] *Ibid.*, p. 278.

factions."[47] This suggestion met a dignified refusal from the Bishop
of Mérida, Boset: the executive, he declared, demanded of him an
injustice; he would never accede to such solicitude, since Guevara
merited no accusation. Guevara's absence from his diocese was due
to no fault of his; he had attempted to return and had been prevented. "I should sacrifice my sentiments and my dignity if I should
heed this demand. I am informed of all that has occurred with
Señor Guevara in Caracas, and I believe that he has been at fault in
nothing."[48] Along with a statement he made in regard to the law
of civil matrimony, this reply of the Bishop led to his exile on March
19, 1873. This incident is an excellent example of the sinister system of intimidation that Guzmán Blanco used in dealing with the
clerical question.

` In the memorial of February 17, 1873, to Cardinal Antonelli,
the Congress, acting under the direction of the Dictator, asked the
Pope to confirm one from the list submitted for provisor and governor of the Archbishopric.[49] But on February 14, Pius IX had
named Miguel Antonio Baralt as apostolic vicar, granting him full
power to raise suspensions, interdicts, and censures imposed by the
Archbishop.[50] Although this expedient was received, no doubt, with
considerable relief by Guzmán Blanco as a temporary adjustment of
the ecclesiastical problem, he was careful to explain that it was unusual and extraordinary. It was contrary, in fact, to the traditional
practice of the Republic with regard to relations with the Papacy.
The fundamental principles of the ecclesiastical constitution established by the Conservative Oligarchy had been accepted without
question by their opponents. In a series of articles in La opinión
nacional, A. L. Guzmán had recently cautioned the government and
the public against any interference in the ecclesiastical question that
might be attempted by the pontifical delegate, Leopoldo A. San-
tanche, resident in Santo Domingo.[51] In his address to the Con-

[47] Documentos, Memoria del Interior, (1873), pp. 29.
[48] This interesting document, with many others on the ecclesiastical question under
Guzmán Blanco, is published by Navarro in his Anales; vide, pp. 277-278.
[49] Memoria del Interior, (1873), p. 29.
[50] Ibid., pp. 38-39.
[51] La lei de patronato eclesiástico de los estados unidos de Venezuela y el supuesto
legado del papa, reprinted (Caracas, 1873).

gress in 1873, Guzmán Blanco stated that he had, "through the pious benevolence of the Pope, permitted an apostolic vicar to enter upon the exercise of functions during the continuance of such an extraordinary state of things."[52]

In the reply of the Congress to this message A. L. Guzmán, as President of the House, expressed the hope that the President of the Republic would spare no efforts for obtaining from the Pope the confirmation of one of the priests proposed by him for governor, thus putting an end to this provisional solution. "In the meantime," he said, "it recognizes that you have proceeded with firm and happy skill in . . . giving consent to a apostolic vicar, named by a nuncio not recognized by our government and of a jurisdiction incompatible with our laws. . . !"[53] Certainly no words were spared to make it clear that the acceptance of an apostolic vicar was an extraordinary procedure to be discarded as soon as possible for the accustomed practice.

And it was an expedient with which Guzmán Blanco was not long satisfied. On June 3 of the same year (1873), the Congress sanctioned a decree declaring the archbishopric vacant.[54] The Dictator exercised in this act a power not assumed by the state, even in the ample Law of the Patronage of 1824. The decree added that the Congress would suspend the election of a bishop until it heard from the negotiation with the Pope.

In his message of February 2, 1874, Guzmán Blanco returned to the question:

The Roman Catholic church continues in charge of an apostolic vicar for the reasons that I explained to you in my message of last year. Such a situation is contrary to the patronage and the laws of the Republic, just as it is to the canons themselves and to the sound traditions of the church of Jesus. But, as the last Congress declared vacant the archepiscopal see of Caracas, it is to be hoped that the

---

[52] *Mensajes presentados por el General Guzmán Blanco como presidente provisional de los estados unidos de Venezuela al congreso de plenipotentiarios en 1870 y como presidente constitucional al cuerpo legislativo en 1873, 74, 75, 76.* (Caracas, 1876), p. 30.

[53] Quoted in Navarro, *Anales*, p. 386. When the pontifical delegate, in accordance with his instructions, asked to be allowed to enter Venezuela to deal with the problem of the church, he met an outright refusal; *vide*, his letter to the Pope of August 28, 1873, Navarro, *Anales*, p. 288-289.

[54] *Leyes y decretos*, vol. v, p. 870.

present will remove that anomaly, electing an archbishop in order that he be able to be presented by the government to the Pope. . . . This is the only means of avoiding the lack of a head, since our laws do not allow the vicarage.[55]

He went on to eulogize the religious liberalism of the age. "In that direction modern societies are going," he declared,

and we should be false to our manifest destiny if we should fail to incorporate ourselves in that movement. Because of this, and because the ultramontanism of the Roman Court is made each day more incompatible with our sacred independence, I judge that the occasion has arrived in which the Congress should dictate a law guaranteeing the rights of the Venezuelan church in the manner that the cultured, democratic, and resolute Switzerland has just done.[56]

Although his later conduct would indicate that this was a mere threat, or gesture, on the part of Guzmán Blanco, it fitted well with his extravagant pronouncements in the same message of his beliefs in his divine mission and his determination to realize his historic rôle.

Following his suggestion, the Congress elected Baralt as archbishop. Under his administration as apostolic vicar the church had shown submissiveness to the Dictator in the celebration of *Te Deums* and in other acts of favor, which brought upon it the severe judgment of the friends of Guevara.[57] But Baralt refused to accept the place as archbishop under an election so contrary to canon law. He went further to issue a dignified protest against the action of the President and Congress, a reply that does him honor. For this refusal and protest he was at once exiled.[58] The Congress chose then José Manuel Arroyo, Bishop of Guayana, for the place. Although he accepted the appointment and took the oath required, he refused to enter upon the duties of the office until a reply should be received from the Pope.[59] Pius IX pronounced his action indicative of an "abjection of spirit and a pusillanimity unworthy of a bishop."[60]

[55] Guzmán Blanco, *Mensajes*, p. 84 *et seq.*
[56] *Ibid.*, pp. 85-86.
[57] Navarro, *Anales*, p. 281.
[58] *Memoria del Interior*, (1875), p. xiv.
[59] *La opinión nacional*, March 28, 1874.
[60] Navarro, *Anales*, pp. 303-4, gives the letter of Pius IX.

The archbishopric was again left without an active head. Only one individual remained in the metropolitan organization, a notary of the court, who was a layman. Upon the retirement of Baralt as vicar, Guevara reassumed the direction and named a *cura* of the city to act as provisor. "The archdiocese," said Castro later, "had only a secret provisor, the venerable Juan Andrés Domínguez. . . . It was like the life of the catacombs."[61] In a short time Domínguez was imprisoned on some pretext. Thus, through the suspensions of Guevara and the proscriptions of Guzmán Blanco, the ecclesiastical organization had been completely destroyed. In the process, too, the Dictator had presumed to exercise spiritual jurisdiction by pronouncing the priests he exiled incapable of exercising ecclesiastical functions. He had insisted, moreover, upon filling pastorates without ecclesiastical intervention. Two priests accepted such "institution"; they were immediately declared suspended by Guevara.[62]

In his message of 1875, Guzmán Blanco returned to the proposal of establishing a national church:

Venezuela must resort to one of two extremes: either abdicate her sovereignty and accept Señor Guevara just as Rome wishes to impose him and allow the nation to be converted into a foreign sacristry; or, assuming the legitimate rights of sovereignty . . . discountenance . . . the usurpation of the Curia and establish the church as exclusively Venezuelan, regulated in accordance with the principles and practices of the primitive religion of Jesus. Would to God that you take advantage of this happy opportunity for assuring our future generations all the well-being of which humanity has been deprived by the Roman church. . . .[63]

He was determined to settle the ecclesiastical question before the end of his Septenio, as a crowning glory to the rule of the *Regenerador*. As the end of that period drew near, its resolution became an obsession with him. The public was, moreover, disturbed by the continued discussion and particularly by the pronouncements suggesting a severance of unity with Rome.

In the same year, however, the Secretary of the Interior an-

[61] *La religión*, May 10-June 13, 1898.
[62] Navarro, *Anales*, p. 283.
[63] Hortensio, (Josá Güell y Mercador), *Guzmán Blanco y su tiempo*, (Caracas, 1883), pp. 33-34.

nounced that the executive hoped to be able to report at the end of the year the solution of the problem through the Papacy.[64] What Guzmán Blanco wished to accomplish was not a break with Rome, but the removal of Guevara. The former was to be used only as a last resort to achieve the latter. He had continued communications with the apostolic delegate in Santo Domingo, now Roque Cocchia, sent by the Pope with ample powers to rule on the Venezuelan question. On April 30, 1875, Guzmán Blanco sent Antonio Parejo on a special mission to Roque Cocchia with instructions to secure the nomination of a capitular vicar and the consent that the one named by Congress as archbishop be allowed to enter at once on the civil functions of his office. These requests were refused. The delegate declared that neither he nor the Pope could

authorize the *cabildo* to name a vicar with faculties for governing the archbishopric. That authorization belongs to the bishop, and nobody in the world is able to usurp it. As to the Pope's accepting the election of a bishop named by the Congress, that is to propose that he accept the deposition of the titular authority by an assembly of laymen and is not, in fact, a matter to be taken into serious consideration.[65]

In the meantime, Roque Cocchia went to Trinidad to communicate with Guevara. He had instructions from Pius IX to secure, if possible, the resignation of the archbishop in order to relieve the situation in the Venezuelan church. Upon his first suggestion of such a solution, he met a firm refusal from Guevara. Such action would constitute a precedent that would bring grave evils to the church in Venezuela, he declared. Presidents would presume to change bishops at their pleasure.[66] Having failed to persuade Guevara to resign, Roque Cocchia returned to Santo Domingo.

In 1878, Parejo was given a new commission to the apostolic delegate. He was to "try to persuade Señor Cocchia that this resolution of the President is unchangeable; that the Illustrious Amer-

---

[64] *Memoria del Interior* (1876) pp. xxxiii-xxxiv.

[65] Parejo, Antonio, *Al público: Hechos históricos en relación con la cuestión religiosa en los años de 1875 y 1876* (Caracas, 1896), pp. 3-5.

[66] Olavarría, *op. cit.*, p. 465.

ican cannot come to the end of his presidential term without the question being resolved."[67]

He was instructed further to attempt to get Roque Cocchia to accept for his "immense services" to Venezuela "a sum that would allow him to secure a rest in his last days." According to the account of Parejo, the delegate suspected that suggestion and forestalled it, warning Parejo in advance not to give offense by offering money.[68] The second mission failed as completely as the first; Parejo was sent a third time to Santo Domingo, but when he arrived the papal representative had left for Trinidad to attempt again to secure the resignation of Guevara.

The exact course of the negotiations in Trinidad in the last days of April and the first days of May, 1876, are yet a matter of dispute. Roque Cocchia secured the resignation of Guevara after a week's delay. Certain churchmen, notably Henrique Fanger, a devoted adherent of Guevara, assert that advantage was taken by Roque Cocchia of his good faith; that the delegate claimed to have a new communication from Cardinal Antonelli in which the Pope insisted upon the archbishop's resignation, but that its authenticity was doubtful; that the friends of Guevara in Trinidad were prevented from seeing him; that he was virtually forced to a resignation by Roque Cocchia, acting as a tool of Guzmán Blanco.[69] Vallenilla Lanz has observed that this battle between the archbishop and the Illustrious American was "a history full of curious *perpetias*, in which the Holy See played a rôle that yet remains in mystery."[70] He expressed the hope that Duarte Level, Venezuelan consul at Puerto España and secret agent of Guzmán Blanco, would relate what he knew of the incident, declaring that he was "personally capable, by intelligence, by character, and by very superior faculties as a detective, of penetrating the most intimate intentions of the sagacious Italian."[71]

Parejo declared that there was no doubt of the existence and

[67] Parejo, *Al público*, pp. 8-10.
[68] *Ibid.*, p. 10 *et seq.*
[69] *El Tiempo*, "*Suplemento*," October 13, 1896. This paper gave a detailed discussion of the incident with many documents. Much is contained also in *La religión*, April 11-16, 1896.
[70] Vallenilla Lanz, *Críticas*, pp. 410-411.
[71] *Ibid.*

authenticity of the letter of the Cardinal, that Pius IX did not urge resignation until he was convinced that it was the only way for avoiding greater evils, that Guevara refused at first, but was urged to give up his office by the counsel of friends, who insisted he should sacrifice himself to save the Venezuelan church.[72] A similar account is given by Olavarría and is supported by statements of Roque Cocchia.[73] Olavarría attributed the decision of the archbishop to the influence of a faithful friend constantly with Guevara on his exile, the Father Nicanor Rivero.

Guzmán Blanco did not have much confidence apparently in the success of the negotiations. In messages to Congress he continued to urge the establishment of a national church. On April 17, he insisted that he could not leave the Cause of April to be implicated in the future by enemies dissembled under the cloak of religion, that if Rome did not accept the decision offered, it would be necessary to take care of the future with a law that would free the Venezuelan church.[74] On May 8, Duarte Level telegraphed from Trinidad the failure of Roque Cocchia to secure the resignation of Guevara. On May 9, Guzmán Blanco sent to the Congress a special message in which he declared:

Yesterday there came to me finally the official report that Señor Guevara has refused to resign. . . . In such a situation all the diplomatic means are exhausted for ruling the archepiscopal question, which we are not able, on the other hand, to leave unsolved to the next government without endangering it and endangering the national cause.

As the representative today of that cause by the repeated vote of the nation, as the one chiefly responsible before history for the consolidation of the work of April, and with the full conviction that our enemies, disguised with the religion of the Christ, would change the splendid future that we are building for the country for the obscure past . . . I ask you for the law that will free the Venezuelan church from the Roman bishopric; and I ask that you order that the pastors be elected by the faithful, the bishops by the pastors, and the archbishop by the Congress, returning thus to the primitive church founded by Jesus and his apostles.

[72] Parejo, La religión, April 11-16, 1896.
[73] El Tiempo, "Suplemento," October 13, 1896; Olavarría, Estudios históricos, pp. 465 et seq.
[74] Gaceta oficial, April 17, 1876.

That law will not only settle our clerical question; but it will be besides a great example for the Christianity of republican America, retarded in its march of liberty, order, and progress by the element, always retrograde, of the Roman curia; and the civilized world will regard it as the most definitive evidence of the regeneration of Venezuela.[75]

The question was introduced in the Congress on the same day. Only one member, José Manuel Montenegro, ventured to oppose the proposal of the President on the floor of the Congress. He suggested the purely personal character of the controversy in asking, "Are we under obligation to punish the people of Venezuela, reforming their worship, because of the conduct of a prelate?" According to his statement, there was much perturbation among the members over taking this extreme step; only two votes, however, were cast against it.[76] The bill passed on to the third reading.

On May 16, Duarte Level reported that Roque Cocchia had secured the resignation of Guevara; Guzmán Blanco was not yet satisfied, however, and the discussion of the law continued. The President feared there might be conditions to the resignation; moreover, he was afraid he might not be able to secure the confirmation of a new archbishop at once. Parejo was commissioned to go to Puerto España to accompany the apostolic delegate to La Guaira.

Never before had a papal representative been received in Venezuela, nor even set foot on Venezuelan soil. According to the report of Parejo and statements of Rojas Paúl and others, it was only with great reluctance that Guzmán Blanco allowed Roque Cocchia to enter. The Legate experienced even more difficulty and embarrassment in securing recognition in his diplomatic character than in obtaining admittance. The Secretary of Foreign Relations, Eduardo Calcaño, in his report of the year, was careful to explain that only the extraordinary situation had led to his admittance and that "as it was not thought that the same circumstances would be repeated, nor that the fact in this case would be invoked at any time as a precedent, the Illustrious American had decided to recognize him during his

---

[75] *La opinión nacional*, May 9, 1876; May 11, 1876; *Independencia de la iglesia venezolana de la Curia Romana*, (Caracas, 1876).

[76] *La tribuna liberal*, January 16, 1878.

residence in the country in the character in which he presented himself."[77]

As Parejo, who attended Roque Cocchia, described the reception, Guzmán Blanco kept the Legate waiting on board the boat for two hours, while he read the correspondence from Trinidad. These communications apparently did not please him. They were, no doubt, those of his agents in Trinidad, who received only hearsay, Parejo observed. If the resignation of Guevara did not give Congress the power to elect an archbishop in this session, it would be imprudent, the President declared, to allow the Legate to enter; nevertheless he might be given residence at La Guaira until decision was made as to his coming to Caracas. Rojas Paúl, Secretary of the Interior at the time, affirmed afterwards that he begged Guzmán Blanco to put aside all sentiment of *amour propre* and go to La Guaira to see the nuncio; that the president agreed to this after he had assembled a *junta* to counsel him.[78] On the next day the President received Roque Cocchia, not in Caracas, however, but at his house in Macuto. The Legate had refused in various notes that had passed on the day before to sanction the election of an archbishop until the Pope declared the see vacant through the acceptance of the resignation of Guevara; nor would he approve the entrance into office of the one chosen before the *fiat* of the Pope was received. "The Law is old," observed the "astute and sagacious Capuchin." At the close of the conference in Macuto, Roque Cocchia left for Saint Thomas to send a cablegram to Pius IX concerning the settlement of the ecclesiastical problem. He returned on June 14 with the answer of the Pope, which declared vacant the archepiscopal see of Caracas.[79]

On June 13, the Congress had closed its regular session. Upon the call of the President it met in extraordinary session on the fourteenth for the election of an archbishop. Baralt was elected, but refused to come to Caracas until everything was settled according to canon law. Guzmán Blanco was indignant, and the Congress has-

[77] *Memoria de relaciones exteriores*, (1877), pp. lxxviii-lxxix.
[78] *Guzmán Blanco y Crespo: La cacareada reacción contra la Causa Liberal, defensa de Rojas Paúl* (Caracas, 1894), pp. 20-22.
[79] Parejo, *Al público*, p. 15 *et seq.*

tened to elect José Antonio Ponte. Only on July 9 was Roque
Cocchia received officially in Caracas.[80]

In his message to Congress on June 19, Guzmán Blanco announced that the question of the patronage might henceforth cease
to be discussed; that the sovereignty of the Venezuelan people had
been vindicated and harmony between the Holy See and the government of Venezuela established. In 1877, he declared that the right
of patronage had been recognized.[81] Urbaneja, Secretary of the
Interior, in his *Memoria* of the year proclaimed as one of the glories
of the Illustrious America his success in obtaining the recognition of
the right.[82] The bull of confirmation of Ponte would seem to concede—not to recognize—the right of presentation, the most significant feature of the patronal rights. It stated that for the provision
of the Metropolitan Church, "in virtue of indulgence and apostolic
privilege, the nomination and presentation of the proper person to be
presented to the Roman Pontiff belongs to the very illustrious man
that is President of the Republic of Venezuela."[83] Navarro has
denied that the right of patronage was recognized; this was merely
another boast of the Guzmanistas, he declared.[84] Olavarría expresses
a similar view.[85] Certainly there was no recognition of the right in
all its extension. Difficulties arose later, moreover, over the right of
presentation that would indicate that not even this right was conceded unconditionally.[86]

In 1877, during the presidency of Alcántara, the decree of exile
against Guevara was repealed. His return to Caracas on August 7,
1877, was attended with great public demonstrations of devotion.
La tribuna liberal declared that the public rejoicing showed that religion was not dead among the people, that "their pious sentiments
had only been suppressed under the domination of the autocracy."[87]
This paper, the organ of the government, represented itself as critical

[80] Navarro, *Anales*, p. 335.
[81] González Guinán, *Historia contemporánea*, vol. xi, p. 237.
[82] *Memoria del Interior*, (1877), p. xix-xx.
[83] *Ibid.*, (1877), p. 41 *et seq.*
[84] Navarro, *Anales*, 337-39.
[85] Olavarría, *op. cit.*, p. 464.
[86] González Guinán, Francisco, *Historia del gobierno del Doctor J. P. Rojas Paúl,*
(Valencia, 1891), p. 395 *et seq.*
[87] *La tribuna liberal*, August 9, 1877; December 29, 1877.

of the administration of Guzmán Blanco, especially on the matter of the church. Its criticism was, however, weak, sporadic, and equivocal. Aside from permitting the return of Guevara the government of Alcántara showed no favor to the church. The anti-clerical legislation stood unchanged. Those prominent in the government were men who had supported Guzmán Blanco in his war on the church. Alcántara, holding the presidency until Guzmán Blanco should choose to return from Europe and reassume it, had been president of the state of Aragua under his administration; Laureano Villanueva, prominent in the new administration, was an apologist of the Masonic advance against "religious fanaticism, the oppressor of the consciences of the people," and the editor of *La tribuna liberal,* Nicanor Bolet Peraza, who welcomed so extravagantly the return of Guevara, had given active support to the government of Guzmán Blanco and had approved the expulsion of the archbishop and the project of the law for separation from Rome.[88]

Efforts on the part of some members of the clergy to take up the defense of Guevara in this interim between the presidencies of Guzmán Blanco were discouraged not only by the political press, but by leaders in the church. J. B. Castro, a churchman of high character, later archbishop, and the foremost figure in the church after Guevara, appeared in criticism of J. N. Urdaneta, whose ardent support of Guevara led him to attack Ponte, the successor. Castro urged that wounds made by a long and fatiguing battle not be opened; he ventured to suggest the future course for the church. "What we need," he insisted, "is integrity of conduct, perfect austerity of life for resisting as much as we can the relaxation of morals and the invasion of modern paganism." He urged that the clergy flee from seeking popularity and abandon attempts to gain political influence or wealth; that it give attention only to the spiritual functions of its office.[89] Similar discouragement of the discussion of the recent political contests came from bodies of the clergy in Caracas, Valencia, and other places.[90]

In the last days of the *Septenio* of Guzmán Blanco, Archbishop

[88] Navarro, *Anales,* pp. 325-326.
[89] *La opinión nacional,* July 23, 1877.
[90] *La voz pública,* July 21, 24, and 26, 1877.

Ponte had added his voice to the servile laudation of the Dictator. He accompanied the President on a tour of the states, speaking on platforms in praise of his "regeneration" of Venezuela, comparing him to Moses and to Charles the Great. He enjoined his parishioners to obedience to the political authorities.[91] All criticism of the government had been driven under cover.

In the contest with Guzmán Blanco the church had lost integrity and spirit; its ministers were reduced to servility or driven into exile. They were, in some cases, made objects of public indignity that destroyed their prestige. Masonic activity sponsored by the Dictator in his program of "national regeneration" discredited the church as obscurantist, as an obstacle to material and educational progress. Never before had the institution been subjected to such unrestrained criticism. Anti-clerical legislation further reduced its power in society. This legislation, much of it at least, would no doubt have been enacted, even though there had been no personal conflict; it had been discussed from the beginning of the Republic. But the personal factor caused its execution to be attended with a publicity and a bitterness that possibly would not otherwise have appeared.

If one may venture to pass judgment, it would seem that Guevara might have served the church more successfully in another rôle than the one he chose to play. No prelate in the Venezuelan church has received such unmeasured praise for his personal qualities or pastoral virtues. Not even his bitterest personal enemies questioned him with respect to his high character. By these attractions, by his zeal, and by his ability to accommodate himself to the changing political situation, he had checked the progress of anti-clerical reform and raised the church in the public esteem. That he could have continued to hold back legislation against the church is doubtful, but he might have saved something of the institutional integrity and of public respect for the church. It is impossible to say. Probably he foresaw the uncompromising personalism and servilism that would follow the success of Guzmán Blanco and believed that he might serve his cause more worthily by remaining in opposition.

[91] *La opinión nacional*, August 4, 1877; the following issues give his pastorals in support of the government. For a defense of Ponte by a devoted colleague, *vide*, Sosa Saa, José Tomás, *Ilustrísimo Señor Doctor José Antonio Ponte*, (Caracas, 1929).

II

MORE DETAILED consideration should be given now to the constitutional provisions on religion and the legislation affecting the church enacted under the Guzmán-Blanco régime. The Constitution of 1874, drawn up under his dictation, made no change in the article on religious liberty contained in the fundamental law of 1864; it provided in Division III, Section 13, that religious liberty should be allowed, but that only the Catholic worship should be observed outside the churches; that is, in processions in the streets or other such public demonstrations. In criticism of this feature, Guzmán Blanco declared that in Venezuela "where all men are equal before law, where all have the right to think according to their own consciences, and . . . the faculty to worship God as it appears best to them, no religion should exercise worship apart from the churches"; all should be guaranteed perfectly; and all should be subject to public inspection.[92] He admitted that he had not asked that such provisions be made for the reason that he did not wish to complicate further relations with Rome. The Constitution of 1883 suppressed this limitation on freedom of worship, returning in Division III, Section 13, to the simple grant of religious liberty accorded in the Constitution of 1858. In Article 98 of the Constitution of 1874 it was declared that the nation was in possession of the patronage and would exercise it according to the Law of 1824. This was the first statement made in the fundamental law with regard to the patronage; up to this time it had been a principle of statutory law only, although, as has been observed, it possessed more stability than the fundamental law itself. This feature of the Constitution of 1874 has been copied in later ones.

A decree of September 7, 1872, restored the chairs of ecclesiastical science to the university.[93] This was followed, on September 21 of the same year, by the closing of the seminaries.[94] In the decree ordering their extinction it was stated in defense of the measure that the isolation of the students in these institutions and the texts

---

[92] Documentos favorables á los reformas de la constitución de 1864 pediadas por el Ilustre Americano, General Guzmán Blanco, presidente de la República y sancionadas por el Congreso Federal de 1870, (Caracas, 1870), p. 678.
[93] Leyes y decretos, vol. v, p. 148.
[94] Ibid., vol. v, pp. 150-151.

and doctrines taught there developed a spirit hostile to the political institutions of the country and opposed to the ideas and progressive advance of the Republic; further, that the prelate had never submitted the constitution of the seminaries to the government for its approval according to the requirement of the law of 1856 separating the Seminary of Santa Rosa from the University of Caracas. The establishment of these institutions had been a part of the Liberal program of ecclesiastical reform, and this group had actively supported Guevara in his efforts to promote them. Their extinction may be regarded as an expression of personal resentment toward him. The decree of 1872 stated that they were not to be reëstablished; their property was granted to the schools of arts. One of the injunctions of Pius IX to Ponte in the bull confirming him as archbishop was that he attempt to secure the reëstablishment of the seminaries.[95] During his administration he was able to obtain permission to organize an episcopal school for the promotion of ecclesiastical education.[96] And in 1891 seminaries were reëstablished.

On May 5, 1874, convents for nuns were extinguished in law and ordered closed.[97] These corporations were pronounced contrary to principles of individual liberty, of equality, and of national sovereignty; moreover, they were declared contrary to the material interests of the country. On these grounds, convents for men had been extinguished in 1837. The property of the convents, Guzmán Blanco advised in proposing the law, should go to the University of Caracas for the promotion of natural science.[98] The nuns were granted a pension varying from eight to twelve *pesos* a month, much less than that granted the monks in 1837. Rojas Paúl stated that when he proposed in 1889 the increase of this pension, which was wholly inadequate for support, he was pronounced a fanatic under the influence of the clergy.[99] There were only five convents existing at the time of the extinction, three in Caracas, one in Trujillo,

---

[95] *Documentos, Memoria del Interior*, (1877), p. 41, *et seq.*
[96] Sosa Saa, *José Antonio Ponte*, p. 136, *et seq.*
[97] *Leyes y decretos*, vol. vi, p. 38.
[98] Guzmán Blanco, *Mensajes*, pp. 85-86. The property of those of Trujillo and Mérida was granted to the national *colegio* of Trujillo; *vide, Memoria del Interior*, (1877), p. xx.
[99] Rojas Paúl, *Guzmán Blanco y Crespo*, p. 137.

and one in Mérida.[100]   These ·contained seventy-nine women.[101] The extinction of the Convent of the Immaculate Conception in Caracas was especially desired by Guzmán Blanco; he wished the site for his new government buildings.   The ecclesiastical authorities opposed the alienation of the property without the fulfillment of certain canonical formalities.   Guzmán Blanco was impatient and ordered the walls broken down.· The nuns were thus expelled by force. "Upon the site of the Convent of the Immaculate Conception there is displayed today the Federal Palace and the Capitol, material beauties of the capital city," observed Juan B. Castro in his biography of the last abbess, ". . . but whose construction we could have wished . . . had been executed by proceedings of justice and of respect for property."[102]   According to the statement of Olavarría, much of the property of the convents went to increase the personal fortune of Guzmán Blanco.[103]

On January 1, 1873, decrees establishing civil matrimony and civil registry were issued.[104]   Guzmán Blanco announced the fact to the Congress of 1873, giving as motives of the action the desire to attract foreign population.[105]   There had been from the beginning of the Republic much support for these institutions.   They were leading features, it will be recalled, in the Project of Ecclesiastical Reform of 1834.   The Academy of Jurisprudence, an association of lawyers of Caracas, had recommended civil matrimony in 1842.[106] And it was ably supported by Luis Sanojo in his scholarly periodical, *El Foro,* in the late fifties.   The Masons had urged it upon congresses in the sixties and were largely responsible for the achievement of the reform.[107]   In addition to this support of the establishment of civil matrimony, Guzmán Blanco had, however, a strong personal

---

[100] Landaeta Rosales, Manuel, *Gran recopilación, geográfica, estadística é histórica de Venezuela,* 2 vols., (Caracas, 1889), vol. ii, p. 91.

[101] Arístides Rojas in his *Estudios históricos,* (2nd series, pp. 298 *et seq.*) has an essay on the convents of Caracas.   According to his statement, there were sixty-three convents of this city.

[102] *La religion,* May 10-June 13, 1898.

[103] Olavaaría, *op. cit.,* p. 467.

[104] *Leyes y· decretos,* vol. v., p. 207; p. 216.   These provisions were included in the new civil code of 1873.

[105] Guzmán Blanco, *Mensajes,* p. 54.

[106] Zuloaga, Nicomedes, *Código civil concordado,* (Caracas, 1899), p. xi.

[107] Ascanio Rodríguez, *Apuntes,* pp. x-xv; *Memoria del Interior,* (1874), p. xii.

motive, the vindication of his minister and friend, Diego B. Urbaneja. The Dictator was married again according to the formalities of the new law.[108] This was done, Olavarría observed, to allow Urbaneja an opportunity to take advantage of it without undue notice.[109] Not yet satisfied, however, Guzmán Blanco instructed Parejo on his first mission to the papal legate in Santo Domingo to ask for a dispensation for Urbaneja's marriage.[110] Reference has been made of the exile of Bishop Boset of Mérida for his instructions to his parishioners that the church would not recognize the civil ceremony, that unless it were followed by marriage by the church those thus united would die impenitent.[111] The *Memorias* of the Secretaries of the Interior under this régime were full in praise of the new law of civil matrimony; it was universally supported, it was declared, and marriages had increased under it. This was, one may easily believe, merely the boasting of the Guzmanistas. There has been much criticism of the law; this will be considered in the following chapter. Along with the establishment of civil marriage and civil registry the Civil Code of 1873 provided, in Article 419, for the secularization of cemeteries. This, too, had been a leading feature of the Masonic program of reform.

In addition to the redemption of the *censos* and the confiscation of the property of the convents and seminaries, there were other laws affecting the property interests of the church. A decree of February 6, 1873, abolished primacies.[112] Of much more serious import, however, was the provision, in Article 710 of the new civil code, which prohibited the church from inheriting property and those in orders, unless they were relatives of the testator within the fourth degree. The church had never been wealthy in Venezuela; these measures so reduced its property and income that its activity and influence were much further restricted. There were suggestions that the appropriations of the government to the church cease. An

[108] González Guinán, *Historia contemporánea*, vol. x, p. 157.
[109] Quoted in Navarro, *Anales*, p. 272.
[110] Parejo, *Al público*, p. 10 *et seq.*
[111] Marriage of the clergy was not prohibited in the civil code of 1873. Several priests took advantage of this omission, causing much public criticism. The restriction was soon reintroduced, providing that clergymen should not marry, if the church to which they belonged forbade it.
[112] *Leyes y decretos*, vol. v, p. 238.

informe, for example, from Barquisimeto in 1872 recommended this on the grounds that it would force the clergy to be neutral in political contests, since they would have to look to men of all groups for private contributions.[113] Such a proposal has not been seriously considered, however; the appropriations to the church are regarded as the chief means for maintaining the Law of the Patronage.

All remaining ecclesiastical *fueros* were abolished by a decree of June 1, 1874.[114] The decree provided that the Federal High Court should take cognizance of cases against the archbishops and bishops, the superior courts of those against vicars and canons, and the ordinary courts of those against other clerics. The Penal Code of 1873 provided in Article 188 an elaborate statement of penalties for crimes of the Catholic clergy against the national jurisdiction and the Law of the Patronage.[115]

Statistics on the church in the census of 1881 indicate the failure of the Republic to remedy the great lack of pastors. Parishes had been multiplied, but more than half of them were without pastors: for six hundred thirty-nine parishes, there were only two hundred forty-one *curas*. These priests served more than two million parishioners.[116] Under the Guzmán-Blanco régime appropriations for the church dropped lamentably. In 1875, only 22,302 pesos were granted. In 1886, the allotments were still much below those of the early years of the Republic.[117]

The administration of Guzmán Blanco gave the death blow to the church as a social power in Venezuela. The Conservative Oligarchy had done much to destroy its intellectual influence with the upper class; Guzmán Blanco reduced it to ineffectiveness even with the masses. It became an object of contempt. If, on occasion, as on the return of Guevara, the public has been stirred by sentiment for a representative of the institution, such expressions are always

---

[113] *Documentos de Secretaría del Interior* (1872), unnumbered.

[114] *Leyes y decretos;* vol. vi, p. 58.

[115] There were some slight changes in the Law of the Patronage. It was decreed that opposition for official canons be fixed at seventy days instead of six months, since communication was easier than in 1824; it was provided further that the President of the Republic, instead of the executives of the states, should approve the posting of edicts for the concourse for the official canons. (*Memoria del Interior*, 1877, pp. xviii-xix.)

[116] Landaeta Rosales, *Gran recopilación*, vol. ii, p. 94.

[117] *Memoria de la Hacienda*, (1878), p. 63; (1886), p. 210.

short-lived. The church is incapable of consolidating the loyalty and devotion of the people. A campaign of intimidation added to hostile legislation has discouraged still further the entrance of able men into the church. Moreover, the government does not desire such. Rarely today are there found superior men like Navarro in the ranks of the clergy; he himself has deplored the unfitness of the majority of the clergy for their work.[118] Although there has been some favor shown the institution under subsequent administrations, reforms have been, on the whole, partial and ineffective. The anti-clerical legislation of Guzmán Blanco stands with little change.

[118] *Anales*, p. 339 and footnote. He wrote of the conditions in the late nineteenth century just after the Guzmán Blanco régime, but they have not changed much in this particular.

CHAPTER VI

SOME OBSERVATIONS ON THE PRESENT STATUS OF THE CHURCH IN VENEZUELA

THE WRITER offers the materials presented in this chapter as a study of the church in Venezuela since 1890 only in respect of its constitutional and legal history. Statements as to the administration of the church and as to its status in society are suggestive merely of the course of its evolution in the period.

There appears to have been little, if any, improvement in the status of the church since 1875. With the exception of the law abolishing the seminaries, the anti-clerical legislation of Guzmán Blanco remains unchanged in matters of importance. The church has gained something perhaps in institutional discipline through closer contact with the Papacy, whose representation has been continued in Venezuela since 1876. But this contact has involved no relaxation in the strict surveillance of the state under the Law of the Patronage. The church has not regained in any appreciable degree economic strength nor social influence. Such concessions as have been made to it for participation in education and public welfare suggest rather the magnanimity, euphemistically speaking, of a supreme power toward a conquered rival from whom resistance is no longer to be feared; they are, in fact, the surest evidences of the complete subjection of the institution. Nor does the state need to proceed cautiously in its relations with the church, as it once considered advisable through fear of potential popular support of the institution; its preponderance of power is as complete in fact as in law. On occasion, it is true, the religious sentiments of this people are stirred to demonstrations of interest and even enthusiasm; as they were, for example, by the return of Guevara in 1877. But such expressions of interest are always ephemeral. The accustomed attitude is apparently one of indifference or contempt.

The Constitutions of 1893, 1904, 1909, 1914, 1922, and 1928, contain little reference to religion except in the grant of liberty of worship. There is, indeed, slight occasion for any statement on the church in the organic law; the Law of the Patronage requires no amplification. All the constitutions mentioned declare the nation to be in possession of the right of the patronage and state that its exercise shall be according to the Law of 1824.[1]

Rojas Paúl, president from 1889 to 1891, showed some favor to the church. He had been Secretary of the Interior under Guzmán Blanco during the conflict with Guevara. Now, however, he was in opposition to the Dictator. According to the interpretation of González Guinán, the attitude assumed toward the church in his administration resulted from a desire to attack the government of his predecessor rather than from a real concern for ecclesiastical interests.[2] In February, 1890, the remains of Guevara were removed at the expense of the national treasury from El Valle and deposited in great state in the cathedral.[3] There was a week of celebration in honor of the victim of the Dictator.

By an executive resolution of January 11, 1889, it was ordered that eighteen Sisters of Charity be brought to Caracas with two chaplains to serve them. These were destined for work in the Institutes of Public Beneficence. Fifty *bolívares*, about ten dollars, a month were apportioned as the pay of each.[4] This was the beginning of a policy, continued up to the present, of bringing, or allowing the entrance, of nuns for work in education and public welfare. Today there are sixteen "congregations" of women engaged in such activities.[5] No change has been made, however, in the law against convents. These groups, as well as groups of men admitted for missionary work, form associations without legal recognition.

A beginning was made in law under this administration toward the revival of the missions for the reduction of the Indians. In 1882, the government had returned to the consideration of the Indian problem. A law of June 2, 1882, gave the executive au-

[1] Mention is made below of certain provisions with regard to the admission of foreign ecclesiastics.
[2] González Guinán, Francisco, *Historia del gobierno del Doctor J. P. Rojas Paúl*, (Valencia, 1891) p. 396, p. 445.
[3] *Leyes y decretos*, vol. xiv, p. 319.
[4] *Ibid.*, vol. xiv, p. 180.
[5] Navarro, *Anales*, pp. 404-410.

thority to distribute land among those who submitted to civil life.[6] Later President Crespo issued an executive order, instructing the states in which unreduced Indians were found to appoint a fiscal to intervene in the division of lands.[7] No provision was made, however, as to means for the civilization of the Indians. In an executive resolution of October 27, 1890, Rojas Paúl gave authority to the archbishop to bring fifty Spanish regulars for service in the missions.[8] Due regard was to be paid to the Law of the Patronage and the prohibition of convents. The order stated that the government realized that Catholic missions were the only satisfactory means of reduction. The regulars brought were to be paid passage and one hundred *bolívares* a month. Under this order eight missionaries were sent to the Orinoco region, but nothing was accomplished toward reduction.[9] By a formal law of May 12, 1894, a system of missions was outlined, to be encharged to the Spanish Capuchins.[10] Through the papal representative, Julio Tonti, the government was to seek from the Pope the appointment of a bishop *in partibus,* or apostolic vicar, to serve as director of the missions. Vicars were to be appointed in each district to act under his direction, all being subject to the orders of the national government through the Department of the Interior. Six regulars were to remain in Caracas under a superior to serve as a medium of communication with the government. The salary of the apostolic vicar was fixed at six hundred *bolívares* a month, those of the missionaries at two hundred each. Further elaboration and extension was made to the law of the missions in 1915 under the administration of Arcaya as Secretary of the Interior.[11] He has shown much interest in the promotion of the work. Through his recommendation the national government published in 1928 a grammar of the dialect of the Guaraunos Indians made by the missionary, Father Olea.[12] This work recalls the an-

---

[6] *Leyes y decretos,* vol. x, no. 2442.

[7] *Ibid.,* vol. xi, no. 2664.

[8] *Ibid.,* vol. xv, p. 192.

[9] Escoriaza, Melchor de, *Crónica de las misiones capuchinas en Venezuela, Puerto Rico, y Cuba* (Caracas, 1910).

[10] *Leyes y decretos,* vol. xvii, pp. 219-220.

[11] *Ibid.,* vol. xxxviii, pp. 154-155. In 1921, another law was passed which made, however, slight change in that of 1915; *ibid.,* vol. xliv, p. 391.

[12] Olea, Bonifacio M. de., *Ensayo gramatical del dialecto de los indios guaraunos,* (Caracas, 1928).

cient studies of Ruíz Blanco and Rivero; the need for such a study indicates the failure of the national government in reducing the Indians to civil life. The work of the Capuchin missionaries continues, but progress has been slow and uncertain. Only in 1927 was the apostolic vicarage finally established in the *pase* given the bull of the Papacy erecting it.[13] Reports from the missions indicate that funds are inadequate, that the Indians resist reduction, that the geographic and climatic conditions prove fatal to the health and even to the life of the missionaries. Most of those brought in stop in the towns or soon return to them. The zeal of the seventeenth-century missionaries is found only in exceptional cases; moreover, the government lacks the enthusiasm of the Catholic Kings. Its intent is utilitarian and something beyond that seems necessary if the difficulties of the task are to be surmounted.[14] It might be observed, too, that what has been accomplished under the republic has been the work of the Capuchins. Efforts purely civil have been without result.

An executive decree of September 28, 1900, provided for the reëstablishment of the seminary of Caracas; license was granted also for the establishment of such institutions in other episcopal centers. The constitutions of these were to be drawn up by the diocesan prelates subject to the revision and approval of the national executive. Schools erected under this law were to be under the inspection of the Minister of Public Instruction. Seminaries may grant the degree of Bachelor of Philosophy, but only the universities can grant that of Doctor of Philosophy. In spite of the efforts of certain churchmen and representatives of the Papacy to promote this work, it appears that slight interest is shown in ecclesiastical education.[15] Religious instruction may be given in the public schools if the parents of ten children of the same faith desire it, such instruction to be restricted to one or two hours a week.[16] Complaints have been made that the execution of this decree has been impeded by inspectors hostile to the

[13] *Leyes y decretos*, vol. xlvi, p. 38.
[14] *Memoria del Interior*, 1928, *et als.*, give reports of the missions; also *Gaceta oficial*, March 1, 1922.
[15] *Leyes y decretos*, vol. xxiii, p. 221.
[16] *Ibid.*, vol. xl, p. 16.

church.[17] Church schools exist but occupy a minor place in secondary education. Ninety per cent of those in schools are in public schools.[18] All schools are under government inspection.

The organization of the church in Venezuela has been expanded considerably under the administration of Gómez. In 1923 four new bishoprics were erected, and that of Mérida was raised to an archbishopric.[19] The number of prebends has been increased. In spite of this enlarged organization and the reëstablishment of seminaries, the personnel of the church is still sadly deficient, particularly in the interior. In answer to a complaint made against him in 1915 for allowing foreign priests to serve in his diocese, the Bishop of Guayana protested that he had no other pastors to fill the parishes.[20] The government has continuously found it necessary to allow foreign ecclesiastics to enter or let the parishes lie vacant. It permits the admittance of foreign priests with reluctance, however, fearing that they will oppose the subordination to which native priests have become accustomed. All foreign ecclesiastics must be naturalized. Deportations of those who fail to comply with this rule are common.[21]

The national support of the church is meager. In 1930, the appropriation for it was only 442,568 bolívares, approximately $90,000.[22] This is less than the average annual appropriations in the first half of the nineteenth century. The prohibitions placed by Guzmán Blanco on the right of the church to inherit property and the restrictions placed on the priests in this respect have not been repealed.[23] Although there has never been a complete expropriation of the property of the church by the state the institution today possesses little. According to a report of the Secretary of the Interior in 1916,

[17] *Memoria de relaciones interiores*, (1922), p. 159 *et seq.*

[18] *Documentos de la memoria de instrucción pública*, (1910), p. 489. The percentage in church schools is probably less today.

[19] *Leyes y decretos*, vol. xlvi, p. 7. There are today ten dioceses including the two archdioceses: Caracas, Mérida, Guayana, Calabozo, Zulía, Barquisimeto, Coro, Cumaná, Valencia, and San Cristóbal.

[20] *Memoria de relaciones interiores*, (1915), p. 237 *et seq.*

[21] *Memorias del interior, passim.*

[22] *Leyes y decretos*, vol. lii, pp. 198-200.

[23] *Código civil de Venezuela*, (Caracas, 1922). Article 829 of this code continues the same prohibitions and restrictions. There has been some discussion of a change of these provisions in the various revisions made of the civil code, particularly in the Commission for Revision in 1916. The suggestion has raised protests that indicate the strong anti-clericalism of most lawyers and legislators; *vide*, for example, Zuloaga, *Bibliografía y otros asuntos.*

its property, exclusive of church buildings was valued at 2,290,828 *bolívares*, about $450,000.[24] This estimate did not include the possessions of the church in several of the interior states, but its holdings in these are probably much less than in those from which the reports came. On account of its loss of social power, the church receives, it is believed, only slight and uncertain support through voluntary contributions from the faithful.

Reference has been made to the fact that Venezuela since 1876 has received the representation of the Papacy. Until 1909 the papal legate to Santo Domingo and Haiti was commissioned to Venezuela also, but he never resided there. In 1909, however, a legate was sent to Venezuela alone. Later the status of the representation was raised to that of an internuncio, 1918, and finally to that of a nuncio, 1921.[25] Venezuela has never celebrated a concordat with the Papacy. Nor has the reception of representatives been attended by any submission to the authority of Rome. This is evidenced, for example, in a contest over the delimitation of bishoprics in 1909, in which Gómez insisted on the absolute control of the state and refused to give *pase* to the bull, because it contained some provisions contrary to the Law of the Patronage.[26]

One feature of the anti-clerical legislation of Guzmán Blanco has occasioned recently considerable discussion; namely, the law of civil matrimony. Some free thinkers and liberals, notably the sociologists, Pedro Arcaya and Vallenilla Lanz, favor a modification of the law as a means of encouraging legal unions. To the restrictions placed on the method for formalizing marriage, they attribute the widespread lack of legal regularization of matrimonial unions in Venezuela, where two-thirds of the children are born illegitimate.[27] Although they do not oppose civil matrimony, they advocate extending to the clergy the privilege of giving legal recognition to the union. Arcaya states that, although concubinage has been common in Ven-

---

[24] *Memoria de relaciones interiores,* (1916) p. 410 *et seq.*
[25] Navarro, *Anales,* pp. 393-404.
[26] Correa, *El General J. V. Gómez, Documentos para la historia de su gobierno,* p. 25; p. 47; *Memoria de relaciones interiores,* (1909) p. 276, *et seq.*
[27] Pietri, Alejandro, *El código civil de 1916,* (Caracas, 1916) pp. vii-xxi. The introduction to this code gives Arcaya's project for the reform of the law presented to the Commission for the Revision of the code. For the views of Vallenilla Lanz, *vide, Revista de derecho y legislación,* vol. iv, (July 1, 1915), pp. 212-217.

ezuela from colonial time, such unions were usually soon formalized; the censures of the church were effective in bringing this about.[28] Vallenilla Lanz points to the incongruous situation which exists whereby a churchman may belong to the Council of State, whose incumbents can perform the marriage ceremony, although as a priest he does not possess the right. Any revision of the civil code that would extend the right to the clergy has been bitterly opposed, however, and no change has been made nor does it seem probable that any will be made.[29]

On the other hand there are certain restrictions commonly placed on the church by anti-clerical legislators that have never been enacted in Venezuela. The institution has never been entirely dispossessed of its property by state expropriation. The clergy may establish schools, although such schools must submit to public inspection and regulation. The political privileges of the clergy have, moreover, been maintained. The maintenance of unrestricted political rights may be attributed, no doubt, to the equalitarian sentiment of the people, which has persisted since 1810.

All Venezuelan historians and publicists recognize the progressive decline of the church from the late colonial period. None is able to explain quite satisfactorily its almost complete loss of social power. Vallenilla Lanz attributes the loss primarily to the popularity in Venezuela of French philosophy—the sentiments of equalitarianism and nationalism. He calls attention to the fact that there has never existed in Venezuelan political life an organized class interest, of birth, wealth, military group, or other with which the church might have identified itself in defense of special privileges.[30] Navarro, the lead-

---

[28] Arcaya, Pedro, "La evolución de matrimonio en Venezuela," *Revista de derecho y legislación*, vol. iv, p. 219 *et seq.*

[29] The revision of the civil code in 1916 brought forth the opposing views on the question of modifying the law of civil matrimony. The commission was divided on the question. Alejandro Pietri, editor of the *Revista de derecho y legislación*, stated that there was considerable support for the modification by the press. In the Senate, however, there was strong opposition to any change that would favor the clergy. Gil Fortoul led in this. He proposed that the marriage by teachers be allowed (*Discursos y palabras, 1910-1915*, pp. 233-244). In the lower house he was ably supported by Crespo Vivas. (*Conversaciones parlamentarias*, Caracas, 1917), p. 7 *et seq.*; Ascanio Rodríguez, *Apuntes*, pp. v-xv). They advocated also suppressing the restriction on the matrimony of the clergy. Zuloaga in the revisory commission expressed views in agreement with those of these extreme liberals.

[30] Vallenilla Lanz, Laureano, *Críticas de sinceridad y exactitud*, (Caracas, 1921) p. 401 *et seq.*

ing clerical student of the institution, emphasizes the reduction of economic power as a chief factor in the decline.[31] These and other views have been recorded in the preceding pages. It should be repeated in this connection that there exists a relatively strong church sentiment in certain centers as Valencia and Mérida; also, that some insist there has recently been a more or less general recrudescence of interest in religion and the church. The writer does not find adequate support for the latter assertion.

The majority of the Venezuelan intelligentsia regard the reduction of the influence of the church as a cause for national congratulation. A few, however, hold a different view. Arcaya and Vallenilla Lanz, for example, attribute not only the irregular matrimonial unions, but other social ills to the loss of moral predominance by the church. Without advocating its restoration to political place, they would like to see it regain social power. "In the psychological state of our people," Vallenilla Lanz asserts, "religion and morals are so closely united that to destroy the one is to attack fatally the other."[32]

Some believe that the next step in Venezuelan anti-clericalism will be the separation of the church and state. Gil Fortoul has been a foremost advocate of such action. He is supported in this view by certain other extreme liberals, notably Raúl Crespo, Bruzual López, and Razetti.[33] Bruzual López declares that the Venezuelan people would regard with impassivity the disestablishment of the church.[34] There has from 1830 been some sentiment in support of such policy; it has, however, always been slight. Anti-clericalism in Venezuela has rather insisted on the union as the only means for maintaining surveillance over the church. Lisandro Alvarado has expressed no doubt the sentiment of the majority of the Venezuelans in opposing separation.[35] The Law of the Patronage has remained the most stable political instrument in Venezuela.

[31] Navarro, Article on the Venezuelan church in the *Catholic Encyclopedia*.
[32] Vallenilla Lanz, *Criticas*, p. 421.
[33] Crespo, Raúl, *La libertad religiosa y separación de la iglesia y el estado*, Caracas, 1906.
[34] Quoted in Navarro, Nicolás, *Tres refutaciones con mótivas de otras tantas conferencias anti-católicas patrocinadas por la masoneria de Caracas, 1909-1910* (Caracas, 1910), p. 29.
[35] *El Tiempo*, April 2, 1910.

APPENDIX

LAW OF THE PATRONAGE

The Senate and House of Representatives of the Republic of Colombia united in Congress, considering:

1. That the government of Colombia not only should sustain the rights that it possesses as protector of the church, but also those that belong to it in the provision of benefices based on the discipline under which the churches of this territory were established, which until now has undergone no alteration;

2. That this discipline has been that of the patronage, of which the Spanish government was in possession and exercise without any restriction or limitation through the centuries that its rule lasted in these centuries;

3. That the exercise of those rights ought to be adapted to the system of government of the Republic and made to conform in the matters that it comprehends to the attributions that the constitution confides to the different powers of the government and to their authorities;

Decree:

Art. 1. The Republic of Colombia shall continue in the exercise of the right of patronage that the kings of Spain had in the metropolitan churches, cathedrals, and parishes of this part of America.

Art. 2. It is the duty of the Republic of Colombia and of its government to sustain this right and to secure from the Apostolic See that it be neither varied nor changed in any respect; and in accordance with this principle the executive shall celebrate with the Papacy a concordat that shall assure forever and irrevocably this prerogative to the republic and prevent complaints and reclamations in the future.

Art. 3. The right of patronage, that of supervision and protection, shall be exercised: (1) by the congress; (2) by the executive with the senate; (3) by the executive alone; (4) by the intendants;

[222]

(5) by the governors. The High Court of the Republic and the superior courts shall take cognizance of contentious matters that shall be sustained in this matter and that shall be detailed by this law.

Art. 4. It belongs to the Congress:

1. To decree the erection of new archbishoprics and bishoprics, to establish their limits, to designate the number of prebendaries that the cathedrals which are erected shall have, and to appropriate the funds that are to be used in the construction of the episcopal and metropolitan churches.

2. To regulate the limits of the dioceses already existing in Colombia and to determine from what funds the expense of the re-building of the cathedral churches shall be drawn when they happen to be destroyed.[1]

3. To settle doubts that shall occur as to the erection of the metropolitan churches and cathedrals that exist in Colombia or that shall be erected in the future.

4. To permit, and even to propose, the celebration of national and provincial councils when the good of the church and of the Republic demands it and to approve the *sinodales* that may be made.

5. To permit or not the foundation of new monasteries and hospitals; to suppress those that exist if it shall be considered useful, proper, and opportune, and to apportion their incomes; and either to establish the regulations that shall rule in the hospitals or to approve those that are presented to it, if the foundation is the work of an individual, of a company or corporation, and the national treasury did not have to have expense in it.

6. To establish the tariff of parochial fees and those that shall be collected in the ecclesiastical courts.

7. To regulate the administration and inversion of the tenth or of any other income established already or that shall be in the future established by the same Congress for the support of the worship and the subsistence of its ministers.

8. To give the proper license to the bulls and briefs that deal with the universal discipline or the reform and variation of the constitution of regulars, in order that their dispositions be observed in

[1] Earthquakes in Colombia were the cause of frequent destruction of buildings.

the Republic; or to resolve and dictate the proper measures, in order that they not be fulfilled nor have any effect, if they are contrary to the sovereignty and prerogatives of the nation, designating the penalties which those shall incur who do not observe and fulfill them.

9. To make all those laws that it shall consider proper for maintaining in its vigor the exterior discipline of the churches of the Republic and for the conservation and exercise of the ecclesiastical patronage.

10. To choose and name those that are to be presented to the Pope for the archbishoprics and bishoprics.

11. To make laws upon the establishment, regulation, and subsistence for the missions of the natives and suitable support for the missionaries.

Art. 5. It belongs to the Executive with the Senate to name the persons that are to occupy the offices of prebendaries and canons that are not official, according to the terms that Article 12 of the constitution provides that employees of influence and rank in the Republic shall be named.

Art. 6. It belongs to the executive alone:

1. To present to the Pope the decrees of the Congress upon the new erection of archbishoprics and bishoprics and upon the establishment of the limits of those that exist in order that, having been ratified by the Apostolic See, they shall be executed.

2. To present to the Pope those named by the Congress for archbishops and bishops.

3. To name the person or persons that, representative of the government, are to attend the national, provincial, and diocesan councils and to give them proper instructions upon matters they are to promote and upon the decisions they are to encourage.

4. To present to the prelates and ecclesiastical *cabildos* those whom he has named, with previous agreement and consent of the senate, for the offices of prebendaries and canons.

5. To name those for the official canonries, prebends, and half prebends, and to present those named to the prelates and the ecclesiastical *cabildos*.

6. To name the pastors of the diocese in which he now presides

or in the future shall reside and to present them to the respective prelate.

7. To give or not his assent to the nomination that the prelates and ecclesiastical *cabildos* have made for provisors and capitular vicars.

8. To give or not his assent to the nominations that the regular communities of the religions admitted into Colombia shall make in the capital of the Republic for their provincials and superiors.

9. To have the ecclesiastical prelates comply with visiting their dioceses, giving them the aid necessary to the fulfillment; to have them give account after a visitation of the measures they have taken; to support those and have them carried into execution, if they were within the limits of the ecclesiastical jurisdiction; and, if not, to amend them and annul them in so far as they have exceeded said ecclesiastical jurisdiction.

10. To resolve the disputes that are sustained in the matter of election between the intendants and the ecclesiastical prelates, and even to name himself those for curacies and sacristries, when the intendants have failed to do it, or arbitrarily and unjustly, have not been willing to name those proposed by the prelates.

11. To dictate proper measures in order that the properties of the archbishops and bishops be assured, that they be administered and applied to their accustomed uses, and that those encharged with their collection and management give accounts.

12. To take care that the funds for the construction of cathedral churches not be misused nor turned from their due and legitimate purpose and to have the prelates and ecclesiastical *cabildos* give account of the objects to which they are destined annually.

13. To have seized the bulls and briefs that have not been approved by the Congress and those that in any manner are opposed to the sovereignty and the prerogatives of the nation; and to turn them over to the Congress, prohibiting, in the meantime, that they be quoted in judgment or apart from it, or that they be applied by any judge or tribunal.

14. To approve definitively the erection of curacies which, in agreement with the ecclesiastical prelates and intendants, have been ordered in any of the dioceses of Colombia.

15. To enforce the laws of Congress by which the existing missions are regulated or new ones established and to resolve what is conducive to this object.

16. To take care that no novelty be introduced by prelates and ecclesiastical *cabildos* in the external discipline of the churches of Colombia nor any usurpation made of the patronage, sovereignty, and the prerogatives of the nation; and to have the corresponding tribunal follow the case and impose the legal penalties on those that shall introduce these novelties or shall make the expressed innovation.

17. To give license to the briefs that are expedited by the Apostolic See in matters of grace and that have been advanced by the channel of the executive himself; and to have seized and declared without effect official and judicial ones that are not permitted in Colombia, because in opposition to its constitution.

18. To dictate administrative rules in conformity with the laws of Congress for protecting religion, the public worship, and its ministers.

Art. 7. It belongs to the intendants:

1. To name and present to the respective ecclesiastical prelates the pastors of the dioceses comprehended in their departmental districts with the exclusion only of those of that one in which the executive resides.

2. To name, without the former limitation, and present to the ecclesiastical prelates the *sacristanes mayores* for the cathedral churches and for the parishes, for the provision of which examination should be held in turn.

3. To give or not their assent to the nominations that the ecclesiastical prelates make for *vicarios foraneos*; and without this requisite no one shall be able to exercise such functions.[2]

4. Having heard the report of the respective ecclesiastical authority, to erect new parishes and to fix their limits, and also those most suitable for those already erected, taking care that the limits of the civil administration correspond to those of the ecclesiastical and be the same; but these erections and demarcations shall not be carried into effect until the executive has approved them.

[2] *Vicario foraneo*—a vicar who serves outside the urban center.

5. To take care that the prelates and ecclesiastical *cabildos* not introduce novelties in the exterior discipline of the churches, nor usurp the patronage and the national prerogatives; to call them to account when they have done so, and if they do not desist, to give account to the executive.

6. To take care that neither the ecclesiastical prelates nor the visitors that shall be named by the *cabildos* in vacant see make resolutions, nor give providences in matters that are not of their jurisdiction, nor demand of the people and of the pastors and individuals any kind of fees that have not been approved as a legal tariff; and to remedy the abuses that are introduced by administrative measures, without preventing that the competent courts administer justice in the complaints upon burdens and exactions that individuals direct to them in these matters, and, also, without preventing that the penalties be applied by said tribunals to those that on these visits have violated the laws and assumed faculties that belong only to the government of the Republic.

7. To take care that the ecclesiastics not usurp the civil jurisdiction, nor evade nor violate the laws, orders, and dispositions of the government; to require the proper judges to restrain and punish those that commit excesses of this nature; and, if these requirements are not fulfilled, to give account to the executive in order that he provide what is proper.

8. To seize any bulls, briefs, or pontifical rescripts of whatever nature and class (with the exception of those that are issued by the penitentiary) that are introduced and circulated in the departments without the permission of the congress or of the executive, and to turn them over to the executive for the legal dispositions.

9. To inform the executive at the proper time what ecclesiastics there are in their departments who by their knowledge, conduct, and morals are worthy to be named for the offices of dignitaries and prebendaries. The intendants, in the capacity of governors of the provinces in which they reside, shall have the faculties that are conceded to the governors in the following article:

Art. 8. It belongs to the governors:

1. To give or not provisional assent to the nominations that the

prelates and ecclesiastical *cabildos* make for provisors and capitular vicars, giving account to the intendants by the proper reports in order that these may make them to the executive. But only the governors who reside in the provinces where the capitals of the dioceses are located shall have this function.

2. To give or not assent to the election of regular prelates, superior or local, that are made in the provinces in which they reside; and when tumults and uprisings are excited in these, to take the measures necessary to quiet them, giving account of everything as soon as possible to the intendants, so that these may report it to the executive.

3. To name the wardens of the cathedral and parochial churches of their provinces and to have them give account of their management in conformity with the law.

4. To appoint upon the nomination of the respective municipalities, the syndics, stewards, and administrators of the hospitals, to place in possession those named, and to have them give account of their management.

5. To admit the *recursos de fuerzas* against the ecclesiastical prelates, if there should not be a court of justice in the province, with the sole object of resolving administratively that the prelate suspend his proceedings and raise the censures that he had imposed, passing the expedient in the shortest time possible to the respective court of justice in order that it provide what is fitting.

6. To permit or not the foundation of chapels and churches that are not cathedral nor parochial, nor belonging to monasteries, which some individual or individuals intend to found.

7. To take the care and the zeal that is encharged to the intendant in the matters of which paragraphs 5, 6, and 7, of the preceding article treat; and to exercise the functions conceded to these in paragraph 8, giving immediate documented account of whatever contravention or excess that the persons comprehended in them commit in those cases, in order that the measures be dictated that are proper.

8. To visit the hospitals themselves or through persons of trust; to remedy the abuses that have been introduced in them and that

make them less useful for the purpose for which they were destined in society; to have them fulfill the laws that govern them; and to propose to the executive, through the intendants, the reforms that should be made in the establishments for improving them.

9. To permit the assembly of brotherhoods and sisterhoods where they are established; to inquire how many there are in each parish, how their incomes are administered, and if they fulfill the purpose of their institution, having them comply in these cases with the laws that have permitted their establishment.

10. To inform the intendants, with documentary evidence, of the places in which, because of their particular conditions, new parishes should be erected, of those that should be united in order that they be better conserved, and of those that ought to be suppressed; in order that the intendants, having heard the report of the ecclesiastical prelate, resolve what is fitting.

11. To admit the *recursos de fuerza* in their jurisdiction and with the object that the intendants do it; but this shall be done only when the governors reside in the capital of the diocese whose prelate gave motive to the *recurso*.

12. To inform the intendants of worthy ecclesiastics that are in the provinces and that could be placed in the offices of dignitaries and prebendaries.

Art. 9. The High Court of Justice shall take cognizance of the following matters:

1. Of cases of infidelity of archbishops and bishops to the Republic; of those that deal with usurpation by these prelates of the prerogatives of the nation, of its sovereignty, and of the right of patronage; and in general of all those for which these same prelates should be exiled and their temporalities occupied.

2. Of the controversies that occur between two or more dioceses concerning their limits.

3. Of the controversies, that proceed from the concordats that the executive shall make with the Papacy.

Art. 10. The superior courts shall take cognizance of the matters that follow:

1. Of the cases of provisors, capitular vicars, dignitaries and

prebendaries, *vicarios foraneos,* pastors, and other ecclesiastics upon crimes of infidelity to the Republic; of usurpation of its sovereignty, prerogatives, and right of patronage; of usurpation of the civil authority and jurisdiction; and for any other excess for which the one who commits it should be exiled and his temporalities occupied.

2. Of the *recursos de fuerza,* in taking cognizance and proceeding, in the mode of taking cognizance and proceeding and in not consenting, that shall be designed against archbishops, bishops, and any other prelates and ecclesiastical judges, having them raise the censures they have imposed.

3. Of the *recurso de protección* of the regulars.

4. Of the *competencias* between the ecclesiastical and civil judges of the territory to which the jurisdiction of the superior court extends.

5. Of the complaints upon impositions that the ecclesiastical prelates make in their exile, or the visitors named by them in occupied or vacant see. If the archbishops and bishops do not raise their censures after they are requested three times by the superior courts, these tribunals shall give account to the High Court in order that it proceed to what should be done. The points of strict patronage in a matter of nominations and elections shall never be able to be reduced to a *competencia* nor be made contentious. The executive or the intendants and the governors in the respective cases shall determine them as matters of administration. If the fulfillment of a bull, brief, or apostolic rescript upon any matter whatever that has not been given the sanction of the congress or the executive shall be sought before the High Court, superior courts, or any other tribunals of justice, they shall seize it immediately.

Art. 11. When metropolitan or cathedral church shall be vacant, the ecclesiastical *cabildo* shall immediately give account of the vacancy to the executive, and he, as soon as he receive the information, shall have it inserted in the official organ of the government in order that the vacancy that is to be provided shall be known in all the Republic.

Art. 12. The archbishops and bishops and, in vacant sees, the ecclesiastical *cabildos* shall inform the executive of the vacancies in the offices of the dignitaries, canons, prebendaries and *medias raciones* for the same purposes that the preceding article set forth.

Art. 13. For the vacancies announced in the archbishoprics and bishoprics, the executive shall be able to recommend to the congress the ecclesiastics of all the Republic that he considers most worthy for the office of the dignitary to be provided.

Art. 14. In its first meeting after the vacancy (occurs), the Congress united in the Senate House shall proceed to the election of archbishop or bishop. The person that obtains two-thirds of the votes of those present at the election shall be the one named for presentation by the executive.

Art. 15. Whenever there is lacking the majority indicated, they shall proceed in conformity with articles 73, 74, 75, and 79 of the constitution.

Art. 16. Before those named by the Congress for the archbishoprics and bishoprics are presented to the Pope by the executive, they shall take before him, or before the person that he delegates for that purpose, the oath to sustain and defend the constitution of the Republic, not to usurp its sovereignty, rights, and prerogatives, and to obey and to fulfill the laws, orders, and resolutions of the government. Two copies of this oath, both signed by the one named shall be recorded and sent, one to the Senate and the other to the House of Representatives, in order that they be kept in their respective archives.

Art. 17. As soon as those named have taken the oath that precedes, they shall be able to enter upon the exercise of their jurisdiction, the executive moving the ecclesiastical *cabildos* to that; but they shall not receive the income that belongs to them until the *fiat* of the Pope [is received].

Art. 18. Before their consecration, which ceremony shall not be able to be deferred more than four months counted from the day on which the bulls of the pope are received, the archbishops and bishops ought to make, with the assistance of the *fiscal*, if there should be one in the capital of the diocese, and if not of the *synodal procurador-general* of the municipality, of the minister of the departmental treasury, or that of the province, and of two prebendaries named by the ecclesiastical *cabildo*, an exact and minute inventory of all their property and income and of their increases, active and passive; of this inventory three copies shall be formed signed by the persons that assist in it and by the archbishop or bishop, and one shall be delivered to the executive, and the other two shall be deposited in the archives of the respective treasury and in the secretary's office of the ecclesiastical *cabildo*.

Art. 19. When the one named for an archbishopric or bishopric shall renounce it before the executive makes the presentation to the Pope, the congress shall take cognizance and pass upon the resignation; but if this is made after the presentation to the Papacy, it shall be handled through the executive, and proceeding shall not be able to be made to a new election until the resolution of the Pope [is received].

Art. 20. The nomination and election of archbishops and bishops can fall upon other archbishops and bishops; but in this case the one named shall not acquire any right in the administration of the diocese to which he has been elected, and he shall remain in that of which he was in possession, until the Pope has dispatched the bulls.

Art. 21. When it is a matter of the provision of a prebend or canonship that is not official, the executive in agreement with his council of government shall designate the one that is considered of most merit and virtues and propose him to the Senate in order that it give or not its consent and approval.

Art. 22. In the nominations for prebends and *medias raciones* the executive shall proceed with his council of government in the terms designated by the preceding article, and those who are named by them shall be presented to the ecclesiastical prelates and their *cabildos* in vaçant see in order that they give them possession and canonical institution. The same shall be done in the case of those named for prebends and canonships, as soon as they have obtained the agreement and consent of the Senate.

Art. 23. The concourse and opposition that have been customary shall precede the provision of the official canonships. The edicts shall be issued in the name of the prelate and the respective *cabildos*, their term shall be six months, and they shall be extended throughout the Republic; but they shall not be able to be posted without having obtained the approval of the intendants, or of the executive, as the case may be, which shall be sought by the prelate or by the ecclesiastical *cabildo* in vacant see at the time they give him account of the canonship that is to be provided.

Art. 24. The executive shall name a person to attend for the acts of opposition and afterwards to be able to inform him of the capacity and talents that the opponents have shown. The prelate and *cabildo* together shall form a list of the opponents and send it to the executive, setting forth the merits, services, and qualities of those that it proposes as they have accredited themselves at the time of presenting themselves for the opposition. Of those proposed the executive shall name the one that appears to him most worthy, without being limited necessarily to those of the first place, and shall present him to the prelate or *cabildo* in vacant see in order that they place him in possession, giving him canonical institution.

Art. 25. If for any official canonship that should be vacant, there is presented no more than one candidate, he being one capable and having the qualities required by law of those that obtain these offices, the prelate and the ecclesiastical *cabildo* shall propose him to the executive, and this one shall present him; but if he lacks ability and fitness and the qualities necessary, the provision shall be suspended, and new edicts shall be posted, account being given to the executive of the result of the first concourse.

Art. 26. In the provision of curacies and likewise in that of sacristries the formalities that *capítulo* 18, *sesión* 24 of the Council of Trent prescribe shall be observed, and concourse shall be opened for the vacant benefices every six months at least. The edicts shall be posted by the ecclesiastical prelates with the compliance of the intendants, or of the executive, as the case may be; and when the prelates do not convoke the concourse promptly, they shall urge them to do it; and if they do not comply with it, shall inform the metropolitan; and if this one should be negligent, they shall notify the nearest suffragan in order that, conformable to the canons, they correct the neglect.

Art. 27. For each benefice the ecclesiastical prelate shall propose to the executive or to the intendant three of the opponents at the concourse, who, after having been examined and approved, have shown their deserts, stating the merits and services that each has given evidence of having made to the church and to the Republic. If there shall be no obstruction, the intendants and the executive, as the case may be, shall present the one of those proposed that appears most worthy; but if they should know that these are not worthy of the benefices, either because of their personal qualities or because the greater merit of other ecclesiastics is ignored, they shall be able to return the list in order that it be revised, indicating to the prelate the reasons they have for not presenting any of those proposed.

Art. 28. If there should be no more than one opponent for the provision of a curacy or a sacristry, the ecclesiastical prelate shall propose him, if he is of capacity and fitness; and the executive or the intendant shall present him, provided that it is evident to them that others have not been opposed.

Art. 29. No one shall be able to take major orders, including the priesthood, under pretext of a curacy or sacristry that has not been obtained in conformity to the two preceding articles; nor seek a definite curacy or sacristry, without having served another for two years in succession, within which time he shall not even have been admitted to the concourse. Those that place themselves in opposition for the first time ought to serve the curacy or the sacristry to which they have been named.

Art. 30. When the curacy belongs to the regular clergy, the superior prelate of these shall name three and propose them to the ecclesiastical prelate in order that they be examined; and if they are found to be competent and approved, they shall be proposed by the ecclesiastical prelate to the intendants in order that he present one of the three. If all or any of those designated by the regular prelate are not suitable, the ordinary prelate shall have others proposed that have the necessary fitness. Edicts shall not precede for the provision of these benefices.

Art. 31. The monks that are appointed by the regular prelates for the work of the missionaries shall be examined by the respective ecclesiastical prelate in the terms that the chapter of the Council of

Trent, already cited, prescribes; and if they are capable and fitting, the ordinary prelate shall grant them the necessary license and inform the intendant of it, or the executive, as the case may be, in order that the license be given to the patent of the regular prelate and that the expense of the voyage and their stipends be ordered to be allowed them.

Art. 32. If the territory of a diocese is comprehended in two or more departments, the ecclesiastical prelate shall inform the intendants that have to do with posting edicts for the vacant benefices; and each one of the intendants has the right of notifying the ecclesiastical prelate for the holding of a concourse and of performing in his turn the measure provided in Article 26.

Art. 33. The inhabitants of new parishes that have built churches at their expense and individuals that have done the same shall have the right of naming the ecclesiastics that shall serve as pastor for the first time; and this one shall be named by the respective intendant or by the executive, as the case may be, and instituted by the ecclesiastical prelate, provided that he be competent and suitable for the ministry.

Art. 34. The filling of the curacies and the sacristries provisionally belongs to the prelates in full right; they shall be able to do it with secular or regular ecclesiastics, but not with proprietary pastors; and the executive and the intendants shall prevent such changes, opposed to the universal discipline of the church, being made.

Art. 35. Pastors that, having placed themselves in opposition for other benefices, have not been approved in the concourse shall not be able to be nominated for the curacy they sought nor to return to their own until they have studied for some time in the diocesan seminaries or the schools for candidates for orders and after this study have been examined again and found competent. In the meantime trustees shall be named in conformity with what the Council of Trent provides; there being reserved for the prelate a part of the income of the benefice for his subsistence. The intendants and the executive, as the case may be, shall take care that it shall be done thus, and to that end they shall ask of the ecclesiastical prelates, and these shall deliver to them at the end of the concourse, a list of the priests that were not approved in the examination,

Art. 36. Neither the executive nor the intendants shall intervene in the removals which the ecclesiastical prelate make, in conformity with the Council of Trent, of pastors whose crimes and excesses have brought upon them this penalty; as soon as the sentence of removal has been executed by the party having consented to it, or by its having been confirmed on appeal, or by any other means legal or canonical, testimony of it shall be sent by the prelate to the executive or the respective intendant in order that they be informed of the vacancy and of the reason that occasioned it.

Art. 37. Those that are named for the dignitaries, the prebends, the curacies and sacristries, with the exception of those comprehended in Article 29, shall be able to resign the appointment to which they have been nominated; if it should be before taking canonical institution, before the executive or the intendant that presented them; but if they had already been instituted the renunciation shall be made before the respective ecclesiastical prelate and he, for its reception or rejection, shall proceed in agreement with the executive, if the presentation belonged to him, or with the respective intendant, as the case may be, sending him to that end the expedient with an indication of his opinion and of the reasons upon which it is based.

Art. 38. No ecclesiastic is able to obtain at one time an office of dignitary or a prebend and an endowed curacy nor two distinct curacies.

Art. 39. Every ecclesiastical benefice, archbishopric, bishopric, dignitaryship, prebend, curacy, sacristry, or any other of whatever nature or class they may be shall be provided necessarily with natives of Colombia or those naturalized into the Republic in conformity with the laws; but the character of natives shall be necessary and indispensable in the archbishops and bishops.

Art. 40. The ecclesiastical prelates, as soon as they take charge of the administration of their churches, and the ecclesiastical *cabildos* within the first eight days of the vacancy, shall name provisors and general vicars, and, before placing the one named in possession, shall inform the executive, in order that he give his assent to the nomination. If the executive should not have his residence in the diocese, the intendants and governors shall do it provisionally in his stead:

but the one thus named shall not be able to continue, if the executive for grave reasons should not agree to his nomination. The nomination of the provisors and capitular vicars shall not be able to fall except on natives of Colombia.

Art. 41. For the nomination of wardens of the churches the ecclesiastical *cabildos* shall propose three individuals, and if they are suitable and trustworthy, the governor shall name one of them; for those of the parochial churches the inhabitants shall also propose three, and if they are suitable and trustworthy, the governor shall name one of them. For forming these lists the inhabitants shall assemble in the parochial churches, presided over by the alcaldes and in the presence of the priest.

Art. 42. Any laws, cédulas, and royal orders that have ruled until now are revoked and annulled in all and each one of the points of which this law treats; if in it there shall be found any lack or anything should occur that has not been foreseen, the congress shall be consulted for its resolution.

Enacted in Bogotá: July 22, 1824, 14—The President of the Senate, José María del Real—The President of the House of Representatives, José Rafael Mosquera—The Secretary of the Senate, Antonio José Caro—The acting Secretary of the House of Representatives, José Joaquín Suárez.

House of the Government in Bogotá, July 28, 1824, 14.

Signed, Francisco de Paula Santander—For His Excellency the Vice-president of the Republic encharged with the executive power— The Secretary of State for the Department of the Interior—José Manuel Restrepo.

BIBLIOGRAPHY

I. Manuscript Collections

Archivo Nacional: *Asuntos eclesiásticos.*
———— *Documentos de secretaría del interior y justicia de la república de Venezuela.*
———— *Documentos de secretaría de la hacienda de la república de Venezuela.*
Archivo de la Catedral de Caracas: *Libros de edictos de los obispos.*
———— *Documentos del cabildo metropolitano.*
Archivo de la Universidad Central: *Documentos del archivo universitario de Caracas.*

II. Published Documents: Political and Ecclesiastical

Academia Nacional de la Historia: *Documentos para los anales de Venezuela desde el movimiento separatisto de Colombia hasta nuestras dias,* first period, 1829-1830, 7 vols., Caracas, 1890-1891; second period, 1831-1840, 4 vols., 1891-1894; third period, 1840, 1 vol., 1909.
———— *Prólogo á los anales de Venezuela,* Caracas, 1903.
Actas de la convención nacional de Venezuela, 5 de julio de 1858 hasta 3 de febrero de 1859, Caracas, 1859.
Actuaciones y documentos del gobierno central de la unidad de la raza en el descubrimiento, exploración, población, pacificación y civilización de las antiguas provincias españoles hoy república de Venezuela, 1486-1600, Tipografia Americana, Caracas, 1926.
Altolaguirre y Duvale, Angel, (editor), *Relaciones geográficas de la gobernación de Venezuela, 1767-1768,* Madrid, 1908.
Anuario estadístico de los estados unidos de Venezuela, Caracas, 1903-1921.
Azpurúa, Ramón (editor), *Anales de Venezuela,* Imprenta "La Opinión Nacional," vol. i, Caracas, 1877.
Blanco, José Félix and Ramón Azpurúa (editors), *Documentos para la historia de la vida pública del Libertador de Colombia,* 14 vols., Caracas, 1875-77.
Case of Venezuela by a special Commission of the Government of Venezuela, Reply to the British Blue Book. Atlanta, 1896.
Castillo, Pedro P. del, (editor): *Teatro de la legislación colombiana y venezolana vigente,* 3 vols., Valencia, 1852.
Censo primero de la república de Venezuela verificado en noviembre de 1873, Caracas, 1875; also, 1881, *et al.*
Código civil de los estados unidos de Venezuela, Caracas, 1922.
Código de instrucción pública, Caracas, 1912.
Código penal, Caracas, 1915.
Congreso de 1823: Actas, Biblioteca de Historia Nacional, vol. xxxvii, Bogotá, 1926.

[238]

Constituciones sinodales del obispado de Venezuela, 3 vols., Madrid, 1761.

Correa, Luis (editor), *El General Juan Vicente Gómez; Documentos para la historia de su gobierno,* Litografía del Comercio, Caracas, 1925.

Cortazar, Roberto and Luis Cuervo (editors) : *Congreso de Angostura: Libro de actas,* Bogotá, 1921.

———— *Congreso de Cúcuta, Libro de actas,* Biblioteca de Historia Nacional, vol. xxxv, Bogotá, 1923.

Decretos expedidos por el poder ejecutivo de Venezuela desde 1830 hasta 1838, George Corser, Caracas, 1839.

Cuerpo de leyes de Colombia . . . desde 1821 hasta 1827, Valentín Espinal, Caracas, 1840.

Cuerpo de leyes de Venezuela, 1830-1850, Valentín Espinal, Caracas, 1850.

Cuervo, A. B. (editor), *Colección de documentos inéditos sobre la geografía y la historia de Colombia,* 5 vols., Bogotá, 1893.

Documentos favorables á las reformas de la constitución de 1864, Imprenta León Hermanos, Caracas, 1930.

Documentos favorables á las reformas de la constitución de 1864, Imprenta "La Opinión Nacional," Caracas, 1874.

Documentos relativos á la cuestión de límites y navegación fluvial entre el imperio del Brazil y la república de Venezuela, Imprenta Eloi Escobar, Caracas, 1859.

Documentos Relating to the Question of Boundary Between Venezuela and British Guayana submitted to the Boundary Commission by the Counsel of the Government of Venezuela, 3 vols., Washington, 1896.

Glorias del ilustre americano Guzmán Blanco, Imprenta "El Democrata," Caracas, 1875.

Guzmán Blanco, Antonio, *Mensajes . . . como presidente provisional de los Estados Unidos de Venezuela . . . y como presidente constitucional al cuerpo legislativo en 1873, 1874, 1875, y 1876,* Caracas, 1876.

———— *Documentos para la historia de Venezuela, Memorandum del General Guzmán Blanco,* Caracas, 1875.

———— *Discursos del General . . .* Caracas, 1883.

Guerra, José Joaquín, (editor) : *La Convención de Ocaña,* Biblioteca de la Historia Nacional, vol. vi, Bogotá, 1908.

Hernáez, Francisco Javier, (editor) : *Colección de bulas, breves, y otros documentos relativos á la iglesia de América y Filipinas,* 2 vols., Brussels, 1879.

Leyes de Colombia, 1821 (without date or place).

El libro nacional de los venezolanos: Actas del congreso constituyente de Venezuela en 1811, Tipografía Americana, Caracas, 1911.

Libro 4 de actas del supremo congreso de Venezuela en 1812: Orígenes de la república, Litografía del Comercio, Caracas, 1926.

Martí, Mariano: *Relación de la visita general que en la diócesis de Caracas y Venezuela hecha por el obispo . . . ,* 3 vols., Caracas, 1928.

Memorias de la hacienda de la república de Venezuela, 1831—

Memorias del interior y justicia de la república de Venezuela, 1831—

Memorias de relaciones exteriores de la república de Venezuela, 1858—

Memorias de la instrucción pública, 1881—

Posada, E. and P. M. Ibáñez, (editors), *Relaciones de mando: Memorias presentados por los gobernantes del nuevo reino de Granada,* Bogotá, 1910.

Recopilación de leyes y decretos de Venezuela, 52 vols., Caracas, 1874-1930.

Recopilación de leyes de los reinos de las Indias, 4 vols., Madrid, 1841.

Relaciones históricas de las misiones de padres capuchinos de Venezuela, Colección de libros raros ó curiosos que tratan de América, Madrid, 1928.

Restrepo, Ernesto Tirado (editor), *Archivo Santander,* 23 vols., Bogotá, 1914.

Rionegro, Froilán, (editor), *Relaciones de las misiones de las antiguas provincias españoles hoy república de Venezuela,* Seville, 1918.

Silva, Antonio Ramón (editor), *Documentos para la historia de la diócesis de Mérida,* vols. i, ii, iii, iv, vi, Mérida, 1908-1922; vol. v, Caracas, 1927.

————— *El patriotismo del clero de la diócesis de Mérida,* Mérida, 1911.

Strickland, Joseph (editor), *Documents and Maps of the Boundary Question Between Venezuela and British Guayana from the Capuchin Archives in Rome,* Rome, 1896.

Solórzano Pereira, J. de, *Política indiana,* 2 vols, Madrid, 1776.

United States Senate Documents, no. 6, 55th Congress, 2nd Session, *Report of Special Commission on True Divisional Line Between the Republic of Venezuela and British Guiana,* Washington, 1898.

Venezuela-British Guiana Boundary Arbitration: The Counter-Case of the United States of Venezuela before the Tribunal of Arbitration, 3 vols., New York, 1899.

III. Memoirs, Letters, etc.

Archivo del General Miranda: Viajes, diarios, documentos, cartas, etc., Parra León Hermanos, Caracas, 12 vols., 1929-32.

Biggs, James, *The History of Don Francisco de Miranda's Attempt to Effect a Revolution in South America,* 2nd edition, Boston, 1810.

Brown, C. C., *Narrative of the Expedition to South America in 1817,* London, 1819.

Cuervo, Luis Agusto (editor), *Epistolario del doctor Rufino Cuervo,* 3 vols., Bogotá, 1918.

Depons, F. R. J. *A Voyage to the Eastern Part of Tierra Firme on the Spanish Main in South America during the Years 1801, 1802, 1803, 1804.* Translated from the French by an American gentleman, 3 vols., New York, 1806.

Díaz, José Domingo. *Recuerdos sobre la rebelión de Caracas,* Madrid, 1819.

Flinter, G. D. *A History of the Revolution of Caracas,* London, 1819.

Heredia, J. F., *Memorias sobre las revoluciones de Venezuela,* Garnier, Paris, 1885.

Hippisley, G., *A Narrative of the Expedition to the Rivers Orinoco and Apure in South America,* London, 1819.

Humboldt, Alexander de, and Aimé Bonpland, *Personal Narrative of Travels to the Equinoctial Regions of the New Continent during the Years 1799-1804,* translated by H. M. Williams, 6 vols., London, 1826.

Lacroix, Perú de la, *Diario de Bucaramanga,* edition of Cornelio Hispano, Paris, 1912.

Lavaysse, Dauxion de, *A Statistical, Commercial, and Political Description of Venezuela, Trinidad, Margarita, and Tobago*, London, 1820.

Lecuna, Vicente, (editor), *Cartas del Libertador*, 10 vols., Caracas, 1929-1930.

Mahoney, W. D., *Campaigns and Cruises in Venezuela and New Granada and in the Pacific Ocean, 1817-1830*, 3 vols., London, 1831.

Morillo, Pablo, *Manifesto que hace á España el teniente general . . .*, Caracas, 1820.

O'Leary, Simón B. (editor), *Memorias del General O'Leary*, 32 vols., Caracas, 1879-1888.

Páez, José Antonio. *Autobiografía*, 2 vols., 2nd edition, New York, 1871.

Plaza, José Antonio de, *Memorias para la historia de la Nueva Granada desde su descubrimiento hasta el 20 de julio de 1810*, Bogotá, 1850.

Posada Gutiérrez, Joaquín, *Memorias histórico-políticas; Ultimos días de la Gran Colombia y del Libertador*, 3 vols., Madrid, 1920.

Pondenx, H. and Mayer, F., *Mémoire pour servir l'histoire de la révolution de la capitainerie générale de Caracas depuis l'abdication de Charles IV jusqu'au mois d'âout, 1814*, Paris, 1815.

Robinson, J. H., *Journal of an Expedition 1,400 Miles up the Orinoco and 300 Miles up the Arauca*, London, 1872.

Recollections of a Service of Three Years during the War of Extermination in the Republics of Venezuela and Colombia by an Officer of the Colombian Navy, 2 vols., London, 1828.

Ségur, Comte de., *Mémoires, souvenirs, et anecdotes*, 2 vols., Paris, 1859.

Semple, Robert, *Sketch of the Present State of Caracas, Including a Journey from Caracas through La Victoria and Valencia to Puerto Cabello*, London, 1812.

Sevilla, Rafael. *Memorias de un oficial de ejército español*, Madrid, 1916.

Urdaneta, Rafael. *Memorias del general . . .*, Madrid, (without date).

Urquinaona y Pardo, P. de, *Memorias de Urquinaona, comisionado de la regencia española para la pacificación del nuevo reino de Granada*, Madrid, 1917.

IV. Special Studies and Ecclesiastical Histories

Abbe de Pradt, *Concordato de América con Roma*, Paris, 1827.

Álvarez de Villanueva, Francisco, *Relación histórica de todos los franciscanos en las Indias*, Colección de libros raros ó curiosos que tratan de América, Madrid, 1892.

Andara, J. L., *La evolución social y política de Venezuela*, vol. 1, La colonia, Caracas, 1904.

Arcaya, Pedro, *Estudios sobre personajes y hechos de la historia venezolana*, Tipografía Cosmos, Caracas, 1911.

———— *Estudios de sociología venezolana*, Madrid (without date).

Arévalo González, R., *Apuntaciones históricas*, vol. i, Caracas, 1913.

Ascanio Rodríguez, J. B., *Consideraciones acerca de la unión matrimonial en Venezuela*, Caracas, 1925.

———— *Apuntes y documentos para la historia del registro civil en Venezuela*, Caracas, 1925.

Astrain, Antonio, *Historia de la Compañia de Jesús en la asistencia de España*, 7 vols., Madrid, 1925.

Ayarragaray, Lucas, *La iglesia en América y la dominación española*, Buenos Aires, 1920.

Borda, J. J., *Historia de la Compañía de Jesús en la Nueva Granada*, 2 vols., Poissy, 1872.

Borreguero, F. López, *Los indios caribes*, Madrid, 1875.

Cadeña, P. I., *Anales diplomáticos de Colombia*, Bogotá, 1878.

Carrocera, Cayetaño de, *La orden franciscana en Venezuela*, Caracas, 1929.

————— *Memorias para la historia de Cumaná*, Cumaná, 1926-1927.

Carvajal, Jacinto de, *Relación del descubrimiento del río Apure hasta su ingreso en el Orinoco*, León, 1892.

Castellaños, Juan de, *Elegías de varones ilustres de Indias*, *Biblioteca de autores españoles*, 3rd edition, vol. iv, Madrid, 1874.

Caulín, Antonio, *Historia corográfica, natural, y evangélica de la Nueva Andalucía*, Madrid, 1779.

Cassani, José, *Historia de la provincia de la Compañia de Jesús en el Nuevo Reino de Granada en la América*, Madrid, 1741.

Cisneros, José L., *Descripción exacta de la provincia de Venezuela*, Colección de libros raros ó curiosos que tratan de América, Madrid, 1912.

Crespo, Raúl, *La libertad religiosa y separación de la iglesia y el estado*, Tipografía Gutenberg, Caracas, 1906.

Crespo Vivas, R., *Conversaciones parlamentarias*, Caracas, 1917.

Dominici, Anibal, *Comentarios al código civil venezolano*, 4 vols., Imprenta Bolívar, Caracas, 1902.

Ensayo histórico sobre el poder temporal de los papas, Translation by J. D. L., Caracas, 1834.

Escoriaza, Melchor de, *Crónica de las misiones capuchinas en Venezuela, Puerto Rico, y Cuba*, Caracas, 1910.

Escriche, Joaquín, *Diccionario razonado de legislación y jurisprudence*, 4 vols., Madrid, 1876.

Frasso, Pedro, *De regio patronato*, Madrid, 1677.

Gil Fortoul, José, *Discursos y palabras*, Caracas, 1915.

————— *El hombre y la historia*, Garnier, Paris, 1896.

Gilii, Filippo Salvadore, *Saggio di storia americana: o sia storia naturale, civile, e sacra de regni e delle provincia spagnuole di Terra Ferme*, 4 vols., Rome, 1780-1784.

Gumilla, José, *El Orinoco ilustrado, historia natural, civil, y geográfica de este gran río y sus caudalosas vertientes*, Madrid, 1741.

González, Eloy G., *La ración del boa*, El Cojo, Caracas, 1908.

————— *Dentro de la cosiata*, Caracas, 1907.

————— *Al margen de la epopeya*, Caracas, 1906.

González, Dávila, Gil, *Teatro eclesiástico de la primitiva iglesia de las Indias occidentales*, 2 vols., Madrid, 1649-1655.

González de Soto, Cristóbal, *Noticia histórica de la república de Venezuela*, Barcelona, 1873.

González Guinán, Francisco, *Tradiciones de mi pueblo, Valencia, Venezuela,* Caracas, 1927.

Guzmán, Antonio Leocadio, *Datos históricos sur-americanos,* Brussels, 1878-1882.

——— *Editoriales de "El venezolano,"* Caracas, 1883.

Guzmán Blanco, Antonio, *En defensa de la causa liberal,* Imprenta de Lahure, Paris, 1894.

Larrazabal, Felipe, *Historia de los seminarios clericales,* Caracas, 1856.

Lea, H. C., *The Inquisition in the Spanish Dependencies,* New York, 1908.

Leturia, Pedro, *La acción diplomática de Bolívar ante Pío VII, 1820-1823,* Razón y Fe, Madrid, 1925.

Level, Andrés, *Informe sobre el estado actual de los distritos de reducción de indígenas en el Orinoco,* Caracas, 1850.

Llorente, Juan Antonio, *Apología católica del proyecto de constitución religiosa escrito por un americano,* San Sebastian, 1821.

Lodarés, Baltazar de, *Los franciscanos en Venezuela,* Caracas, 1922-1931.

Machado, José E., *El día histórico,* Caracas, 1929.

Marcano, Gaspard, *Etnographie pre-colombienne du Vénézuéla,* 2 vols., Paris, 1889-1890.

Medina, J. F., *Historia del tribunal del santo oficio de la inquisición de Cartagena de las Indias,* Santiago de Chile, 1899.

Méndez y Mendoza, Juan de D, *Historia de la universidad central,* 2 vols., Caracas, 1911.

Michelena y Rojas, Francisco, *Exploración oficial,* Brussels, 1867.

Navarro, Nicolás E., *Anales eclesiásticos venezolanos,* Tipografía Americana, Caracas, 1929.

Olavarría, Domingo A., *Estudios histórico-políticos,* Tipografía Artistica, Valencia, 1894.

Parra, Caracciolo, *La instrucción en Caracas, 1567-1725,* Parra León Hermanos, Caracas, 1932.

Parras, Pedro Joseph, *Gobierno de los regulares de la América,* 2 vols., Madrid, 1783.

Picón-Febrés, Gabriel, *Datos para la historia de la diócesis de Mérida,* Caracas, 1916.

Pierson, W. W., *Lectures on the Church in Hispanic-America,* University of North Carolina, 1929-1930, unpublished.

Pietri, Alejandro, *El código civil de 1916,* Litografía del Comercio, Caracas, 1916.

Pocaterra, José Rafael, *Gómez, the Shame of America,* Paris, 1929.

Restrepo, Juan Pablo, *La iglesia y el estado en Colombia,* London, 1885.

Ribadeneyra, Antonio Joachím, *Manuel compendio de regio patronato indiano,* Madrid, 1755.

Rivas, Angel César, *Ensayos de historia política y diplomática,* Madrid (without date).

Rivero, Juan, *Historia de las misiones de los llanos de Casanare y los ríos Orinoco y Meta,* 2 vols., Bogotá, 1883.

Rodríguez, Teófilo, *Tradiciones populares: colección de crónicas y leyendas nacionales por varios escritores patrios*, Caracas, 1885.

Rojas, Arístides, *Estudios históricos*, 3 vols., Tipografía del Comercio, Caracas, 1917-1927.

———— *Orígines de la revolución venezolana*, Caracas, 1883.

———— *Estudios históricos: Orígenes venezolanos*, vol. 1, Caracas, 1891.

Rojas Paúl, Juan Pablo, *La cacareada reacción contra la causa liberal*, Curaçao, 1894.

Ruíz Blanco, Matías, *Conversión en Píritu de indios cumanagotos y palenques*, Colección de libros raros ó curiosos que tratan de América, Madrid, 1892.

Salas, Julio C., *Civilización y barbarie: estudio de sociología americana*, Barcelona, 1919.

———— *Tierra Firme*, Mérida, 1908.

———— *Los indios caribes*, Barcelona, 1921.

Samper, José María, *Ensayo sobre las revoluciones políticas y la condición social de las repúblicas colombianas*, Thunot, Paris, 1861.

Simón, Pedro, *Noticias historiales de las conquistas de Tierra Firme en las Indias occidentales*, Bogotá, 1882-1892.

Tamburini de Brescia, P., *Verdadera idea de la Santa Sede*, Caracas, 1832.

Terrero, Blas José, *Teatro de Venezuela y Caracas*, Litografía del Comercio, Caracas, 1926.

Talavera y Garcés, Mariano de, *Apuntes de historia eclesiástica de Venezuela* —edited by Nicolás E. Navarro, Tipografía Americano, Caracas, 1929.

Urquinaona y Pardo, P. de, *Resumen de las causas principales que preparon y dieron impulso á la emancipación de la América española*, Madrid, 1835.

Urrutia, F. C., *Páginas de historia diplomática: Los Estados Unidos de América y las repúblicas hispano-americanas, 1810-1830*, Bogotá, 1917.

Vallenilla Lanz, Laureano, *Críticas de sinceridad y exactitud*, Imprenta Bolívar, Caracas, 1921.

———— *Cesarismo democrático*, El Cojo, Caracas, 1929.

Vélez Sarsfield, Dalmacio, *Relaciones del estado con la iglesia en antigua América española*, Buenos Aires, 1889.

Villegas-Pulido, G. T., *Los extranjeros en Venezuela-su no admisión-su expulsión*, Litografía de Comercio, 2nd edition, Caracas, 1919.

Zahm, J. A., *The Quest of El Dorado*, New York, 1917.

Zamora, Matías Gómez. *Regio patronato español é indiana*, Madrid, 1897.

Zubieta, Pedro A., *Apuntaciones sobre las primeras misiones diplomáticas de Colombia*, Bogotá, 1924.

Zuloaga, N., *Códigos, leyes, y decretos concordados por*—Imprenta Bolívar, Caracas, 1896.

V. PAMPHLETS

Acta del clero secular y regular de la ciudad de Bogotá, (Bogotá, 1824), reprinted, Caracas, 1851.

Acta solemne de concordia entre al estado y el sacerdocio y para proveer los ejércitos que obran contra los enemigos que invade el territorio de Venezuela, Caracas, 1814.

Arias, Buenaventura, *Á los señores de las camaras del congreso de Venezuela*, Caracas, 1831.

———— *Exposición sobre patronato eclesiástico dirigida al primer congreso constitucional de Venezuela*, Caracas, 1831.

Á "El arzobispo de Caracas," ó sea la refutación al impreso así titulado, unos orthodoxos, Caracas, 1851.

Autoridad episcopal independiente del soberano temporal, un católico, Caracas, 1837.

Ávila, José Cecilio. *Contestación del dr . . . al autor de los "Variedades de Iris." No. 102.* Caracas, 1824.

———— *Contestación dada al señor fiscal de la hacienda pública de Caracas . . .* Caracas, 1820.

Azuero, Juan Nepomuceno, *El doctor Merizalde y El Noticiozote*, Bogotá, 1825.

Breve impugnación del folleto intitulado "Reforma de la política eclesiástica" ó sentimentos de la provincia de Carabobo. Caracas, 1834.

Las bulas, ó sea lo que se debe hacer en el cuestión acerça del arzobispo electo, Caracas, 1851.

Burke, William, *Additional Reasons for our Immediate Emancipation of Spanish America*, London, 1808.

Cartas de un alemán á S. E. el vicepresidente, Caracas, 1826.

Castro, H. M., *El matrimonio civil en Venezuela*, Barinas, 1858.

La cátedra del espíritu santo convertida en ataque al gobierno de Colombia bajo el nombre de mazones, Caracas, 1825.

Un Católico á "El patriota" en la "cuestión arzobispo de Caracas," Caracas, 1851.

Contestación á la hoja suelta titulada "Al público" que ha circulado en estas últimas días sobre la cuestión arzobispo, Caracas, 1851.

El dean, y cabildo de Caracas sobre las asignaciones eclesiásticas y su cuenta, Caracas, 1833.

Defensa del celibato eclesiástico, ó sea compendio de doctrinas ortodoxas sobre el matrimonio de los clerigos mayores (Published 1838 by the Archbishop of Bogotá; ordered reprinted by Domingo Quintero, Dean of Metropolitano Cabildo of Caracas), Caracas, 1873.

Dilate de la corte suprema, Valencia, 1849.

Disertación refututoria del artículo "El arzobispo de Caracas" inserto en "El Republicano" no. 291, Mérida, 1850.

Documentos oficiales que dan el justo concepto acerca de la expulsión de iltmo. Sr. Dr. Ramon Ignacio Mendez, dignísimo arzobispo de Caracas y sobre otras circumstancias interesantes que ocurrieron en ella, Caracas, 1830.

Documentos oficiales que dan noticias exactas de las ocurrencias del iltmo. Sr. Dr. Buenaventura Arias, obispo de Jérico desde que tome posesión del vicariato apostólico . . . hasta . . . estuvo . . . en la isla de Curazao expulsado por orden del gobierno . . . Caracas, 1830.

Epistola primera sobre la unidad católica, Caracas, 1851.

Exposición que hace el clero de Caracas al supremo congreso de Venezuela, reclamado contra el artículo 180 de la constitución federal, Caracas, 1812.

Fortique, Mariano F., *Pastoral instrucción* Caracas, 1847.

Guevara y Lira, Silvestre, *Observaciones sobre el concordato de Venezuela celebrado en Roma de julio de 1862 y ratificado por Su Santidad en el palacio del Vatican, 1864,* Caracas, 1865.

————— *Primera carta pastoral,* Caracas, 1853.

————— *Instrucción pastoral á su clero,* Caracas, 1864.

————— *Pastoral,* Caracas, 1865.

————— *Instrucción pastoral sobre la usura,* Caracas, 1867.

————— *El Arzobispo de Caracas á sus diocesanos,* Caracas, 1855.

Gómez, Antonio. *Ensayo político contra las reflexiones del Sr. William Burke sobre el tolerantismo,* Caracas, 1811.

La iglesia y la masonería: Casos de conciencia suscitados por un francmason y resueltos por el arcediano de esta santa iglesia metropolitano, Caracas, 1865.

Independencia de la iglesia venezolana de la curia romana. Caracas, 1876.

La intolerencia politico-religiosa vindicada; ó refutación del discurso que en favor de la tolerancia religiosa público D. Guillermo Burke . . . por la universidad real y pontifical de Caracas. Caracas, 1812.

Landaeta Rosales, Manuel. *Sacerdotes que sirvieron á la causa de la independencia de Venezuela,* Caracas, 1911.

Larrazábal, Felipe. *Colección de artículos sobre la cuestión arzobispo de Caracas y Venezuela publicados en "El patriota."* Caracas, 1852.

La lei de patronato de los Estados Unidos y el supuesto legado del papa, Caracas, 1873.

Méndez, Juan de Díos. *Contestación á la protesta que contra el acuerdo del cabildo metropolitano de la catedral de Caracas de 21 de junio último han publicado los Srs. canónigos Sucre, Alpizar, y Castillo.* Caracas, 1864.

Méndez, Ramón Ignacio. *Pastoral del arzobispo de Caracas.* Caracas, 1829.

————— *Contestación del iltmo Sr. arzobispo de Caracas al informe de un cura dè la arquidiócesis la cual se publica para que sirva de preservativo y desengaño contra la herética y fatalisima máxima de que cada uno puede salvarse en su religión, repetida por D. Guillermo Burke en la Gaceta de esta capital el año de 1811.* Caracas, 1829.

————— *Exposicion 2° sobre el patronato eclesiástico dirigida al excmo. Sr. libertador presidente.* Caracas, 1830.

————— *Exposición sobre diezmos por el arzobispo de Caracas al gobierno de Bogotá.* Caracas, 1829.

————— *Exposición sobre el patronato eclesiástico hecha al supremo congreso de Venezuela por el iltmo Sr. arzobispo de Caracas.* Caracas, 1830.

————— *Exposición sobre diezmos que hace el arzobispo de Caracas al soberano congreso de Venezuela.* Caracas, 1830.

————— *Exposición del arzobispo de Caracas al soberano congreso de Venezuela.* Caracas, 1830.

————— *Observaciones que al arzobispo de Caracas hace al soberano congreso de Venezuela sobre el proyecto de constitución.* Caracas, 1830.

————— *Juramento de la constitución del estado que el arzobispo de Caracas presta en manos del Sr. gobernador de la provincia en en despacho hoy 7 de noviembre de 1830.* Caracas, 1830.

———— *Al excmo señor General José Antonio Páez, presidente del Estado de Venezuela.* Curazao, 1831.

———— *Reflexiones que el arzobispo de Caracas y Venezuela Dr. Ramón Ignacio Méndez dirige á sus diocesanos sobre varias errores que se propagan en la diócesis.* Caracas, 1832.

———— *Reflexiones que el arzobispo de Caracas y Venezuela Dr. Ramón Ignacio Méndez dirige á sus diocesanos sobre varias errores que se propagan en la diócesis.* Caracas, 1834.

———— *Instrucción pastoral que el arzobispo de Caracas dirige á sus diocesanos.* Caracas, 1836.

———— *Contestación que el arzobispo de Caracas da al gobierno de la provincia sobre la erección de nueva parroquia en la iglesia de capuchinos.* Caracas, 1834.

———— *El arzobispo de Caracas á sus diocesanos.* Caracas, 1836.

———— *Continuación del impreso titulado "El arzobispo de Caracas á sus diocesanos."* Caracas, 1836.

El Ministro de Relaciones Exteriores de Colombia en 1826, reprinted Caracas, 1851.

Navarro, Nicolás E., *Los conventos y las garantías constitucionales de los venezolanos.* Caracas, 1895.

———— *La masonería y la independencia.* Editorial Sur-América. Caracas, 1928.

———— *Tres refutaciones con mótivas de otras tantas conferencias anticatólicas patrocinadas por la masonería de Caracas, 1909-1910.* Caracas, 1910.

———— *La iglesia y la masonería sen Venezuela,* Parra León Hermanos. Caracas, 1928.

———— *La influencia de la iglesia en la civilización de Venezuela.* Imprenta "La Religión." Caracas, 1913.

Noticia rezonada de lo ocurrido en la expulsión del M. R. Arzobispo de Caracas, Dr. Ramón I. Méndez. Caracas, 1831.

Observaciones que al congreso nacional eleva el cabildo metropolitano de la santa iglesia de Caracas sobre la ley de 22 de julio de 1824. Caracas, 1825.

Observaciones sobre el proyecto de desafuero eclesiástico archivado en la legislatura de 1834 y revivido en el senado de 1848. Mérida, 1848.

Opiniones sobre el préstamo á interés y justificación de ellas. Caracas, 1867.

Parejo, Antonio. *Al público: Hechos históricos en relación con la cuestión religiosa en los años de 1875 y 1876.* Caracas, 1896.

Piñeyro, C. *Objecciones del desafuero y soluciones del fuero eclesiástico.* Caracas, 1851.

El presbítero maestro José Macario Yépez al público. Caracas, 1840.

Reflexiones imparciales acerca del folleto titulada "La serpiente de Moisés." Caracas, 1826.

Reforma de la política eclesiástica. Caracas, 1834.

A la reimpresión del "Á vosotros." Caracas, 1851.

Representación que el clero de Caracas preparo para darla al soberano congreso de Venezuela con motivo de la expulsión de su digno prelado el iltmo. Sr.

Dr. Ramón Ignacio Méndez ocurrido el 30 de noviembre de 1836, Caracas, 1837.

Representación sobre patronato eclesiástico dirigida al congreso de Venezuela por el obispo de Trícala, vicario-apostólico de Guayana, Caracas, 1832.

Respuesta al papel titulado "Las Bulas." Mérida, 1851.

Rosillo, Andrés, *Venganza de la justicia por la manifestación de la verdad en orden al patronato,* Caracas, 1824.

Saldanha, José de la Natividad. *Discurso teológico-político sobre la tolerancia en que acusa y refuta el escrito titulado "La serpiente de Moisés,"* Caracas, 1826.

Santana, Miguel. *Día que no se contará entre los de Colombia, el 18 de marzo de 1826, en que se comenzo á hallar en Caracas la libertad de la imprenta.* Caracas, 1826.

Segunda representación que el clero de Caracas hace al soberano congreso de Venezuela sobre la vuelta de su benemérito prelado el iltmo. Sr. Dr. Ramón Ignacio Méndez y la justicia que demanda la concordia entre el estado y la iglesia. Caracas, 1832.

La serpiente de Moisés. Caracas, 1826.

Sobre diezmos—dirigido á los señores que se dignen leerlo. Maracaibo, 1832.

Suárez, Antonio. *Defensa practicada el día 19 de los corrientes ante S. E. la corte superior.* Caracas, 1852.

Torrés, Aureliano. *Separación de la iglesia y el estado.* Barquisimeto, 1875.

Filisofía de la historia—abolición del poder temporal de los papas: pocas palabras al público. Caracas, 1886.

Urbaneja, Diego B. *El arzobispo Guevara y Lira.* Caracas, 1870.

Urdaneta, Amenodoro. *El poder temporal de los papas.* Caracas, 1897.

———— *La fe cristiana: consideraciones sobre "La revolución religiosa" de D. Emilio Castelar y otras obras heréticas.* Caracas, 1881.

Valdivieso Montaño, A. *Introducción de la masonería en Venezuela.* Caracas, 1928.

Verdadera idea del poder de la iglesia según las escrituras, la razón, la historia, y la política, ó repuesta por ahora al Fanal, Gaceta constitucional, Tamburini, el elector Pallero, al papel "Á vosotros cualesquera que seais, salud," y otros folletos que han corrido de algunos meses á esta parte— unos eclesiásticos al iltmo Sr. Dr. Ramón Ignacio Méndez. Caracas, 1832.

Á vosotros cualesquiera que seais, salud. Caracas, 1851.

Yépez, José Marcario. *Origen de las dos potestades civil y eclesiástica—La independencia de la una respecta de la otra y sus consecuencias.* Barquisimeto, 1852.

Zuloaga, Nicomedes, *Bibliografías y otros asuntos.* Caracas, 1925.

VI. PERIODICALS

El Agricultor, (Caracas), 1844-1845.
El Argos, (Caracas), 1825.
Boletín de la Academia Nacional de la Historia, (Caracas).
Boletín de la Biblioteca Nacional, (Caracas).
Boletín eclesiástico de la arquidiócesis, (Caracas).

El Cojo Ilustrado, (Caracas).
El Conciso, (Caracas), 1832-1835.
Correo Constitucional de Caracas, 1835-1836.
Correo del Orinoco, (Angostura), 1818-1821.
El Copiador, (Caracas), 1830.
Crónica Eclesiástica de Venezuela, (Caracas), 1855-1857.
Cultura Venezolano, (Caracas).
Diario de Debates, (Caracas), 1853-1855.
Diario Oficial, (Caracas), 1855-1862.
El Federalista, (Caracas), 1863-1867.
Gaceta de Caracas, 1808-1810.
Gaceta de Colombia, (Bogotá), 1822-1830.
Gaceta del Gobierno, (Caracas), 1827-1830.
Gaceta Oficial, (Caracas), 1872—
Gaceta de la Sociedad Republicana, (Caracas), 1830-1831.
Gaceta de Venezuela (Caracas), 1831-1855.
El Heraldo, (Caracas).
El Independiente, (Caracas), 1860-1863.
Iris de Venezuela, (Caracas), 1822-1824.
El Liberal, (Caracas), 1836-1837.
La Opinión Nacional, (Caracas), 1870-1880.
El Patriota, (Caracas), 1845-1846.
El Patriota Venezolano, (Caracas), 1832-1833.
El Publicista de Venezuela, (Caracas), 1811.
Revista de Ciencias Políticas, (Caracas).
Revista de Derecho y Legislación, (Caracas).
El Reconciliador, (Caracas), 1827.
Recopilación Oficial, (Caracas), 1862-1868.
La Religión, (Caracas), 1893-1909; 1915-1931.
El Republicano, (Barcelona), 1844-1849.
El Tiempo, (Caracas).
La Tribuna Liberal, (Caracas), 1877-1879.
La Voz Pública, (Valencia).
El Venezolano, (Caracas), 1840-1846.
El Vigilante, (Caracas), 1824.

VII. Articles in Periodicals

Bolton, H. E. "The Mission as a Frontier Institution in the Spanish American Colonies," *American Historical Review,* Vol. xxiii, pp. 42-61.

Leturia, Pedro. "La célèbre encyclical de Leo XII sobre la independencia de Hispano-America," *Razón y Fe,* May 1925.

Leturia, Pedro. "León XII y Bolívar," *Razón y Fe,* November 30, 1930.

———— "El ocaso del patronato española e americano," *Razón y Fe,* May, 1925.

Parra Pérez, C. "Las idées religieuses et philosophiques de Bolívar," *Bullétin de l'Amérique latine,* vol. vii, pp. 257-271.

Salas, Julio C. "Las misiones de Indios," *Cultura venezolano*, vol. iii, (July, August, 1919).

Vallenilla Lanz, Laureano. "Cesarismo democrático y cesarismo teocrática," *Cultura venezolano*, vol. vii, (1920), pp. 149-158.

Villanueva, Carlos, "Bolívar et l'église en Amérique." *Bullétin de la bibliotéque américaine.* Paris, 1912.

VII. BIOGRAPHIES

Azpurúa, Ramón. *Biografías de hombres notables de Hispano-América*, 4 vols., Imprenta Nacional. Caracas, 1877.

Becerra, Ricardo. *Ensayo histórico documentado de la vida de don Francisco Miranda*, 2 vols. Caracas, 1896.

———— *Vida de Don Francisco de Miranda*, 2 vols. Madrid (without date).

Cuervo, Angel y José Rufino. *Vida de Rufino Cuervo y noticias de su época*, 2 vols. Paris, 1892.

Dávila, Vicente. *Próceres merideños.* Caracas, 1918.

———— *Próceres trujillanos.* Caracas, 1921.

Gutiérrez Ponce, Ignacio. *Vida de Don Ignacio Gutiérrez Vergara y episodios históricos de su tiempo*, 2 vols. London, 1900.

Hortensio (José Guell y Mercador), *Guzmán Blanco y su tiempo*, Imprenta "La Opinión Nacional." Caracas, 1883.

Fanger, Henrique. *Biografía del señor Doctor Silvestre Guevara y Lira, dignísimo arzobispo de Caracas y Venezuela.* Caracas, 1893.

Larrazábal, Felipe. *Vida del Libertador, Simón Bolívar.* Madrid, 1918.

Mancini, Jules. *Bolívar et l'émancipation des colonies espagnoles.* Paris, 1912.

Monsalve, J. D. *El ideal político del Libertador, Simón Bolívar*, 2 vols. Madrid, (without date).

Parra-Peréz, C. *Bolívar: contribución al estudio de sus ideas políticas.* Paris, 1928.

Petre, F. L. *Simón Bolívar, "El Libertador."* London, 1909.

Ponte, Andrés F. *La revolución de Caracas y sus próceres.* Caracas, 1918.

———— *Bolívar y otros ensayos*, Tipografía Comercio, 1919.

Robertson, W. S. *Life of Miranda*, 2 vols. University of North Carolina Press, Chapel Hill, N. C., 1930.

Silva, Francisco. *El Libertador Bolívar y el Dean Funes en la política argentina.* Madrid.

Sosa Saa, José Tomás. *Ilustrísimo señor Doctor José Antonio Ponte, VI arzobispo de Venezuela*, Impresa Gutenberg. Caracas, 1929.

IX. GENERAL HISTORIES

Aguado, Pedro de. *Historia de Venezuela*, 2 vols. Madrid, 1918-1919.

Alvarado, Lisandro. *Historia de la revolución federal en Venezuela.* Caracas, 1909.

Arcaya, Pedro. *Historia del Estado Falcón*, Tipografía Cosmos, vol. 1. Caracas, 1920.

Austria, José. *El bosquejo de la historia militar de Venezuela.* Caracas, 1853.

Baralt, Rafael María. *Resumen de la historia de Venezuela desde el descubrimiento hasta 1797.* Paris, 1841.

Baralt, R. M. and Ramón Díaz, *Resumen de la historia de Venezuela desde 1797 hasta 1830.* Paris, 1841.

Becker, D. J., and J. M. R. Groot. *El nuevo reino de Granada en el siglo xviii.* Madrid, 1921.

Briceño, Mariano de. *Historia de la isla de Margarita,* 2nd edition. Caracas, 1885.

Codazzi, Agustín. *Resumen de la geografía de Venezuela.* Paris, 1841.

Damirón, Antonio. *Compendio de la historia de Venezuela.* Caracas, 1840.

Duarte Level, Lino. *Cuadros de la historia militar y civil de Venezuela.* Caracas, 1911.

Gil Fortoul, José. *Historia constitucional de Venezuela,* 2 vols., 1st edition, Heymann, Berlin, 1907-1909; 2nd edition, Parra León Hermanos, Caracas, 1930.

González, Eloy G. *Historia de Venezuela desde el descubrimento hasta 1830,* 2 vols. Caracas, 1930.

———— *Historia estadística de Cojedes desde 1771.* Caracas, Tipografía Americana, 1911.

González Guinán, Francisco. *Historia contemporánea de Venezuela,* 15 vols. Caracas, 1909-1925.

———— *Historia del gobierno de la aclamación, 1886-1887.* Caracas, 1899.

———— *Historia del gobierno del doctor J. P. Rojas Paúl.* Valencia, 1891.

Groot, José María. *Historia eclesiástica y civil de Nueva Granada,* 5 vols., 2nd edition, enlarged. Bogotá, 1891.

Humbert, Jules. *Les origenes vénézuéliennes.* Paris, 1905.

———— *Histoire de la Colombie et du Vénézuéla des origenes jusqu'a nos jours.* Paris, 1921.

Landaeta Rosales, Manuel. *Gran recopilación geográfica, estadística, e histórica de Venezuela,* Imprenta Bolívar, 2 vols. Caracas, 1889.

Level de Goda, L. *Historia contemporánea de Venezuela, política y militar, 1858-1886,* Imprenta y Tipografía Cunill Sala. Barcelona, 1893.

Mac-Pherson, Telasco A. *Diccionario histórico, geográfico, estadístico, y biográfico del Estado Lara.* Puerto Cabello, 1883.

Montenegro y Colón, Feliciano. *Geografía general,* 4 vols. Caracas, 1837.

Oviedo y Baños, José de. *Historia de la conquista y población de la Nueva Granada.* Madrid, 1885.

Oviedo y Valdés, Gonzalo Fernández de, *Historia general y natural de las Indias, Islas, y Tierra Firme de Mar Oceano,* 4 vols. Madrid, 1851-1855.

Primer libro venezolano de literatura, ciencias, y bellas artes. Caracas, 1895.

Restrepo, José Manuel. *Historia de la revolución de la república de Colombia en la América meridional,* José Jacquín, 5 vols. Besançon, 1858.

Rojas, José María de. *Bosquejo histórico de Venezuela.* Paris, 1888.

Sánchez, Manuel Segundo. *Bibliografía venezolanista.* Caracas, 1914.

Sucre, L. A. *Gobernadores y capitanes generales de Venezuela.* Caracas, 1928.

Tavera-Acosta, Bartolomé. *Rionegro.* Maracay, 1927.

Tavera-Acosta, Bartolomé, *Anales de Guayana*, 2 vols. Ciudad Bolívar, 1901, 1913-1914.

———— *Á través de la historia de Venezuela*. Ciudad Bolívar, 1912.

———— *Historia de Carúpano*. Caracas, 1930.

Tejera, Miguel. *Venezuela pintoresca é ilustrada*, 2 vols. Paris, 1875.

Torrente, Mariano. *Historia de la revolución hispano-Americana*, León Amarita, 3 vols. Madrid, 1829.

Vejarano, J. R. *Orígenes de la independencia sur-Americana*, Editorial de Cromos. Bogotá, 1925.

Villanueva, Carlos, A. *La monarquía en América: el imperio de los Andes*, Ollendorff. Paris (without date).

———— *La monarquía en América: Bolívar y San Martín*, Ollendorff. Paris, 1901.

———— *La monarquía en América: Ferdinand VII y los nuevos estados*, Ollendorff. Paris (without date).

Villanueva, Carlos A. *Napoleón y la independencia de América*, Ollendorff. Paris, 1911.

Yanes, Francisco Javier. *Compendio de la historia de Venezuela*. Caracas, 1840.

INDEX

ACADEMY of Jurisprudence, on civil matrimony, 210

Acosta, Cecilio, 181

Acuña, Antonio González de, Bishop, 43, 46

Aguado, José Suárez, 134

Aguado, Pedro, 16, 41

Alberdi, Juan Bautista, 130

Alcántara, President, 205

Alcega, Antonio de, Bishop, 38, 43

Alegría, José Manuel, 137, 158

Alexander VI, Pope, 88

Alvarado, Eugenio de, commandant in Guayana, report on missions of Caroní, 16-17, 22 et seq., 28

Alvarado, Lisandro, 221

Álvarez de Villaneuva, Francisco, 15

Álvarez, Ignacio, 60

Andalucía, 10

Andújar, Father, 38

Angostura, church in, 29; capital of Guayana, 34; Congress of, on church, 80-81; grants of land to foreigners, 109; on government of church, 94; communications with the Papacy, 118. See also Santo Tomás and Ciudad Bolívar.

Angulo, Gonzalo de, Bishop, 38, 43

Anti-clericalism in Venezuela, colonial tendency, 47 et seq.; in early republic, 83 et seq., 103 et seq.; under Conservative Oligarchy, 125 et seq.; under Guzmán Blanco, 184 et seq., 208 et seq.; in recent times, 214, 220-221

Antonelli, Giacomo, Cardinal, 192, 196, 201

Apure, 13, 90, 155, 158

Aranda, Count, 17

Araure, 129

Arcaya, Pedro, quoted on colonial episcopate, 40-41; on colonial church, 42-43; Secretary of Interior, policy on missions, 216; on law of civil matrimony, 219-220

Argentina, 89

Argos, 113

Arias, Buenaventura, canon in cathedral of Mérida, 59; in Revolution, 69; appointed Bishop of Jericho and Apostolic Vicar of Mérida, 122; protest against Constitution of 1830, 135; controversy with governor of Mérida, 135; exile, 135; death, 138 and footnote

Arias, Esteban, 135

Arroyo, José Manuel, Bishop, 198

Arteaga, Francisco de, 43

Augustinians, 8, 18

Ávila, José Cecilio, 137

Á vosotros, 97, 167

Ayala, Ramón, 132-134

Azuero, Juan Nepumuceno, 96, 103

Azuero, Vicente, 107, 110

BALLESTEROS, Miguel Gerónimo, Bishop, 42

Baluffi, Cayetaño, Monseñor, 141

Baños y Sotomayor, Diego de, Bishop, 38, 41

Baralt, Miguel Antonio, apostolic vicar of Caracas, 196; elected archbishop, 198; exile, 198

Baralt, Ramón María, 65

Barcellona, Father, 16

Barcelona, 8, 55, 60, 131, 155; Constitution of Province of, 80

Barinas, 59, 129, 155

Barquisimeto, petition from, 137; bishopric of erected, 176-177; informe from, 211-212

Bastidas, Rodrigo de, Bishop, 41-42

Becerra, Ricardo, 53, 60

Bello, Andrés, 38-39

Benedict XIV, Pope, 89, 98

Bentham, Jeremy, 106-108, 114, 126, 129, 150-151

Berrío, Francisco de la Hoz, Governor, 42

Betoyes, 18

Biggs, James, Captain, 56

Blanco, José Félix, in Revolution, 58, 65, 67; on Council of State, 174